THE EMERGING PERSONALITY

THE BOSTON CHILDREN'S MEDICAL CENTER
Publications for Parents

THE EMERGING PERSONALITY
Infancy Through Adolescence
*George E. Gardner, M.D., Ph.D., and
Members of the Staff of the Boston Children's Medical Center*

WHAT TO DO WHEN "THERE'S NOTHING TO DO"
*Members of the Staff of the Boston Children's Medical Center
and Elizabeth M. Gregg*

CURIOUS GEORGE GOES TO THE HOSPITAL
*Margret & H. A. Rey in collaboration with
Members of the Staff of the Boston Children's Medical Center*

ACCIDENT HANDBOOK—A New Approach to Family Safety
(A PAMPHLET; ALSO AVAILABLE IN SPANISH AND
IN A PURSE BOOK EDITION)
Members of the Staff of the Boston Children's Medical Center

HOW TO PREVENT CHILDHOOD POISONING
A New Approach (A PAMPHLET)
Members of the Staff of the Boston Children's Medical Center

THE
EMERGING
PERSONALITY

Infancy Through Adolescence

GEORGE E. GARDNER, M.D., Ph.D.
and Members of the Staff of
The Boston Children's Medical Center

A SEYMOUR LAWRENCE BOOK
DELACORTE PRESS / NEW YORK

TO BEATRICE

Copyright © 1970 by the
Children's Hospital Medical Center
All rights reserved. No part of this book may
be reproduced in any form or by any means
without the prior written permission of the Publisher,
excepting brief quotes used in connection with
reviews written specifically for inclusion
in a magazine or newspaper.
Library of Congress Catalog Card No: 78–130749
Manufactured in the United States of America
First Printing

TYPOGRAPHY AND DESIGN BY *Barbara Cohen*

Preface

For a number of years, I had been giving lectures on psychology for undergraduates at Harvard and Radcliffe Colleges and the first-year class at the Harvard Medical School. Under such titles as "Childhood Behavior Problems," "Emotional Development in Childhood," and "Behavioral Growth and Development," the lectures (plus a rather formidable reading list) were intended to cultivate appreciation of the processes of personality growth and to prepare the ground for the later studies of those students who were aiming for the professional services concerned with child care—pediatrics, child psychiatry, clinical child psychology, psychiatric social work, and education.

As might be expected, my lectures laid quite heavy emphasis upon the parent-child relationship, especially the relationship of mother and child, and its effects on the psychological development of the child. Since this is a topic of major interest to the Department of Health Education at the Children's Hospital Medical Center of Boston, its former director, Mrs. Harriet Gibney Coffin, approached me about the possibility of putting the content of my lectures in some form that would be available to parents. My lectures, of course, had been written for and delivered to committed students. On the one hand, simply to put them between covers would only produce another textbook, which might have some merit in the classroom but would hold no appeal whatever for a general audience of parents. On the other hand, I was well aware of the hazards that await the professional when he tries to water down and sweeten the technicalities of his specialty in the hope of turning out an instantaneous best seller. We had in mind an intelligent and concerned audience who would seem to deserve better treatment.

In the end, we decided to make an attempt to preserve as much as possible of the give-and-take atmosphere of a well-conducted seminar while combining with it a reasonably comprehensive exposition of the psychological concepts involved, in language accessible to the modern mother. We gathered together a representative group of mothers from the Boston area, and I met with them regularly over a period of several months, answering their questions, encouraging them to find answers of their own, and striving to explain when explanations seemed worthwhile. All the sessions were taped, and out of the stack of transcriptions this book has been compiled. Mrs. Joanne Bluestone, of the Department of Health Education, was in charge of organizing this seminar, and much of its success is due to her efforts, not only in finding the mothers and bringing them together, but also in keeping a steady but diplomatic pressure upon the author to complete his editorial tasks. John Durston was extremely helpful in the final editing of the manuscript. That the seminar was a success from my point of view is beyond question, for I found the experience not only enjoyable but also very instructive. If the professional in this field has any tendency to wander in the intellectual clouds of his own theorizing, he will soon discover that the acute questions and observations of intelligent mothers engaged in the day-to-day realities of child rearing will bring him sharply back down to earth.

A few words about the composition of our seminar and its procedures are in order. We began with fourteen mothers, and it was gratifying that all but two, who became ill, stayed the full course, which lasted nearly four months. We made an effort to get a fair cross-section of the population in respect to social, economic and educational backgrounds and to have immediate contact with all the stages of childhood. That is to say, the collective children of the women in the seminar ranged in age from infancy to adolescence. We wanted the mothers to be able to acquaint (and confront) us with the significant questions and problems that actually do arise in the everyday tasks of all the most demanding years of motherhood. Diversity of immediate interest therefore was a notable characteristic of our group. The common denominator of the mothers was intelligent curiosity and a willingness to express it in the presence of others.

I had intended to limit each session to discussion of a single topic or concept and so to proceed, in neat steps, through the stages of childhood. I would open by outlining the theoretical concepts, then hear and answer questions, and in summary try to relate the substance of the questions to the theory. To some extent, this tidy plan had to give way to the pressing nature of the mothers' concerns of the day. They needed answers to take home with them that same evening, whether their problems fitted our academic schedule or not. And so, in accordance with their wishes, some of our sessions did evolve into periods of free-ranging questions and necessarily specific answers. Though we have been at pains not to disturb the content of those particular sessions, we have taken the liberty of rearranging the questions in the interest of making an orderly book.

Whether our project has had a lasting effect, beneficial or otherwise, on the child-rearing practices of every mother in our group we cannot say. The eagerness of the mothers to ask questions and contribute to the discussions and their expressed reluctance to have the seminar come to an end would suggest that they found their participation a worthwhile experience.

A mother formerly employed as a laboratory worker wrote that from having had a "clinical" approach to her children, she had come to realize the importance of an atmosphere of love, happiness, and warmth. Another woman said that her husband greeted her after each session with the same eager question, "What did the doctor have to say today?" All the participants expressed enthusiasm for sharing our Thursday afternoon experiences with a broader audience.

GEORGE E. GARDNER, M.D., Ph.D.
PSYCHIATRIST-IN-CHIEF
The Children's Hospital Medical Center
PROFESSOR OF PSYCHIATRY
Harvard Medical School
DIRECTOR
Judge Baker Guidance Center

Contents

IV. The Leap into Adulthood

V. Continuing Developmental Tasks

I. EARLY
INTERPERSONAL
DEVELOPMENT

1

The Tasks of Infancy

OVER THE PAST fifty years, mothers have been showered with information about how the child should grow and develop physically, about how to keep them healthy. What we hope to do now is to encourage appreciation of the other, equally important forms of growth. These have to do with emotional adjustment, personality development, and intellectual maturation. Most mothers know today, for example, what they can expect of the child physically—a first tooth somewhere around six months, some unsteady steps around a year, and a linking of words that resembles a short sentence by the time he is two. They may not be quite so certain about the

3

early tasks that have to do with the child's emotional and social development. When should he notice certain things in his environment? When should he be able to make a distinction between the significant and the not-so-significant people in his life? When does he begin to generalize his positive feelings to others outside the home? These events, like the appearance of the first tooth or the taking of the first step, also occur at fairly specific times, but there is a wide range of normality within which each child will keep to his own pace.

There are not a great many useful books for parents on the way in which a child's personality develops. Some of the available books arouse parental anxiety: "Can it be that we are harming these budding personalities?" I may say at the outset that my job is to allay anxiety, not to create it. I wish to dwell on the normal development of children rather than on the abnormal or the atypical. While it is true that we in the hospitals occupy ourselves mainly with the child who is ill or not maturing as well as he should, our ultimate goal is that there should be as few of these children as possible. In other words, we are trying to do ourselves out of a job.

We hope you will keep in mind that within normality there is a particularization, if you will, a specificity in development, for each individual child. Perhaps your older child began to talk at nine months, whereas your younger child isn't talking on his second birthday. The lag probably means nothing more than that the two children have different "timing." There is a great deal of variation within the family group itself.

I need not tell those of you who have both boys and girls that there's a quite marked difference in their development. Boys, as a general rule, mature more slowly. They have a tough time in life. Their difficulties arise in both the physical and psychological realms and in the main are due to the cultural influence on the expectations we have for a boy. We expect a boy to be active, outgoing, strong, aggressive, and masculine. We expect him to show his muscle, to be able to run, jump, and play, and to take part in games. If he departs from this standard in any way, we have a feeling that he is not quite a boy. These expectations sometimes can be so great or so unrealistic when applied to an individual child that they impose a heavy burden. In general, you will find that among the children having difficulty in taking the forward steps in development, boys predominate. My point here is to urge you to try to understand and make allowances for these differences between the sexes.

There are a number of ladders of development. We call them the "parameters" of development. There is a ladder of development for physical growth and another for intellectual growth. A third ladder carries upward the personality development of the child. We call this the interpersonal ladder of development, and it is perhaps the longest ladder the child will climb. I have in mind here those steps a child takes to bring himself into close relationship with other people in his world. He will begin by differentiating himself from all the objects around him: the crib, the blanket, and the people. The next rung for him will be the differentiation of people from those objects which are not human. These are the basic rungs of the ladder, and in my profession when we note an infant has taken these two steps successfully, we feel he is well on his way to establishing that "relatedness" which we want him to have with the people around him.

We all have the notion that most of the significant things, good or bad, that happen to people are those that have to do with other people. The word "personality" really describes how one person reacts to another person. It tells us what kinds of interchanges, or "transactions," if you will, go on between people in their efforts to keep their adjustment or happiness at the highest possible level with the least amount of criticism, conflict, and distress.

It is interesting to note that the child of seven or eight is already a quite sociable individual. He relates to human beings reasonably well. He is able to leave the significant people in his life at home while he goes off to school or to play by himself without showing undue anxiety or giving way to panic. Our seven- or eight-year-old sets out on these adventures with some sense of security for himself. He seems to have a trust in human beings and a reasonable amount of positive feeling toward his own peer group and toward those who are in authority over him. If you look back to your child at eighteen months, however, you will remember this was not the case. When you left him, he began to whimper, perhaps to cry. When you went out of the room, he started to be very uneasy and unsure of what might happen to him. His communication was still limited to gestures, facial expressions, some not-very-intelligible vocalization, and screaming. How has it come about that this child was able to acquire, in a few short years, all the attitudes and habits that are so necessary for living with other people?

The personality of the individual child ripens through a relatively long series of steps or stages in the development of his reactions to other human beings in the family group. We must not overlook, of course, that each child starts with his own particular constitutional background. He's "wired" in his own individual way even before birth. There are differences and perhaps even limitations set by his heredity. The particular environment into which the child is born will have a large influence in determining how rapidly and how far he will develop. For each of us this environment is different, even for closely spaced children of the same family.

If, for example, a five-year-old child is trying to work out the problem of separating from Mother, and if events in the home at that time interfere with his efforts, he may always be afraid, even as an adult, of leaving people. I do not mean that just because a child has difficulty overcoming the anxiety of separation, he automatically will be disabled by this stress, but he may always feel a twinge when in the future he is left by people who are important to him. This kind of stress varies from person to person, but I doubt that any of us gets over having some anxiety from being left by a person who means something to us.

There are tasks in development that children have to solve. It is really problem solving of a kind, and we know that finding the solutions will be beneficial for the child. That is, if he has to learn, for example, to separate from Mother without becoming anxious and panicking, he is probably going to accomplish it between the ages of four and a half and six. We have that stage quite well placed. So we say that if a boy or girl at the age of six has solved this particular problem, he or she has advanced within the average range. He may solve the problem somewhat earlier or he may solve it somewhat later, but this in general is the scheme.

These tasks begin in infancy. Certain of them arise one after the other, and the solutions will depend on what has happened in the mastery of previous tasks. Some of these earlier problems may have been solved beautifully, others with minor faults. You might think of a house with a slight fault in it somewhere; it's nothing disastrous, and the house stands up for a hundred years. Certain structural faults, which will show as lesser traits or idiosyncrasies when the child is older, are always present. We want to make sure that those faults will be only little ones and not big ones that later will disable him. There is a very real difference between a developmental fault and a developmental disability. The latter may have to be dealt with psychiatrically. While the small faults do not bother us very seriously, we in preventive psychological medicine are concerned to keep them from becoming built-in, minor though they may be.

We have to begin somewhere to make this child a social being. So we begin with the newborn. What is his first task? Obviously, he has to sleep about twenty hours a day and take in a certain quantity of food. He has to grow physically. His central nervous system must mature a bit before he can do much of anything. This type of development is another of our "ladders," and we will assume that when each task is presented to the child, he is ready, in respect to the development of the central nervous system, to solve it. I say "assume" because we can't get inside the head of a young baby to figure out what's going on there. Over the years, we have observed thousands of children whose development has been rapid and others whose development has been at a slower pace. From those observations we have to make assumptions of what should be going on in a particular child's mind. We depend on the evidence of what a child does or does not do—especially what he does not do—to tell us whether or not he has taken any particular step in his development. By this method we build our growth schemes. Just as we make comparisons in regard to height and weight, so we make comparisons in psychological development.

On the ladder of personality development as we see it, the first task the child must solve in early infancy is to make himself into an individual—an object apart and distinct from all the other objects in his environment. (I keep talking about "him," but obviously I mean to include "her" as well.) What we want him to do is to get a clear-cut sense of himself as an individual. While the picture may not be sharp for a few years, this child nevertheless is at work to differentiate himself from his environment, including other people. Of course, he is not using the word "individual"—he's not using any words, as a matter of fact. We watch this process of differentiation from a purely behavioral point of view, noting how he looks at his world and deals with it and how he himself gets the notion of being a recipient of certain things good and bad. The assumption we make is that the very young baby has no clear-cut notion of what is "me" and what is the outside world. The blanket that he clings to so tenaciously seems to him almost as much a part of himself as the fingers that hold it. Through the long series of experiences of the first six or eight months, the baby begins to get the notion that he is a separate object in the center of a whole universe of other objects.

The next important thing to learn is that his universe includes human objects, as well as such material objects as his blankets and bottles and toys. This step is important because it is the first of a long series of tasks in which the child will have to sense *differences* in things and perceive ever-differing *classes* of objects. It is not only important that he appreciate that he is a different and separate individual; the very practice of this *method* of separating different classes of objects is in itself a great step forward.

If you accept the basic notion that from the start there are certain things in life that are very pleasurable and others that are unpleasant, you can get an inkling of how important the pleasure-pain principle is in motivating growth. This principle is not the only motivation, but it seems to be the important one. The child learns that he experiences certain pleasurable feelings from various parts of his body. He gets them from the warmth of a blanket, from the warmth and the smell and sounds of his mother, and from movement. In later years, we sometimes forget the pleasures of muscular action, but to a small child physical movement is highly pleasurable. He gets many of his most pleasurable feelings from his mouth, from the sucking with which he takes in his food, from the warmth of the food, and from the comfortable fullness he feels when he has eaten.

If we are going to trace the development of a personality, we must start with the body as a physical system. We surmise that somewhere in the central nervous system, in the brain, these pleasurable sensations from various parts of the body come in, are registered, and seem to become related. While his mother holds him close, speaking in soft tones, the baby sees something moving and feels a nipple placed in his mouth. All these different pleasurable feelings are coming in at the same time, and we postulate that in the brain they tend to become associated the one with the others. The sight of pleasurable things that come and go and come back again, the varied taste and feel of things, and the motion of objects seem all to be part of himself as though the stimulus could not be separated from the feelings it brings forth. Only gradually does the baby learn that it is the stimulus outside his body that evokes the feeling within him. Through this gradual and repetitive process he begins to sense where his own body ends and the rest of the world begins.

Now, all these sensations that are pleasurable have the potential of becoming painful. While feeding, the baby experiences wonderful oral pleasures, but if he continues to feed too long, he is going to experience pain. The baby may take great delight in waving his hand, but if he waves long enough the sensation is not going to be pleasurable anymore; it's going to become painful. If the baby experiences hunger but cannot get this wonderful pleasure-giving device, plus the food, inside his mouth, then the deprivation is painful. By the same token, if he cannot move his arm because his hands are pinned underneath the blanket, the inability to experience this pleasure is painful. And so we see that either an excess or deprivation of these very primitive pleasures of the baby can be painful.

As these feelings occur, the child learns that there are two attitudes you can have toward your body. One is that it can give you pleasure, the other that it can give you pain. In later years we see that some people are certain their bodies function well for them, others feel their bodies work poorly, but everyone has certain dual feelings toward his own body and body structure. It is not unusual to meet people with heart, or uterus, or skin trouble who regard the offending organ as an outside alien enemy and not as part of themselves.

At any rate, the child soon gets the notion that things both pleasurable and painful are happening to him and that in some ways they may all be cross-related and interrelated. A wordless conclusion is formed. Later, when he's able to make verbal conclusions, he puts the name of self, or myself, to this complex. The process of "individuation," this differentiation of himself from other objects, begins to crystallize. He at last knows that the rattle he holds is not an extension of his own body. He is now prepared to learn that the rattle, here only a second ago, has fallen from his grasp and is gone. The bottle is here for fifteen minutes and then it disappears. The blanket was here, but it has fallen off and he is cold. From the continual repetition of appearance and disappearance of the objects around him, he begins to get a notion of the permanence of the body and the "impermanence" of external objects. The rattle comes back, because somebody has picked it up off the floor, but the next moment it's gone again. The wonderful person who comes and does all these things for him comes and goes, too. The continual *wagging* back and forth of these objects, human and material, establishes their permanence as only relative, whereas his thumb and tongue are always here. The first stage of differentiation probably develops in this fashion.

Now, once the child has arrived at the point of knowing where his body ends, that it has limits, his progress toward a realization of what is mine and what is thine, what is permanent and what is impermanent, goes on apace through the rest of the first year of life. The child soon learns that most of these pleasures—waving the hand, rolling the head back and forth on the pillow, rocking—can be self-initiated. He can do them all by himself.

The next step in personality development, after he has become aware of the permanent and the impermanent, is to create a hierarchy of values. He begins to put objects outside himself on different levels of value. Where one child puts the rattle near the top of the list and his pillow down at sixth or seventh place, another child may reverse the rating.

But there is one object in this world of his that he invariably puts at the top because of the amount and the quality of the pleasure it provides. This is his mother.

What the child is doing here, of course, is classifying the objects of his world, and this process of classification will go on for the rest of his life. In other words, he is asking himself what objects are of the greatest worth. "What objects give me the most pleasure? The least pain? No pain at all?" He not only is differentiating these various objects in the world but also is taking a further step. He is beginning to relate to a human being. His first task in infancy was to get a fairly definite notion of where he began and ended as a unit, as a distinct individual, but now his major problem is to relate to human beings in preference to objects of the material world. And while he is working at these tasks, remember, he is also fixing levels of value for the various body pleasures. This hierarchy of pleasures will probably stick with him the rest of his life. The mouth and the tongue and the teeth (when he gets them), in sum, the oral cavity, get a certain very high value. Muscle movements get a certain level of value also. At the other end of the gastrointestinal tract, the processes of elimination, by urination and defecation, have a value, too. Banging the head has a value. There is also a place on his list for the pleasures of sight and sound. In other words, he is beginning to draw up his own particular accounting of pleasure preferences.

Although in the early months Mother usually elicits his most charming response, a child will also respond well to other individuals who approach him. By the time he is eight months old, however, I would be surprised if he has not shown a certain amount of what we call "stranger anxiety." A stranger coming into the room, even if the "stranger" happens unfortunately to be Father home from work, may at that age arouse some fearfulness. What this stranger anxiety really signifies is that at this point in normal development the child has put *one* person at the very top of his preference list of objects. His relationship to her—his mother, of course, is positive and intense. There is, therefore, a stage beginning between six and eight months when his reaction to people is a variable kind of thing. He may relate to only one or perhaps two people, including his father with his mother but nobody else, or he may suddenly begin to act as if his father didn't belong to this exclusive club. This rejection, I might say, is very distressing to most fathers. Up to this stage they have been getting along very well with the baby; then suddenly the child begins to react in a negative way. It's a perfectly normal stage of development and not an occasion for the father to withdraw or to be jealous of his wife because she has captured the child's entire attention. If each partner is not aware of what is going on, these developmental stages can sometimes alter, even disrupt, the marital relationship.

By the time he is relating to a human being the child is on the third rung of this important ladder of personality development. He has the firm notion that human beings are not, in a material sense, objects. I cannot stress too strongly how important this developmental stage is. It is the beginning of all the experiences that depend upon a positive feeling of love, affection, and trust toward other human beings.

The many pleasurable experiences the infant has very early in life with his own mother, or the one person who is responsible for his care, generate these feelings of trust and security. From his relationship to her, he generalizes his sense of trust to those like her—to the other human beings in his world. If he has these well-established feelings of trust, we can be reasonably certain that he will not have many problems in relating to others during childhood or as he becomes an adult. But if he does not sense that he can always rely upon this one person, or if his relationship with her is more painful than pleasurable, he may well have a more cautious, even a distrustful, approach to others.

You and I know many persons who would rather deal with things than with other people. It is reasonable to assume that their early experiences with other human beings must in the main have been not pleasurable nor satisfying but frustrating or even painful. Hence, they tend to withdraw from relationships with people and prefer the safer world of material objects. By this withdrawal they feel they may avoid further pain.

The adolescent boy in distress says, "I'll have nothing more to do with this world of humans. I'm going out to Wyoming to a horse ranch." Though he may be a quite well-adjusted person, his words complain that people sometimes have done him in, that people should but won't give him all the things he wants, that people are not to be trusted to any great degree. The best of all possible worlds for this kind of lad would seem to be a world of horses or a world of trees and wide-open spaces rather than the world of human beings. This is a transient sort of fantasy that all adolescents have once in a while. We call it the "desert-island fantasy." Maybe you have it once in a while yourselves! Everything would be fine if you could just get to a desert island away from everybody in the world, except usually one other person. The bananas and the coconuts would drop into your hands; you would have no cooking to do, nothing to do at all. No need to worry about hairdos, clothes, or anything like that. Fantasies of this sort are perfectly normal and may help to tide us over some of the rough spots of even adult life. But for the growing child we want these fantasies to be no more than transient phenomena. We don't want to see them become locked into a permanent attitude of doubt and mistrust.

QUESTIONS

Mrs. _____: You mention the three developmental ladders —physical, intellectual, and emotional growth. In older children, we sometimes see a marked discrepancy on these three levels in the same child. Could you say something about the early causes of these discrepancies?

Dr. G.: There are differences and discrepancies in the levels of growth and achieved maturity in any child. His physical or intellectual growth is rarely altogether compatible with his emotional or social development. In our culture we most often see children whose emotional and social development lags somewhat behind their physical and intellectual growth.

The reasons for these differences are not difficult to discern. The determinants of physical and intellectual growth are largely related to inborn, or constitutional, factors. But bear in mind that genetics, which has to do with inherited characteristics, is a very young science. The big breakthroughs have been made in only the last ten or fifteen years. Genetics obviously is on the threshold of very important discoveries, and what they may tell us about the child's inherited psychological constitution we cannot, of course, predict.

The determinants of personality and social growth are related more directly to the experiences that the child has had, or been subjected to, in respect to other human beings in his early home and school environment. It is the event, or a huge number of events, in the child's home, community, and school life in association with *people* that, in large measure, will determine his personality or "emotional self." If these events or transactions with human beings have been positive and secure, he will probably establish a trusting and positive feeling toward others. He will be outgoing, friendly, and sociable. If these relationships with people—parents, siblings, classmates, playmates, teachers, and others—have carried associations loaded with pain, frustration, derogation, and punishment, he will tend to withdraw from contacts within the world of people. He may well become accusative, unfriendly, uncooperative, "blaming," and, indeed, possibly suspicious of the alleged good intentions of people. For his pleasures and real satisfactions, he is likely to turn to the "companionship" offered by a world of activities that do not require close personal relationships with others.

Mrs. _____: Dr. Gardner, you mention the difference in the rate of development between boys and girls. Is the difference something that is noted in early infancy, and is it related only to physical development or to the mastering of the other developmental tasks you have discussed?

Dr. G.: Among pediatricians and others who have made intensive studies of infant and child development it is a recurring observation that the girl baby and child, on the average, is ahead of the boy baby and child in development. To be sure, the girl baby's average weight at birth is 7 pounds, while the average newborn boy weighs 7 pounds and 6 ounces. Nonetheless, the girl baby soon catches up to and surpasses the male in development. This "supremacy of development" in girls not only is evidenced along the physical ladder of development but also is observed in relation to girls' intellectual, emotional, and social development. It is based, presumably, upon genetic or inborn constitutional factors wherein nature, over millions of years, has determined that the female sex shall develop along these various ladders at a faster rate than boys.

Nevertheless, the boy, and the parents of the boy, need not despair, for in midadolescence—between fifteen and seventeen—the development of the boy, at long last, renders him, in respect to all of the ladders of development, equal to the girl, and in respect to some phases of development never again to be the slower one.

Mrs. _____: Related to what you have said about the various kinds of pleasures associated with the individual's body systems, could you tell us more of what is known about why certain people experience these pleasures so differently? Does this have its source in his very early experiences or in the way he was handled? For instance, why are oral pleasures of such great importance to some people and not to others?

Dr. G.: In the very early months of life, certainly by the end of the first year, the infant has classified, or established a preference for, the various body pleasures he experiences. They may be the pleasures offered by the mouth and oral cavity (most usually); the muscular system; the sensory, or tactile (touching), system; or the external genitals.

It is difficult to determine in the individual child why he, and not his brother or sister, should have chosen one type of pleasure as being to him, but not to them, of paramount importance. Presumably, either an extreme *over*stimulation or an extreme *under*stimulation, or the absence altogether of these bodily pleasures, in the overall child-rearing practices of the mother could account for these individual preferences or differences.

In the first year of life oral pleasures are undoubtedly the greatest for all children. Anything at all you hand him will go straight into the mouth. But many tend to overlook the almost equal pleasure children take from moving and touching. To a degree varying with the individual, something within this system compels the child to move, to touch, and to be touched. If you try to restrain a child who is learning to walk, he'll kick up a real furor. At that stage, he reacts to objects by crawling or running to them. We are all aware of this activity, but often we fail to see it in its rightful place in the psychological hierarchy of pleasures. From reading popularizations of psychological theories we get the idea that only the oral pleasures and perhaps the anal pleasures have any psychological significance. This is an unjustified assumption.

We suspect that something from the child's hierarchy of pleasures carries over into adult life, but we really do not know. The priority of the pleasures does vary according to the phase of the child's development, at least through the preschool years. These phases are certainly not fixed chronologically for all children but are in the ascendancy at different ages.

Mrs. _____: Does the child's basic intelligence have anything to do with how quickly he learns to distinguish his own body from the environment?

Dr. G.: It goes without saying, of course, that the innate intelligence of the child will determine, to a significant degree, how soon he will learn to distinguish his own body and its limits in space from the other objects in his environment. It must be remembered, however, that the environment, both human and material, must be so constituted as to make it possible for the child, whatever the degree of his innate intelligence, to arrive at a concept of this important differentiation. Otherwise, in even the most highly endowed child this very important basic sense of differentiation will not take place.

Mrs. _____: At what age would you say a baby begins really to recognize another person?

Dr. G.: Some time around three months, when he develops the capacity to focus his eyes and thus to see as we adults think of seeing. The baby's eyes react to light right after birth and will even follow a moving light, but we cannot draw a justified inference from this fact on what the baby actually is *seeing*. At a very early age babies give every indication of being able to detect movement. Is that seeing as we adults see? We can't say. Once he has learned to focus, however, there is no question. The first time he looks into his mother's eyes the difference is unmistakable. Recognition seems to begin at that moment. It's almost startling. The most fascinating thing about it is that it must be the other person's *eyes*, not the chin or the top of the head. The first eye-to-eye contact is a very significant moment in the differentiation of the baby.

Mrs. _____: And this period of stranger anxiety you've mentioned—why do some children have more of it than others?

Dr. G.: Usually, stranger anxiety seems to intensify between six and ten months. In this phase children want only Mother. Some children do suffer more than others who will let anyone pick them up. Perhaps they have particularly strong personal needs for bodily contact. Perhaps they have been handled by more people. There's much about stranger anxiety we don't know. I doubt that the amount of stranger anxiety reveals a great deal that is significant about the mother-child relationship.

The beginning of human relationships is really a problem in stages. First, there's the recognition of people as people, followed by a particularization in which the baby favors perhaps one or two people. Then comes a further generalization in which he extends to all the people the relationships he has developed with one or two favored ones. Why the middle step of stranger anxiety should interrupt this process we cannot say. Why shouldn't babies from the very beginning progress to relating to everyone? No one yet has found the final answer, but we have to assume that stranger anxiety is important in the developmental process.

Mrs._____: Could you say more about the early sources of a person's feeling about his own body image? His feeling of ease or unhappiness about the way it functions? Is there a connection here to people who develop hypochondriacal symptoms later in life?

Dr. G.: It would seem reasonable to assume that the early experiences of the child in respect to the pleasure and pain associated with the different body processes would influence the emphasis these processes will have in later life. These processes, and the organs involved, may become the focus of his anxieties concerning the functioning or malfunctioning of the body. They may even become the locations of supposed disease. Thus there could be a relation between these early primitive pleasure-pain feelings and the much later symptoms in the so-called psychosomatic anxieties or concerns that plague adults.

I shouldn't want to sound dogmatic here. We don't know a lot about this supposed relationship. We do know that people who have psychosomatic symptoms of the upper gastrointestinal tract seem to be of different personality types than those who have symptoms in the lower GI tract. Something must set the stage for this selection, which is a basic question for us in psychiatry. For all we know at this moment, the explanation may turn out to be a genetic one. Similarly, we know little about why one person tends to be compulsive, another hysteric, and so forth. Our inheritance must have a place in all this. It would also seem that some of these psychosomatic symptoms have something to do with early rejection, lack of love, existence of hatreds. And while I am on this subject, let me add that when I speak of psychosomatic symptoms I mean those in which there seems to be a demonstrable relationship between actual physical disorder and the emotional state. In contrast, the psychogenetic symptom arises in the mind alone and no objective physical evidence for the symptom can be found.

But these speculations, remember, must be stated with great caution. The establishment of body systems vulnerable to anxiety or to hypochondriacal expression is still a hypothesis that requires more investigation. The speculation is sensible, but proof is yet to be demonstrated.

Mrs. _____: What are some of the practical things a new mother can do to encourage the establishment of basic trust in her baby?

Dr. G.: This is an interesting, vital, and often-asked question. What are some of the *practical* things a new mother should do? If ever there was a situation where the adage "Do what comes naturally" applies, it is in respect to the mother's role in early infancy. Even though the *attitudes* of mothers toward different children differ somewhat, depending on a host of factors in the total situation, the basic feelings of mothers differ very little—if only they can allow themselves the freedom to express those feelings hour after hour, day after day, when the child is awake.

The basic, perhaps even inborn, attitude almost universal among mothers is a feeling of deep compassion toward, and sincere sympathy with, one who needs help or sustenance. Babies are people who, in short, need "mothering" in the most constructive, and not merely sentimental, sense. It was this innate compassion in mothers, carried outside the home, that led to the establishment of some of the most significant social programs for child care. It has always seemed to me that mothers are far better able to understand the liberal position in government and politics. Most women have instant compassion for the underdog and feel it far more acutely than we men do. I think history will prove me right in this analysis. This is a digression from the question, but I want to emphasize the natural feelings of mothers, or at least of most mothers. These natural feelings directly concern the practical question of what a mother can do to instill in the young infant a sense of basic trust. From my professional point of view I would cite the following as important to establishment of this basic feeling of trust in children:

1. In the first place, there is the mother's good and adequate physical care of the child. Specifically, this care includes the attention to the child's physical needs for food in adequate amounts, for warmth and dryness, together with immediate attention to all the child's genuine cries for help.

2. Second, and to my mind of equal importance in personality development, is the necessary response to the child in respect to his emotional needs. The baby and young child need plenty of "nearness" on the part of the mother. He or she needs a lot of physical closeness, cuddling, and contact, accompanied by an unmistakable expression of the mother's

positive feeling. Even before the child is able to talk, there is a definite "feedback," or rapport, with his mother that tells him how she views her contact with him.

3. Our observations indicate that consistency—that is, unchanging response—in these respects on the part of the mother is seemingly of great importance to the child. It is almost as if the child early poses this question: "Can I *count* on this object (Mother) beyond me to respond to me in this way? Can I trust her in respect to the fulfillment of these very important needs of mine?" Or again, "Can I count on her, not just in my relatively brief feeding and diapering moments, but also in those longer periods when I am awake and exploring all the interesting things in the world about me?" Perhaps it is presumptuous for us to think that we can enter the infant's world and assume that these are his feelings and thoughts, but our observations of infants indicate that if we could do so, we would find these to be his basic questions and concerns.

4. Finally, I feel the goal of this effort to give the child a feeling of basic trust should not end in his trust in the mother alone. It must become generalized to include Father and the other "human objects" in his environment. This requirement calls for the presence of the father and for the child to have access to other people, both inside and outside of the family. Next in importance to the parents, of course, are the child's own brothers and sisters.

Years ago, as you know, we could rely on what is known as the "kinship" relation to help a child to find his place, and indeed his basic feelings of security, within his world. Family members representing two or even three generations were available to the child, and their presence enabled him to enlarge and expand his feelings of basic trust. In the comparatively rural areas of our country today—in what is left of the villages and small towns—opportunities for the extension of this vital feeling of the child still exist. In the urban environment of the majority, however, these kinship conditions no longer are readily available to the maturing child. This fact presents a very important problem to parents in their attempts to develop the sense of trust until it extends not only to those significantly close to the child but also to those who are somewhat removed from his immediate life space.

It is my feeling that whatever can be done to counteract this condition of absentee relatives is in the best interests of the child. Our intensive work with orphaned or essentially abandoned children in our clinics indicates that they long for the establishment and continuance of a *blood* relationship with someone, however remote the kinship may be. If this is true of children who essentially are disenfranchised of relatives, we can easily assume its vital importance in respect to the establishment of a sense of trust and security in all children.

The individual child's sense of trust, security, and feeling of belonging through kith and kin is of vital significance to him. If you have ever stopped to think of the sense of aloneness that a person who lacks a single blood relative in this world must feel, you will recognize, I am sure, the value to the child of being a part of an extended family.

I know, of course, that these prescriptions may be difficult for mothers to carry out in this modern world, but it is my feeling that they are important and warrant our attention.

Mrs. _____: Is there such a thing as a child having too much basic trust?

Dr. G.: In spite of all I have said, I suppose there is the possibility of a child's having too much basic trust. You are right in your implication that the child has to learn that *all* human beings are not to be trusted. You are right also that it is possible for a child to develop in such a way that he would trust everybody, even those who might harm him or take advantage of him. In short, such a child would be the "patsy," the inevitable victim, of the nefarious ends some people have as their purpose in dealing with others. Your question suggests that this child would have too much basic trust; to this I would agree. Short of *exposing* them to such human beings, I suppose all children should be warned in later childhood that not-to-be-trusted people do exist. Usually, in the early years of the child's first excursions beyond the home, he is exposed to such people—usually peer-group members—and lessons relative to the comparative good or bad intentions of others become obvious to him. It is a painful experience for a child but one that must be faced. The function of the parents, however, when these experiences occur is to strengthen his *basic* feelings that in general most, if, unfortunately, not all, human beings can be trusted not to injure or take advantage of him.

In short, the problems set for us is to make sure that our children are not, in the light of their *basic* trust, either fearful or suspicious of people in general; nor do we want them to be completely without power to discriminate the "good" from the "bad" in those they meet. This is no easy task for either children or their parents, but it is one we all share.

Mrs. _____: How important do you feel the first five years are in the development of the personality of a child? I've read that some authorities take the view that it is *the* most important time, but I assume there are others who are not so certain.

Dr. G.: I think most psychologists and psychiatrists would say that the first five years are very, very important. Some would even say that those years are so crucial and critical that no beneficial changes in personality can occur thereafter. To say that the personality is absolutely fixed by the time they enter school, to my mind, is not correct. There are a lot of the basic feelings and attitudes established by that time: for instance, the relationship that the individual has and will have with other human beings. In the first year of life, you will remember, it is extremely important that the child be able to relate to other people and to relate with a certain amount of trust, that is, with a sense of security in other human beings. I think it would be not quite true to say that nothing happens in the development of personality after five or six. I don't think that children are as rigidly set then as we believed twenty or thirty years ago.

If you are thinking about real behavioral pathology or abnormality, you do have to seek out the earliest possible associations and the earliest possible traumas if you are to comprehend the basic ingredients of the adolescent or adult difficulty. There has been much emphasis, particularly in the professional literature, on the preschool years. You could guess that much from the trend of our discussion here. When I talk about the first four or five years of life, it is relatively easy to pinpoint the working out of the tasks in development almost to the month. When we get into the age from five to eleven we encounter many more complex kinds of behavior, and we're not quite so definite about the time of the mastery of these tasks. When, for example, should a child stop stealing? At five and a half a child is not thoroughly socialized. When does he begin to blossom, or to relate well, to people beyond the home? We cannot pinpoint these steps so well. The emphasis on the early years has led many people to believe that after five or six there is nothing more one can do. I don't think that's true at all. Everything we do, whether it motivates relearning or new learning, is important, and it is important at all ages.

Throughout history there has always been some magic age, perhaps five or seven or thirteen, at which the child in the eyes of his society becomes a "little adult." People believe that by the time the child has reached some particular year certain things will have happened. My observations tell me that it just doesn't work that way. Children go forward and backward and forward again. There is a lot of flip-flopping. We cannot underestimate the importance of getting a child started off well in these early years, but as long as he lives, he'll still be learning and changing.

Mrs. _____: I sometimes wonder whether educated people have more trouble in raising children and whether our education doesn't make life difficult for our children sometimes. Are there any guidelines that parents might set up about "going by the book"?

Dr. G.: The most important guideline for a mother is to trust her own feelings. We hope that the feelings will be of a positive nature and she will do the right thing intuitively. Most mothers have picked up a lot of information about child care, and we can't say for sure how they have arrived at their own stands on things. There could never be a book that would offer the right solution to every question on child care. Whatever mothers read must be used in conjunction with their feelings. To slavishly follow a routine because it has been written down just will not work. Nevertheless, I do think that the more information you get, the stronger base you have on which to make rational decisions. These decisions, of course, will be altered for the particular problem presented by the particular child and tempered by your own intuitive feelings. Like good teachers, some mothers seem to be "born" and not "made" for motherhood. Yet I never have seen one of either group who hasn't learned something from what they have read.

There are people who say, "Why are you telling mothers all these things? You'll make them nervous." It is interesting that no one objects to women reading articles about food preparation or how to keep their children physically healthy. But when it involves parent-child relations, people are a little uneasy about learning things from books. It seems to me a pity that they should set off this one area and assume that mothers should know all these things intuitively.

Common sense is a wonderful thing, but it isn't hindered when bolstered by facts. Some people immediately sense how to handle the practical aspect of things. Others see more clearly the abstract issues. I really don't know how much progress we would have made in the field of human behavior if we had relied only on common sense. The work of professionals has opened broad horizons for us. Because each child, as we have noted again and again, differs from the other, one must vary the application of all that we know. What will work with the first child in a family may not work with the third because it is not the same child nor is it the same family situation any longer. Perhaps I get a little bit irked when people say, "Just let them use their common sense." I should say, too, that we forget that much attributed to "common sense" in the mother's practices is in reality *learned* behavior. She learned not only from books but also from her own mother. Furthermore, she has learned from the same source many times what *not* to do.

I do think we could say that people who have a lot of information about child development are more aware of the problems that appear, but I feel that's all to the good. They may be able to act before the situation gets out of hand. We would also hope that this knowledge helps in a preventive sense.

Mrs. _____: My four-year-old child was ill about three weeks ago. She started off with a strep throat and she was given oral penicillin. She was unable to swallow, and both my husband and I got very concerned. Besides being unable to swallow, she held her jaw so rigidly. She had had a lip injury about a year and a half ago, and at that time she had also held her jaw in a rigid fashion. This injury was so severe and went on for so long that she had trouble eating and drinking. When this latest episode occurred, we began to assume that her behavior was motivated by her memory of last year's illness. We certainly felt she was overreacting. It turned out that she was a very sick little girl. She had developed *herpes stomatitis* in her throat and it was acutely painful. This is a case where I looked for a *psychological* rather than *physical* explanation.

Dr. G.: But you didn't do her much harm, did you, by thinking of that as a possibility? In addition to the specific medication, your approach probably was helpful.

Mrs. _____: I don't think it was harmful at all.

Dr. G.: I don't think you should feel guilty because you happened to think that this might be related to her other illness. After all, we do know children use this sort of response.

Mrs. _____: Our pediatrician has another little girl in his practice who is emotionally disturbed. Every time she gets a sore throat she can't swallow and holds her lips open and drools in exactly the same way, so perhaps that's why he went along with our theory for a while.

Dr. G.: This last item has been an interesting example of what we were discussing in this session, but I still feel that being well informed does not have to cause problems. In summary, I think we can agree that it is not the volume or depth of the information in these matters that "causes problems" in childhood. Rather, it is the rigidity and obsessiveness in the interpretation and in the application of such learning that may get us into difficulties. Instruction and formal learning in these matters constitute guidelines, but in the aggregate it is best that they do not become a bible!

Mrs. _____: My question is in several parts. I've read a theory that says that a child is born a specific physical type. He is either an endomorph, an ectomorph, or a mesomorph. The endomorph is the fat, jolly, easy-going one; the ectomorph is tall, thin, and angular; and the mesomorph is husky and heavily muscled. Those who hold to this theory feel that each child is born with a personality type according to his body build and that most people are some mixture of these types but with one dominating. My question is this: Is it preordained that your emotional type is largely due to your physical build? I have four children. Three of them could be described as ectomorphic. I never put too much stock in this until I had my fourth child. He is completely different from the others in build, emotional development, and personality type. I'd like to know what your feeling is on this.

Dr. G.: This is a very interesting question and a fundamental one, I might add. Can you tell us in what ways the children differ?

Mrs. _____: Well, the three older ones are all tall, thin, angular, and mild-mannered. They are easy-going most of the time, but this last one is definitely mesomorphic. I sometimes think I got him mixed up in the hospital because he's so different. His build is husky, he's heavily muscled, and his temperament is simply terrible! I mean he's so different from the other children that even close members of my family and my friends say, "How did you ever get one like that? The other three are so alike."

Dr. G.: Are these three girls or boys?

Mrs. _____: One is a boy fifteen, one is a girl twelve, and the other is a boy seven. This little one I'm talking about is just two; he's a boy. In all his upbringing from infancy to two, everything he's done has been the hard way. When he gets sick, he's badly sick. I'm trying to toilet-train him now, and I have never had such problems. I think he'll be wearing diapers when he's five! He's a very fussy eater. He has violent fits of temper, yet he can also be very lovable. He's extremely attached to me and yet he's very aggressive. The pediatrician said he is hyperactive. He had an immature digestive system when he was born and had colic until he was eight months old. I don't think he slept the night through until he was nine months old. Sometimes I feel so frustrated because I don't know how to cope with him. I will say that

I do think he's a little spoiled, but not any more than the other children were, because I'm a rather indulgent mother. I am not the disciplinarian in my family—my husband is. I more or less go along with him. This little one's very smart. He's smarter than the other three were at his age.

Dr. G.: In what way is he smart?

Mrs. _____: Oh, he understands very quickly what you are saying to him. I tell him to go get a certain article of clothing in his drawer or to go get a specific article in a different room and he goes and gets it immediately. He knows all the articles in the grocery store and he speaks very well. He has a set of cards with animals on it, and since he was a year and a half he has been able to recite those cards with the corresponding animal. You can't mix him up.

Dr. G.: He's more difficult than the others?

Mrs. _____: Oh, he's terrible! He really is. My husband says it's my fault. I say no, it isn't my fault. I do think that having three older children who adore him makes a difference. They are heartbroken when I spank him for doing something wrong.

Dr. G.: Your question can be summarized along this line. Are we born with a certain body type and this certain body type expresses itself in turn with a certain kind of personality? Then, is there any sense in assuming that what you or I do as parents will have an effect on the personality of the child? Well, what is the personality of the older children? I see they're more tractable than this baby. But do they tend to withdraw from the world? Are they more quiet and sedate, less active?

Mrs. _____: Well, they are more of a mixture, I think. They are outgoing like me, but they also have a lot of their father's traits. He is very quiet and withdrawn. I find their emotional outlook very interesting and am looking forward to watching them grow up. My husband has had two nervous breakdowns, one ten years ago and one just recently. I am watching very closely to see just how much of him they've got in them and how much of me.

Dr. G.: There is an obvious anxiety on your part because you wonder if the personality is associated with a certain body type and thus determined before we're born, or if the environment and the parental practices of child rearing shape us into certain types of people. You mentioned traits, for example. Are people born with certain traits? Let me give you some of the background for the notion that there are certain body types that tend to have certain types of personalities. This, by the way, does not mean that they have the same types of personality disabilities. As Shakespeare says, there are "the lean and hungry types." They tend to be the intellectuals. They also tend to withdraw from the world. But again let me say that the social behavior of any person has a wide range of normality within which to operate.

If one were to classify the great thinkers of the world according to body type, I think most of them would probably fall into the ectomorph group. They are known as aesthetic individuals. The mesomorph is usually the more athletic type of individual. He usually is highly motile and given to action in his response to events. The endomorph is the plump, jolly, St. Nicholas type. He tends to be outgoing and sociable. The only trouble with this system of classification, as with almost everything in life, is that it doesn't *always* come out the way you think it will. There is a great deal of overlap between types. The thin, tall fellow will not inevitably turn out to be a scholar. He may turn out to be a great basketball player, or something like that, because society also has an influence upon him. So, although there have been many attempts to establish a one-to-one relationship between the body types and the personality type, they do not quite fit in every instance. When theorists have also tried to make a relationship between the body types and the incidence of emotional difficulties, they often don't fit either. The point is that even if a person does fit one or another body type, his experiences in growing up, what occurs in his rearing, will have a great deal of influence upon his destiny. But many people, I think, get anxious about this theory because of the questions it raises.

There are very few families where there hasn't been some deviant individual in the background, some kind of atypical behavior or eccentricity. When a child shows eccentricity of any kind or a consuming interest in a particular pursuit, people start poking around in the family background for an explanation. What they may come up with is one of these unfortunate identifications that parents sometimes make. They hit upon the fact that this child is just like old Uncle Joe. But Uncle Joe was a happy-go-lucky, everyday fellow who didn't turn out to be much; he never went to college, wouldn't even finish high school. This identification process leads parents to unfortunate conclusions. The child is tagged with Uncle Joe's shortcomings whether he deserves them or not.

It is often easier to put people in pigeon holes than it is to think about them as individuals. You are always in peril of thrusting upon the child an identity that isn't valid, but the very act of so classifying him will alter the child-rearing practices you'll use. Once you've tagged the boy as "Uncle Joe, the nonlearner," let's say, then your behavior toward him changes. Herein lies the danger in slotting a person by his body type. You may force a premature identity. Children are very quick to pick up the identity that you're thrusting upon them. The child reasons somewhat like this: "My mother says that I am like Uncle Joe. The best way to please her is to make sure that she is never proved wrong." You see what this is doing to his thinking? Deliberately, or maybe unconsciously, he tries to live up to your expectations by assuming the personality that you feel he has. Quite desperately, he may want to be something else.

We do not know really how or to what degree the genetic, constitutional factors work in regard to the complex items of the personality. We know that genetics will have something to do with the body configuration, with height, with the color of the hair, and even with the amount of it a man has left when he is fifty. But when it comes to the complexities of human behavior, the individual's performance in the tasks of learning, his interpersonal relationships, at this time we can say only that genetic predetermination has not been proved. I think your question is a basic one. Almost everybody, at some time or other, tries to evaluate the family tree, particularly when something goes wrong with a child. We do have schemes in regard to body types. These are large general categories. The exceptions are many and the overlappings very great. What concerns me about unproved ideas like this is that uninformed acceptance of this sort of information does alter a parent's attitude toward the child. Your son is probably going to be all right, a happy youngster who will bring you a lot of pleasure.

Mrs. _____: Oh, he does already. He is a very sweet child.

Dr. G.: You see, there are a lot of factors that we don't know anything about. Do I recall rightly that your child is two and his brother seven?

Mrs. _____: Yes.

Dr. G.: There is a five-year gap there that might make a difference. There are three children ahead of him. What does this mean to him as he tries to gain his position in the family? He has three siblings to contend with. They are all doing things that he would like to do, too. When he has to go to bed and the seven-year-old doesn't have to go to bed, you see, it is a struggle for him.

Mrs. _____: Oh yes!

Dr. G.: And then, from your point of view, four children are more to take care of than three. That compounds your cares a little bit, and so it goes. The constellation around each child differs. You have to look at them and react to them as individuals rather than identifying them with a particular person or with the other children. It would be surprising to me if your four children were all alike. This would be statistically incredible! Make the most of their differences!

II. THE AGE OF EXPLORATION

2

Developmental
Tasks Between
Two and Five

OUR EXPECTATIONS regarding psychological development
must always be measured against the background of the individual child. Is his society willing and has it the capacity
to give him opportunities to learn? By his society I mean his
parents primarily, of course, but also the other persons of
his immediate environment. Will his curiosity and his explorations bring him useful and instructive feedback from
them? The amount of feedback flowing from adults to
children varies not only from family to family but also from
social group to social group, too often depending, sad to say,
upon their economic and educational status. How much

stimulation the child gets from his environment will influence the rate at which he will progress along the several ladders of development: physical, interpersonal, intellectual, and moral. Often when a particular child appears to be retarded in his development, we question his innate ability to succeed. In fact, we find the real lag has been in the amount of stimulation he has received from those around him. For this reason, we hestitate to set chronological boundaries for the stages at which the various tasks of development will be or should be accomplished. When it comes to classifying children as "retarded" or "not normal" for their failure to take some developmental step at the supposed "average age," we have learned to be careful. All the records from studies in child development urge caution and flexibility in setting up these standards.

Nevertheless, if we can persuade ourselves that a schedule needn't be absolutely inflexible, without leeway at either end, we can sketch an outline, using a rough measure of months and years, to lay out the stages at which we will look for certain outstanding characteristics of psychological growth. For example, we can classify the period from two to five years as the stage of almost perpetual locomotion, incessant exploration, and tentative—but not always cautious!—experimentation. Though school is still in the future, learning in a broad but very real sense already has begun and should be making significant progress. And it should be noted that at this age the emotional responses that accompany the process of learning are surprise and delight; at times, indeed, they verge on ecstasy! In the words of the philosopher Alfred North Whitehead, this is the human being's period of "romantic learning." Unfortunately, however, we must agree with Whitehead's conclusion that the romance does not seem to carry over into the period of "precision learning," where the formal lessons of the schoolroom take place. Something has been lost along the way from the period where insatiable curiosity drives the child onward in his craving to know. His energy then has seemed boundless. It is as if he couldn't get up early enough in the morning to explore all the new worlds opening to him every day, on every side.

Besides mastering rapid locomotion, the child at this stage is establishing more control of the coordination of eye and hand. These accomplishments enable him to extend his explorations and to sharpen the precision of his inspections and manipulations of the objects of the physical world. As we say, he is forever "getting into things." Thanks to his increased ability to move about and improved muscle action, he has discovered a whole new spectrum of pleasures. Muscular movement affords him new joys that supplant or supplement his hitherto exclusive reliance on the oral pleasures of sucking, eating, mouthing, and biting. Now, racing about, jumping, rolling on the ground, climbing without goal or purpose become sufficient pleasures in and of themselves to keep the child continually on the go. That we adults intuitively understand these primitive pleasures of movement is attested by the gifts we pick for children of this age. The rocking chair, the express wagon, the scooter, the tricycle, the pedal-operated car are all evidence of our own residues of the childish love of movement for movement's sake.

Still, it is not uncommon for parents to become alarmed at the endlessly repetitive, so it seems, activity of the preschool child. The child is almost never quiet. Even when he is being read to, his attention holds for only a few minutes. Is this some "abnormality" or the first signal of some "abnormality" to come? We in the various professions concerned with child care may have contributed to this parental alarm with our more or less public discussions of the clinical syndrome called the "hyperactive child." This condition not uncommonly accompanies, or results from, damage to the brain, but it is not what I have been talking about. Essentially all children in the preschool and early grade ages are hyperactive in the ways I have been describing. They deliberately drive themselves to hyperactivity for the sheer physical pleasure of it.

So let us see our preschool child not as "hyperactive" but as a normal youngster, his powers of locomotion perfected, his energy boundless, and his questions endless. Why? How? When? Where? Who? He is "into everything," as we say, turning, testing, and investigating. If any new object or relationship is familiar to him in one of its facets but unfamiliar in others, then his curiosity is excited, to remain at fever pitch until all his questions are answered. No longer need he wait for the new to be brought to him; now he can seek it out under his own power. It is at just this point in the life of the preschool child that external stimulation becomes of very great importance in respect to the future course of his development.

Before he goes to school, this child must learn that there are many, many "worlds" in this society of ours beyond the tiny, restricted personal "world" he has up to this point inhabited. We must confront him with facts and ideas that will expand his relationship to this larger society and give him a glimpse at least of the multitude of objects and events existing beyond his own little circle. If he is not exposed to this information and to a diet of varied experiences, he may find when he arrives in the schoolroom that he is suffering from an informational deficit that he will never, literally *never*, be able to overcome. From ten to twenty percent of American children today are deprived of the sort of psychological and intellectual stimulation that is so necessary for emotional, social, and mental growth and is an absolute prerequisite of readiness for precision learning.

When the family milieu is adequate to stimulate the child to exploration and experimentation in this period from two to five, we see a remarkable flowering of his intellectual powers. Basic to this growth, of course, is his increased competence in the use of language. Typically, the child of two years or so has learned to form some sentences of perhaps two or three words, but he still relies heavily upon gestures, facial expression, and total body movement, in addition to grunts, squeals, and shricks, for communication. Gradually, over this period, these more primitive communications fade from the scene. The child begins to produce statements and questions of many words, and, to one's amazement, he produces them in correct, or nearly correct, syntactical arrangements. Pronouns used in proper reference to their antecedents begin to appear, and, suddenly, our three- or four-year-old has acquired the startling ability to alter verbs to convey his meaning in respect to the tenses, past, present, and future!

How the child acquires his grammatical usage is not altogether clear. To be sure, he has the speech of the other members of his family as a model, but if his usage were restricted to repetition of only the sentences he actually heard spoken, his conversation would not burgeon as richly or as speedily as in fact it does. Somehow, before he receives formal instruction, he gets the idea that the sentences he invents should follow the forms of the sentences he hears, and he proceeds to build accordingly. If you think about it for a moment, you will agree, I am sure, that even when his usage may not be quite correct, the child's recognition of "shall" or "will" as signifying future time and his ability to form the past tense by tacking "ed" on the end of verbs in the present tense represent a considerable accomplishment.

The building of his vocabulary is one of the child's most important developmental tasks in this period. We cannot emphasize too strongly how vital it is for him to have acquired at least the average vocabulary by the time he is five and a half years old. It has been shown to be crucial to his performance in school and to his intellectual growth. His acquisition of words will depend almost entirely on the amount of feedback he gets from his parents in response to his interminable questioning about the events and objects of his world. The short answer, the inadequate answer, or no answer at all will defeat the efforts of any but the most exceptional child to gather information and build a vocabulary.

In contrast, fortunately, the methods that will be successful in helping little children acquire a satisfactory use of language are fairly well established. By repeating a word time and again to refine the child's almost correct pronunciation of it, and by acclaiming the child for putting together a compound or complex sentence or for using an adverb properly, parents can stimulate the building of a vocabulary and a feeling for grammar. In the absence of this type of supportive behavior the child may suffer a language deprivation as detrimental to normal development as the deprivation of food or love on the parallel physical and emotional ladders of development.

While the child is gathering information at a steadily increasing rate and enlarging his vocabulary, his manner of incorporating this knowledge into his thinking and reasoning processes will pass through several stages. At the start all his thinking is essentially egocentric. That is to say, he refers every item of information to his own inner drives or wishes. In consequence, throughout this period and into his early months of school, his thinking, his talking, and his action responses will demonstrate a curious, but to him highly satisfying, mixture of reality and fantasy. To fill in the gaps in his information about the real world and to ameliorate the repeated frustrations he necessarily incurs in his first encounters with society, the child has recourse to an imagined "world" of his own. Sometimes there are a succession of these "worlds" that are satisfying to him and not intolerable to his parents. The creation of these fantasies probably constitutes his best method of coping with the anxieties that arise from his frustrations and from his lack of reassuring information about reality.

Whatever the origin or the motivation, we see the existence of fantasy in all preschool children. The "animal world" is one we see most often. A sure bet for an appreciated gift for children everywhere is the toy animal. This is probably evidence enough that parents intuitively understand their importance to children. The child will include these animals in his special world as role players. Because animals, in their structures and functions, approximate human beings—in certain ways, yet not exactly or completely—they can be made into valuable characters in his fantasy world. These attributes allow the child to establish a partial but not total identification with the animals or to identify them, favorably or unfavorably, with the humans of his real world. His animals can be friendly, loving, and kind or aggressive and vicious, controlled in behavior or wild, submissive, or demanding. In short, as he plays out the fantasies to suit his own purposes of the moment, his animals can act and feel as he himself and other people act and feel. Above all, these toy animals, unlike the humans of the real world, remain at all times under his complete control!

There is also the world of dolls, the "playhouse world," the "hospital world" of "doctor and patient," and others that grow from his steadily broadening experiences or from the stories that are told or read to him. In this era of his growth they all become grist for his mill of fantastical creation. This is the stage of development at which "magical thinking" attains its maximum peak. Never again will the processes of "wish-fulfillment" occupy so prominent a share of the totality of his mental activity. In this world or these worlds of fantasy, where he retains complete control of all the actors, he is again almost all-powerful, as he was in earliest infancy. Yet you will note a significant difference. No longer is his thinking altogether egocentric. He is now dealing with other humans, with mothers, babies, doctors, policemen, firemen, soldiers, as well as his animals, and he is applying to them a quasi logic. They now begin to reason and act in the ways he has observed humans to reason and act, and intermittently he allows facts from the real world to intrude upon his play. Either his own small knowledge of reality brings forth to him the absurdity of some magical role he has assumed or has projected onto others or the actual events of the world at this particular moment have called him back to reality. His fantasy is abruptly broken or distorted to another course, but the child is no longer "egocentric bound," as our professional vocabulary has it. The child can switch back and forth easily between his magical thinking and his rational discourse with the real world.

From this point on, the store of information he compiles and the observations he makes modify the egocentricity of his thinking. He is being pushed toward logic, which in the schoolroom will compose the rules and regulations governing his efforts in problem solving and, indeed, his approach to the real world.

In this same age period, from two to five, the child also takes important steps up the ladder of his moral development. By "moral development" we mean, of course, the inculcation of basic notions of right versus wrong, of "do" versus "don't." The mechanism of control that we call the "superego," which is destined to become unconscious and automatic in its operation, is established. We can think of the superego as that process of our inner self which reviews our primitive impulses and evaluates them against the demands and prohibitions of society. Does the external world allow or disallow expression of this urge or impulse? If not, what control or modification is required? In short, we are talking here about the development of the human conscience.

The earliest encounters between primitive impulses and persistent demands for regulation are likely to come, as we will discuss in some detail later on, in relation to the control of physiological processes: the ingestion of food and the emptying of bowels and bladder. Hence, the successes, failures, and meanings that these first efforts at regulation hold for the child will affect significantly the directions taken by his personality development. Cleanliness versus dirtiness, neatness versus untidiness, retention versus giving—all these issues, according to currently prevailing theory, will show up in later life in association with certain personality traits and in relation to what is right and what is wrong, and all will have their basis in those early struggles around society's demand for inner control of behavior at the primitive level.

It should be noted that in the mind of the child at this stage of development the superego has a highly personalized frame of reference; that is, the child seems to carry in his mind a "picture," if you will, of the person—usually his mother, of course—who is demanding control. In the earliest stages this picture tells him, "Mother says you shall do this. Mother says you shall not do that." But gradually, as we will see, his inner "control device," the process that points out right versus wrong to him, becomes impersonalized and dissolves into an abstract moral code devoid of specific reference to individual persons.

As this controlling mechanism develops, the child begins to develop feelings of guilt. When he fails to follow the admonitions of others or when, later, he ignores the dictates of his own code of control, these feelings assail him. Not infrequently, even at this tender age, feelings of guilt can set up an unconscious wish for punishment that will push him to act in a way certain to bring punishment. This relieves him of the burden of his own control.

A final issue in this phase of moral development is the emergence of the concept of truth versus falsehood. The child begins to get a notion of the values that our society attaches to telling the truth, and he learns that punishment is visited—in theory, at least—upon lying. Let me hasten to interject that there is nothing "unnatural" about lying in childhood. The child who never told a lie would be a rare one indeed, and it seems harsh to apply so stern a word to the usual fabrications of this period. We can classify this "story telling" in three categories: In "protective lying" the child seeks to protect himself from punishment for detected wrong doing and frequently tries to shift the blame onto another. "Aggressive lying" is a deliberate attempt to bring punishment upon another, usually a sibling, for an act that never happened. "Fantasy lying" is the concoction of imaginary accomplishments that are supposed to enhance the child's prestige. The normal child employs all these devices at one time or another, and they are best met with consistent, firm, but sympathetic rejection. In time the child will get the idea that the child of most worth in the eyes of his parents is the one who can be depended upon to tell the truth.

As we scan the years from two to five the most general observation we can make is that this period is fraught with struggle. On the one side, there is the drive for independence, for autonomy. On the other, we find the residual dependence on parental care, love, and indulgence. The child still wants the exclusive love of his parents and he wants them to gratify his urges immediately. But this is the time of family growth. A majority of all boys and girls between two and five will have to bear with the arrival of baby brothers and sisters, perhaps more than one. Superseded as the baby of the family, the child between two and five suffers a loss of preferred position. His prestige, he thinks, is diminished, and his sole ownership of his parents is gone forever. He will need patience, understanding, and tolerance.

At this time, the parents should be prepared for regressive behavior. That is, on the advent of a new baby in the family the two- to five-year-old may himself revert to babyish conduct. In respect to his use of language and his control of bowels and bladder he may lose some of the gains of recent months. He may even refuse solid food and demand to have his bottle back. He may go so far as to return to creeping and crawling. The only response a parent can offer to these demonstrations of injured feelings is to make every effort to let him know that he is still loved, that they respect him for the individual he is, and that they recognize and appreciate the strides he already has made in undertakings quite beyond the capabilities of the new baby.

But even apart from the complications introduced by new siblings, negativism is likely to characterize the first half of this period from two to five. This is the phase of the big "No." If you offer his favorite food—he will spurn it. If you try to help with his coat—he will fling it aside. If you expect him to walk, he will demand to be carried. If you pick him up, he will shriek in protest. He wants his own way in everything, and his way may often not be yours. For parents this can be a depressing phase, but it will pass. It is as if the child recognized this as his last opportunity to stage a defiant struggle for infant omnipotence. He seems to be saying, "You want me to become independent? Then, by heaven, I *will* be independent! You deprive me of my dependence on your loving care and attention. Now I will demonstrate this independence by allowing you to regulate my life *not at all!*"

Parenthetically, it may be noted that this preschool phase of extreme negativism, the repudiation of parental help and advice, is not unlike the phase in adolescence when teenagers exhibit the same infantile response to parental authority. Can it be that in the adolescent we are observing a reactivation of, that is, a regression to, a response of earlier childhood? The similarities are certainly striking. We can't say that the theory has been proved, but it is worth pursuing further.

And finally, toward the close of this period, at four to five years of age, there emerges, at least in our culture, a phase of development that will have considerable bearing upon the child's future interpersonal relationships, his sexual identification, and indeed upon his own image of his worth as a person. This development is the establishment of the Oedipal complex. Sigmund Freud was the first to describe this complex in which the child invests his or her libidinal (love) drive in the parent of the opposite sex and strives to exclude the other parent from the relationship. That is to say, a son seeks total ownership of his mother, and a daughter strives to capture the exclusive love of her father.

Freud's identification of this complex, seventy-five years ago, has led to endless debate. Is this complex universal? Is it inevitable for every child? Does it affect the children of other cultures, especially primitive ones? From the beginning Freud's Oedipal theory met resistance, and he himself said of the opposition he encountered, "Only the *mothers* of Vienna really knew what I was talking about and believed me." Whether or not they subscribe to orthodox psycho-analytic theory, the overwhelming majority of child psychologists, on the basis of their clinical observations, will testify to the existence of some process which in its most important manifestations is very like Freud's Oedipal complex. To some degree at least, at some point in their lives, children do "fall in love" with the parent of the opposite sex and exhibit strong jealousy, if not hatred, of the parent of the same sex. The appearance of this complex should not cause alarm, for even though it is not fully understood, it is a natural drive.

Almost needless to say, these Oedipal strivings for the exclusive ownership and love of the parent are doomed to failure, but out of this struggle evolve identifications and attitudes that will be elements of the child's personality forever after. It is successful resolution of this complex that interests us. We will deal with this subject at some length in connection with the next period of development, which we will call the "age of mastery."

The child's ability to solve the developmental tasks in the years ahead will depend a great deal on the psychological events of his preschool years. The stresses and threats he must deal with in this early period are particularly important in determining how he will learn to cope with the everyday events in his life. Not only the number but also the *kinds* of stresses matter.

I think the first serious stress that the child really does understand and react to is the threat of abandonment or desertion. By this I mean the fear of a possible breakdown of the relationships between himself and the significant people in his world—most specifically, his mother and father. This threat of desertion, abandonment, or rejection can impede or prevent altogether the solution of these tasks we want the child to undertake. The child of four or five must take a step outside the home, however short a step it may be. He will go, we hope, to nursery school or to kindergarten for increasing lengths of time each day. He will be left alone; that is, his mother and father will leave him in the care of some other person. The child becomes able to tolerate this separation, but his learning to accept it without fear, without panic, comes gradually.

The abandonment or desertion that I am speaking of is an interpersonal abandonment. It is possible to abandon a child even within his own home. Let's say that another child seriously handicapped by a chronic disease is demanding the mother's attention. It is possible that the mother will have to give so much of her time and herself to this sick child that the other will feel virtually abandoned. There are, of course, many other kinds of abandonments and desertions and rejections, but whatever the circumstances, to a child this threat is very important.

The child's experiences in these early years in respect to this stress will have much to do with how he reacts to separations later on. In everybody's life, beginning in earliest infancy, it is a vital issue. When you are abandoned or deserted later, let's say by a boyfriend or your girl when you are nineteen or twenty, you may react to your loss in a very infantile manner; you may feel as if the whole world had gone to pieces or as if your own destruction were imminent. This is not an unusual type of response. People vary in their ability to withstand such losses, but from early infancy the threat is always present. If this fear is an overwhelming one for a child, the solution of any of his developmental tasks becomes all the more difficult. The fear of abandonment, I would say, is one of the first big threats or stresses we all have had to encounter.

Besides the dread of abandonment, various other fears or phobias emerge around the age of four or five. The quite normal child may exhibit, in succession, fear of the dark, fear of large animals, fear of "monsters," fear of bodily injury or death—any of a hundred threats, depending on his experiences. I call this period the "era of the normally phobic child."

The causes of these passing phobias have puzzled professionals as well as parents. The most pertinent explanation, it seems to me, is the simple one: In this period of exploration the child has it dinned into him that certain acts and certain things are dangerous, potentially mutilating if not death dealing. For example, falling, electricity, bodies of water, animals, automobiles—all can hurt or kill him. He acquires a conception of the *possibilities* of harm, but his experience is too limited to give him an idea of the *probabilities*. Thus, he knows that parents can die, but he has no way of knowing that the probability is heavily against the death of his own parents. He knows that a tiger can eat little boys and girls, but does he really understand that there isn't any tiger around loose? Does he know the odds against a specific lightning strike? To my mind, it is this imbalance of his feeling for possibility and probability that makes for this anxiety in childhood.

Children experience a stress that has to do with the ability to maintain the integrity of the body. This stress ranges from fear of being harmed or mutilated to fear of death itself. Obviously, the concept of death is not clear in early childhood, but there are lots of symbolic substitutes for death in a child's mind before he acquires a realistic notion of the facts. You probably have heard your own children voice these threats. As the child gets older, there is an increasing fear of disfigurement or scarring of the surface of the body. The cosmetic implications become more and more significant, I suppose, in a girl's life than in a boy's. Nevertheless, this is a continuing stress, a worry, because young persons see it as an attack upon their physical equipment and their status as complete human beings.

Though most of these worries about the body do not develop until later than the age we have been discussing, as long as we have opened the subject, we may as well go into it a bit more. We find that the possibility of surgery, such as removal of the appendix or repair of some difficulty inside the body, becomes a source of increasing concern. Fear of internal dissection is among the prevalent fantasies. The children from whom we hear these notions are by no means only those who are having emotional problems. We hear them from youngsters who in their mental and emotional development are completely normal.

The notions children in the hospital express in respect to what has been done to them in surgery of the abdominal cavity open to us a particularly fertile field of their fantasy. Girls often feel they will not be able to have babies because of what has been done to them. Boys have fears and dreads, too. Though we try to explain exactly what's being done and why, the fantasies nevertheless are there. One of these is that all the pain or discomfort is a punishment for something they have done—some "evil" action committed—some hatred or even an expressed death wish. They look upon their suffering as just reward for their misbehavior.

Some fantasies of retribution have to do with sex. Most children have been rebuked for touching certain areas of their body. If they are old enough to have experienced the pleasurable feelings these organs evoke, they may feel their investigations have brought on this punishment. Or a child may feel that the unpleasant things that happen to him in the hospital are due to his having transgressed his mother's wishes. The fear of physical disabilities resulting from surgery constitutes a threat far beyond the sickness or the surgery itself. The child's interpretation may seem quite fantastic to you as an adult and a parent, but I am sure that each of us when very young had fantasies no less unusual or vivid.

Another stress that has to do with body integrity is the fear of disease, sometimes a specific disease. It doesn't take a child long to learn the dangers to which he is exposed in this world. He understands quite early that illness can end in death or in some kind of physical disability. Children learn about these matters not only from what they are told but also from what they can see. They note physical disabilities in other children. Comparisons follow naturally. In other words, the fear or stress embodied in a negative comparison of their own physiques with those of other children of the same age is always a threat.

Another task for the preschool child is that of learning to separate the significance of the gifts he receives from his estimation of whether or not he is loved. Children tend to regard gifts as proof, or at least an indication, of love. "Didn't you bring me a present?" is the frequent cry. There is in their minds a close association between your giving or your not giving something material and your caring or your not caring for them. By the time the child gets to be five and a half he probably won't state this equation anymore. Somewhere earlier, we hope, he will have made the differentiation. But some children never do. It is an important step in development to be able to go beyond equating material things with the love of a significant person in your life. Many parents, and grandparents, too, play into this business and keep it going. Some grandparents can never appear on the scene without bearing a gift. This largesse may irk the mother and father, and it tends to prolong the thought, "She loves me because she gives me presents. When she stops bringing me a gift I'll know she doesn't love me anymore." To straighten out this twisted association is a task. One might think it a superficial task with not much significance, but it is of great significance. There are many people, you all know some of them, who never really get beyond the equation of material things and love—hence, all the jokes about mink coats and diamond necklaces. There are people who never can tell the difference between the gift-bearing person's love and the love of a person who doesn't bother to bring any gift except himself. Although we all like people who give us things, I suppose, children do eventually learn to make the distinction. However, it can be a difficult task.

There is also the old "mine and thine" problem. Children do have to learn to share things with other people. The first step usually comes with the joy a child gets from "compensatory sharing." An exchange of toys takes place. "You can hold Teddy if I can sit in your fire engine." At first, such a trade is tolerated for a relatively short time—only as long as the fair exchange is satisfying. Then the shared toy is snatched back. When at length the child begins to learn that the shared object is not irretrievably lost or "stolen," there is a gradual lengthening of the time he is able to share something important to him and a lessening of his insistence on the "exchange" demand. Slowly, after many positive experiences, a more adult type of sharing or loaning of objects emerges. The first ingredients of the satisfaction of bringing pleasure to others with no expected compensation begin to appear.

Reluctance to share varies from child to child, but in even the child who is a model in this respect there is always some tendency to be frightened as to whether what is shared will come back again. The ability to share is achieved gradually and at times is subject to severe regression. I'm certain you are all familiar with the child who suddenly snatches the teddy bear away yelling, "Mine, not yours," and stamps off, leaving the other child quite bewildered. Difficult as it is for many, the willingness to share should begin to be in evidence as a partial "task solution" when the child is between three and five years old. Gradually, the child will be able to understand that to share doesn't necessarily mean to lose. Inability to grasp this principle is at the bottom of most of the difficulty. Again, you will note that many people never solve this problem. They find it all but impossible to share and never develop a sense of the real joy of giving.

Around this same age, children come up against another problem for which we hope they will find a reasonable solution. This involves the control of their aggressive drives. Aggression is an impulse that seems to operate in some people without visible provocation or it may operate only in response to other people's aggression. In either event, it is a very powerful drive! It has two parts which concern our thinking about developmental tasks. The worst type of aggression is when a person attacks the body of another. We call it, technically, "somatized aggression." (*Soma* is a Greek word meaning "body.") The aggression of the very young child is almost exclusively directed at the body. It is aggression against the body integrity of another. This is one of the forms of behavior that we desperately want the child to overcome. The very young child's physical aggression when frustrated is due to his inability to express his disappointment or fears adequately in words. He necessarily has to rely on "body language."

If you have a number of children in the family, much of your time is spent seeing to it that they control their aggressions of a body-directed nature. They can yell and stamp about, perhaps, but actual assault upon a sibling must be stopped at the very start. Children have the right to be protected against the aggression of their siblings. This is one guarantee that should be in a "Child's Bill of Rights." You must protect the children against the attacks of other children in the family as you would protect them from the physical aggression of the children outside the family. Many children's fear of aggression comes *not* from their experience in the playground, unfortunately, but from the unhappy situations where a parent has not protected them from the physical assaults of their brothers and sisters. All these acts do not take place surreptitiously. You all know about the stuck-out foot that trips and about the elbow that nudges. So, the first step in this task is to get the child not to attack the body of another. You try for a cessation of punching, knocking down, and kicking. This is the first step in the child's control of his aggressive instincts.

At a very young age children cannot talk out their differences. They should be told to ask for an adult to act as a mediator. Gradually, however, they should be encouraged to verbalize their anger—to talk about what is bothering them, to discuss their differences. Verbal aggression can be hurtful, too, but not in the same damaging way that physical abuse is hurtful.

The ultimate phase, which comes much later, is to try to get the child to impersonalize his aggression. For the present, we want him not to direct this aggression against the body of an individual. Later, we hope that he will not need to direct any form of it against people at all. In other words, we want him to learn to rechannel these feelings. It makes little sense, when aggressed against, to respond by letting out one's own aggressive drives. Our goal is to get the child to direct his aggressive thinking not against the people in his world but against the evil things that are going on in the world. This kind of aggression we want to develop within the child at the earliest age possible. We want him eventually to fight, not against people and certainly not against the body of a person, but against the ills and evils of the world—sickness, or dirt in the street, or the maneuvers by which one group of people tries to master another group of people. We want children when grown up to be aggressive but in the sense of being aggressive for goodness. This is an impersonalized kind of aggression. It is not an attack upon people. It is an attack upon circumstances that are evil and bad, unhealthy and injurious, to be fought without hurt to anybody but rather for the betterment of everyone.

We can see some of the steps the individual will have to take in mastering this task of control over his aggressive drives. I don't mean to say that the impersonalization of aggression is easy; there is always a tendency to respond aggressively when thwarted. This task is never finished altogether. If it is going to be solved at all, I think the solution has to start within the home where the person lives as a very young child. Development of the control of person-directed hostility and aggression—effective, constructive control—is probably the first or second most important psychological task that faces members of the human race.

We have all kinds of ways of fostering this development, both at home and in the community. The most important in childhood, I think, is play. Of all the socializing devices we have to offer children, play is the most important because it requires the child to learn the rules and regulations. In play, from even so simple a game as ring-around-the-rosie up to the bone-crushing tackles of professional football, everything depends on rules and regulations to desomatize the activity. In football or basketball the worst breach of the rules is to assault an opponent on the playing field or court. You can pick up your marbles and go home if you must, but in the games we devise for children you cannot break the rules by hitting someone. There are technical fouls, when your offense is to step over the line, but the personal fouls penalize the players for primitive attack upon the body of another. To have the child learn that certain things go according to rule and regulation by which he must abide is to make great progress toward the constructive use of aggression. Even more important, the process of learning to accept that things go by regulation, that there are certain rules to be followed, is probably the most effective preparation for other types of learning. Here I refer, of course, to the precision learning of the schoolroom.

Many of the children we see in our psychoeducational laboratory have never learned the significance of rules. They are perfectly normal youngsters, some even with superior intelligence, but they cannot seem to get hold of the idea that inexorable rules govern certain regions of our lives. They can't remember that you always make *A* this way or *B* that way, that a word can be spelled just one way and no other. The inviolability of rules is one of the concepts the child must grasp if he is to do well in precision learning.

In the survey of major tasks in emotional and personality development I have had to be somewhat selective. It is well to note that I have by no means covered all the tasks that are presented to the preschool child but have concentrated upon the development of the child in respect to his interpersonal relationships—relationships with his mother and father, siblings, and peer-group members—and the to-be-expected stresses and threats that arise in everyday life. These stresses have a marked influence on the child's ability to find satisfactory and satisfying solutions to the tasks he faces.

Over the past twenty years or so, various theories and studies regarding the chronology of child development have had great influence on American parents. First, the Gesell studies suggested that certain quite specific forms of behavior can be looked for in most children as they reach this month or that year of their lives. More recently, we have heard a great deal about the Swiss psychologist Jean Piaget, who has advanced the theory (originally developed from close observation of his own children) that the child's ability to progress from one level of thinking to the next higher level is a function of his development as a biological entity. It cannot be forced by concentrated tutoring or any other means. In other words, while a child may be able to memorize and parrot some abstract idea, he will not really understand it until he has reached the stage at which any idea of that particular abstraction is understandable. The time at which this stage arrives varies from child to child.

In line with this approach, it is natural to ask whether there are certain ages at which children are most vulnerable to the different stresses we have been talking about. I may have emphasized somewhat too heavily the bad and handicapping effects of these stresses, but I do want to point out that some of them can, and very often do, have beneficial effects as well. Stresses and even blocks can be stimulating. To be able to master while under strain brings the joy of achievement, and the value of motivation to achieve cannot be overemphasized.

QUESTIONS

Mrs. _____: If a child has an emotionally unstable parent and it is noticed that many of that parent's traits are showing up in the child, will he have the same difficulties in adult life as the parent does?

Dr. G.: Categorically no! This is, of course, a blanket generalization. I know nothing of what the problems are but I'll still say "No," because the environment that produced the problems in the parent is always altered for the child. An entirely new set of circumstances pertains. It's the individual's adjustment to his own environment that is important.

Mrs. _____: Now, about children who are afraid of the dark. What gives them the idea that the dark is frightening? Does it just come? What do you feel about using a night light?

Dr. G.: No, I don't think it "just comes." Their inability to see their surroundings allows a lot of room for fantasies to appear. I'm not opposed to night lights. A child who wakes up may have difficulty getting oriented and may need a light to readjust himself. He may have been having frightening dreams. I don't think everybody should routinely use a night light, but there shouldn't be a rule against it. We have talked about some of the gruesome fairy tales and nursery rhymes. These may spur some of the bad dreams. Bad dreams are hard to handle even when the lights are on, let alone in the dark.

There is too much fuss about whether a child should always sleep in the dark. I just don't think it's that important. A night light may give him at least a semblance of familiar surroundings so he can hold on to reality. If you wake up, you know where you are. I don't see any great problem about it. We'll probably never find out why a given child has needed a night light at a particular time. As long as he doesn't seem to be generally fearful, I wouldn't worry too much about the request for a light. This is another one of those phases that comes and goes if not much is made of it but tends to linger if a mother creates an issue over it.

Mrs. _____: Some children seem to insist more than others on equating love with material gifts. Does this evaluation of theirs reflect the attitudes of the adults around them, or does it stem from their own nagging needs for reassurance that they are loved?

Dr. G.: This craving for gifts may show, of course, that the child actually is deprived of the emotional nurturance and love that are his due. He must depend on the gift to provide a token of this love. The equation "gifts = love" is perhaps a partial substitute for what is wanting in his life. It is not infrequent for adults themselves to set the stage for this expectation by always bringing gifts. In this situation, the child may by no means be lacking for love and attention; he only has established a wrong assumption that love always is demonstrated, or accompanied, by a material gift. For children with this idea the practice of "overgiving," or "ever-giving," should be modified gradually and with sympathetic explanations. These children need to dissociate affection and material gifts.

Contrary to what one might expect, the distribution of gifts among all the children in a family at the same time may create another issue for each child. Who has received the best, the prettiest, the most valuable, the most wanted gift? Disappointments and wrangling often result from this sort of not-so-subtle competition. A gift should be picked for the individual child and should be chosen in relation to the child's need of the particular moment. Next time, the other children will have their turn. In my experience, however, it seems to me there is a glaring exception to this rule: the father's return from a trip! All the children should be recipients at such times. It is important they know that in his absence Daddy was thinking of each of them.

Mrs. _____: It's the same with learning to share. Why do some children seem to find this so much more difficult than others?

Dr. G.: I suppose differences in sharing depend basically on the sharer's general sense of security. Whether he is a preschooler or older, his feelings will bear some relation to the good or bad results that have been visited upon him in the past when he has shared objects with others. It has been my experience that of two preschoolers the older will be the more distrustful and more concerned about getting the shared object back.

An older sibling may feel more challenged by the younger one in the sense that the latter is threatening him on many fronts of development. The younger one is always striving to do those things which the older has accomplished, and to get those things which the older already has. In this situation the older child vigilantly asserts his unquestioned ownership and protects his sole use of the object. Associated with this fear of loss of ownership there is also fear that the shared toy will be broken or damaged by the sibling. Experience has taught the older sibling that this fear is not entirely unrealistic!

It is interesting, I think, to note that these childish fears of sharing are not entirely overcome at any age. Even when we adults share our lawn mower or car, our clothes or books, our seeming willingness is usually guiltily tempered by concern that if returned, the shared object may not be in the same condition as it was when loaned. Hence, being able to share is presumably one of those many minor mental-health tasks which one has to solve and solve again throughout the years. It is not solved once and for all in childhood.

Mrs. _____: A few weeks ago you spoke of aggression as one of the central drives in development. I have a little girl who will be four in another month and twin boys who are twenty months old. Recently I have noticed an increase of slapping and biting among the three of them. I am wondering just how much I should allow, or just where to draw the line, if a line can be drawn.

Dr. G.: This is an age-old problem. You say the older one is going to be four. And she tends to be rough with the others?

Mrs. _____: Yes.

Dr. G.: Well, I am sorry that you brought that up. I have a granddaughter exactly the same age, and she has a little sister who is a year and six months old. We all have noted that she is really giving this little one a rough time. What's appearing—and this I think you have to watch out for—is a tendency on the little one's part not to grow or mature as fast, not to try things out as early as the other one tried them when she was queen of the nest. I think she is a little bit afraid that the older one—they are both girls—is going to *do* something to her if she does. For example, she can walk perfectly well, but sometimes she is pushed over by the older one. So she delays walking. She'll walk, but she'll walk more readily and do more talking when the older one is out of the room. We often see this situation in families. I think the younger ones really have to be protected against this kind of aggression. You try to reassure the older child that she is still loved, that she doesn't have to be a baby and get down and crawl up the stairs instead of walking. She doesn't have to yell and shout as the young one does to get your attention. Intellectually, of course, the older one knows all this, but two hours later, you'll find that when somebody comes in the house and pays attention to the younger one, the regressive kind of activity begins all over again. It is a tough battle the older ones are fighting, I am sure, and they get to know all of the attention-getting devices. They can do everything that the little ones can do because they have done it already, and received acclaim for it. So they resort to these old tricks.

As I've said, I do feel strongly that parents have the obligation to protect children from the aggression of their siblings. I think this is a rule that has to be followed rather religiously because it makes a tremendous difference on all sides if children are allowed to abuse each other. This doesn't mean that you have to spank them or make their lives miserable. But I think the general attitude of not accepting a bullying kind of behavior has to be reaffirmed again and again. Allowing physical abuse to continue has a bad effect. Not only does it delay the growth of the one who is doing it; but it also has an effect on the maturation of the one who is being abused.

Mrs. _____: I hate to see either one of the twins coming after Anne has begun to play with them, but it seems that playing develops into something more angry. They seem to come running to me for protection.

Dr. G.: You are their only protector. I think it is fairly well accepted that we expect the teacher, the athletics coach, the policeman, indeed everybody else in society, to protect our children from bullies outside the home. Well, I think we also should expect the parents to be the protector of the child against sibling aggression within the home. Of course, it depends on how you go about it. You have to proceed carefully and consistently to show that you just don't like that kind of behavior.

Mrs. _____: I have only one child, but I wonder whether sibling rivalry is a problem in most families. I bring it up because I have a neighbor with a three-year-old son and a seventeen-month-old girl. The son cannot be left alone with her; he hits and hurts her. His mother has tried everything. She scolds him, she tries to reason, she has spanked him but tries always to show him affection. She feels all of this is due to sibling rivalry.

Dr. G.: Well, the situation certainly sounds like sibling rivalry! The question comes up: Why should the rivalry and the envy be so acute in the mind of the older child? Why should he feel so displaced by the younger one? There is no question that even a small child is quite pressured. He must do this thing now and that thing next. If he doesn't progress in just a certain way then there is trouble. I think it's always well to look at what the mother's attitude is toward the child who is envious of another in the family. We must look for a clue in what she is doing in regard to that child. I don't mean that the things she is doing are bad. I think it is normal for a child who is three and a half years old to feel some kind of resentment when he is displaced by another child. Now, some parents recognize the inevitability of this resentment and go all out to make sure that the temporarily displaced child's feelings of security are maximized. The child may not be able to verbalize his feelings, but he feels hurt when his mother seems to give all her attention and love to the younger one. Even when the older one gets a lot of verbal affection, he misses the cuddling.

Competition is a very important drive in the American culture. We may encourage this competition unwittingly to give us a measure by which we can gauge how well our children compare with their peers, to see if they are solving their developmental problems readily and fully in reference to other children in their environment. Competition, you see, is not altogether bad. There are positive ingredients in competition. If everything is just handed to a child on a silver platter and he doesn't have to do anything for his rewards, he won't show much progress. I should mention again that we don't want person-directed competition or aggression, but it is difficult to expect a three-and-a-half-year old to impersonalize his feelings. He will tend to direct his aggression against the mother or the other child by hitting or kicking them. Sometimes a child like this gets a lot of help from going to nursery school where he becomes involved in new interests and new relationships.

Mrs. _____: The child I speak of has just started nursery school.

Dr. G.: That may take off some of the pressure. He'll gradually learn he can do more exciting and interesting things than the baby can, and he'll develop new relationships with children his own age. He'll be able to come home from nursery school with pictures and little tokens of achievement that his mother can praise, and he'll know full well the baby can't do what he's done.

Mrs. _____: I think there are techniques that the mother can use to ease the situation. My babies are eighteen months and two months, and I find that whenever I want to cuddle the baby, I can still talk to the other one. The minute I pick up the little one, I can see the older one freeze and start thinking of something to attract my attention. Often I will talk to the baby about the accomplishments of the older one. "Why can't you be as big as brother?" It is the tone that counts with the baby, not what you say. I can see her just beaming, yet the older one is happy, too. I know that I am going to have a difficult time later on, but for the moment it seems under control.

Mrs. _____: This leads me to a more generalized kind of question. You know, at a certain point I think this "psychologizing" can become very irritating, especially if the child doesn't respond to it one hundred percent.

Dr. G.: What do you mean by "psychologizing"?

Mrs. _____: Well, you know, you're playing a trick. When I pick up my baby I don't want to talk about the other child. It would just be a gimmick for me to do that.

Dr. G.: It might bring results—gimmick or not.

Mrs. _____: You know, I think later on there will be a point when the older one is going to understand that this kind of behavior is false. Are these little psychological tricks really helpful in the long run?

Dr. G.: Well now, let's look at the situation. We are concerned about the older child. The younger one really doesn't understand the words. He only knows about the warmth and the holding and cuddling. You are giving that child enough security. It is the other one that you are really concerned about. You are trying to help him to make this transition from being your only child to a position where he can share your attention. Right? The baby benefits from the sound of your voice and the older one from what you say. It's an example in sharing—a deliberate attempt at good mothering, I would say, rather than a "trick." Only mothers—and certainly not psychologists—can come up with such beneficial devices!

Mrs. _____: But it's what happens later on that I question. What happens when they can see through such plots? Maybe I, as a mother, will become dependent upon gimmicks rather than on more forthright relationships with him.

Dr. G.: Perhaps this is just one more area where your feelings about what you are doing provide the key. If you feel you are just tricking this child, obviously you shouldn't do it. If you really wanted to, you could classify many child-rearing practices—and some of the best of them—as tricks or gimmicks. I prefer to think of them as imaginative solutions to real problems, devised by mothers like yourselves who really care and who are dedicated to doing the best job they can. Most parents give a lot of attention and intuition to finding the answers to what is going on with their children. I feel they should be encouraged, and I salute Mrs. _____ for her handling of what is a very real and painful situation for her little boy.

Mrs. _____: I have a seven-week-old baby who is colicky. Our twelve-month-old was not too bothered until she switched to daytime crying. Now just hearing the crying seems to have an effect on him.

Dr. G.: It distresses him?

Mrs. _____: He was doing great until recently. He was drinking from his cup, but now he won't even touch it. Everything is centered on the bottle now. He sucks his thumb from one end of the day until the next, which he never did before. I've tried getting him outside with other people, but he doesn't want to leave me for an instant. I've taken to shutting the door and keeping the baby in another room. Which is better, to send him out with another person or to keep him inside with me?

Dr. G.: I don't think I would send him out. I think I would keep him close to you. You have brought up several issues. One is this regression that he has shown in demanding a bottle.

Mrs. _____: We have reached the point now where if I give him his juice in the afternoon, he won't take that from a cup either. He still has the bottle and brings it over to me and wants me to fill it. He won't hold it by himself either. I have to hold it for him!

Dr. G.: Here is a very good example of what we have been talking about. What you need to do is to encourage him, of course, to get back on the rails and be the big boy. Not in the sense of chiding him, but rather to motivate him to want to grow up and to emphasize through rewards and attention that growing up is pleasurable and of great importance to you.

Mrs. _____: The baby was crying at night in the beginning. I would get down on the floor with the older one and we'd play and look at pictures. And this was fine. He didn't really hear the crying then, I think. But now that she has switched to daytime, it is not working out too well for him, and I just don't have the same amount of time to devote to him.

Dr. G.: He is probably trying to project what he thinks this baby is feeling or suffering. So, he is very anxious when the baby cries, and not just because her crying is going to get your attention away from him. It may also be that he knows that if you have a pain in the tummy you cry, or if you are hungry you cry, or if you are cold you cry, or if there's a pin sticking in you. He knows at his twelve months that certain bad things cause crying. It may be that he doesn't want you to spend so much time with the baby when the baby's crying, or perhaps he fears that something will happen to the baby because she is crying and needs to be taken care of. I would imagine it is a subtle combination of both. This regression that you mention is common. All you can do is to encourage him to grow. It really is a task that he's working on. "Don't grow up because if you do you'll lose your favored position!" And yet each child does want to grow up. The wish should be encouraged at every possible turn.

Mrs. _____: The scene where he won't hold on to a bottle of apple juice or milk is amazing. He hangs on to my legs when I am holding the baby. It's chaos!

Dr. G.: Sometimes you really have to suppress a laugh. On the surface it all seems so ludicrous. A child progresses up to the second year and is doing everything he is supposed to do when suddenly he goes into reverse. I know it isn't funny when you have to cope with it, but I would be very sympathetic with the child who is going through this stage. He feels rejected and hurt.

Mrs. _____: I was wondering about this thing with the cup and the bottle. Should I forget about getting him to drink from a cup? If I have not given him a bottle for lunch, then the next time I feed the baby he is frantic. He wants that bottle even though he has the same amount of milk in his cup.

Dr. G.: I think I would keep offering the cup but be prepared to give him the bottle for a while. Don't let him forget that he had once mastered the cup.

Mrs. _____: When I had my second baby the person who helped me most to understand my older one's behavior was his nursery-school teacher. "Just imagine," she said, "that your husband brings home another woman and announces, 'I still love you. You really are great, but I love this other woman, too. And not only do I love her, but you have to be nice to her. I can't spend as much time with you as I used to because I have got to spend a lot of time with her, too.' " When I thought of it that way, I was certainly able to empathize with the older child.

Dr. G.: I think the nursery-school teacher who said this to you is a very astute person. She doesn't need a job, does she? She puts it very beautifully, I think. If you can just imagine your husband's pulling a dirty trick like this you may be able to imagine what you would do, too.

By way of summary, it seems clear that sibling rivalry derives basically from a sense of loss of prestige. The child feels his mother's love and attention have been diminished or lost to him. This feeling, of course, can arise from actuality or from pure fantasy. Children suffering from such feelings are prone to *interpret* their loss as a total, not partial, one, and their response is in turn of a "global," or total, nature. The two most characteristic responses are (1) regression to infantile habits, accompanied by the surrender of some developmental progress; and (2) expression of aggression (physical aggression) toward the brother or sister who seems to them to have captured the ascendancy in the family, particularly in the eyes of its most significant member, the mother. A sympathetically voiced refusal to accept either of these "defensive" extremes, regression or aggression, seems to be the treatment of choice.

Mrs. _____: My sister has a son who must be right in the middle of the Oedipal phase. She finds it rather difficult to handle. She doesn't want him to feel she's rejecting him, but his obvious preference for her upsets his father. Are there ways to help a child who seems overly attached to the parent of the opposite sex?

Dr. G.: It seems to me your sister is going to have to educate both father and son. Her husband must learn that the boy is passing through a normal stage of development where he not only is going to prefer his mother but also is actually going to try to possess her to the total exclusion of his father. It is curious that mothers seem to instinctively understand this stage in the development of boys and girls, but fathers have more difficulty in accepting it. They have to be taught to understand their own natural jealousy and at the same time to understand and tolerate the feelings of their sons during this phase. Above all, they should never taunt, or even worse, punish, the little boy for his preference of his mother. Many fathers tease the child, call him a "sissy" or a "mama's boy." This is certainly not helpful.

It is the mother's role, and not the father's, to sympathetically but firmly convince the boy that he is not going to own her and that his father is *not* going to be excluded from her affections. In carrying out this aspect of the boy's education the important thing is to ensure that the boy does not terminate the phase of inevitable frustrations with associated feelings of loss of worth or value in the eyes of either of his parents.

Mrs. _____: We hear so much now about the destructiveness of excessive guilt feelings. Do these have their roots in the years when the child's conscience is developing? If so, is there a way to encourage a firm sense of what's right and what's wrong without making the child feel too guilty when he crosses the line?

Dr. G.: Guilt feelings can be destructive if they overly inhibit an individual or convince him of his own worthlessness and inadequacy. Although the inculcation of both a sense of right and wrong and the establishment of inner controls is accomplished in part through generating guilt feelings, it does not mean that such feelings should be excessive or destructive. The amount of guilt or remorse necessary to mediate and ensure correct, or indeed protective, behavior varies with the behavior itself and the context in which it occurs. The generalizations that parents make in a moment of anger often indicate to the child that he is totally bad or evil. This must be avoided. To be avoided, too, are statements that indicate that his misbehavior will doom him to eventual damnation or permanent isolation or loss of love. Such threats are terrifying, for they are taken literally by young children. It probably is too much to hope that a child can be reared by a parent without some utilization of engendered feelings of guilt, but unwanted or dangerous behavior can certainly be corrected without generating an excess of such feelings.

3

Toilet Training

As you know, getting a child to go to the bathroom when and where he should is much more than a mechanical problem. The side effects are many and varied and are related to the ego development of the child, that is to say, the development of his personality. It's the ego, you know, that tends to mediate between one's inner impulses and the demands of the outside world, and one of its functions has to do with control.

By the time the child is a year or eighteen months old, he has accomplished certain tasks, solved certain problems. He's learned where he ends and the outside world of objects begins. He's able to differentiate between the material objects and the human beings in his world, and he's developed a very definite attachment to the really important person or persons around him. If he's moving about, he's probably learned or begun to learn what to touch and what not to touch. But basically the first really difficult demand we put on him is that he shall control his bladder and bowels.

What we do when we get the child to go to the bathroom at a particular time in a particular place is to motivate him to give up certain physical pleasures which until now he has enjoyed whenever he wished. We ask him to delay these pleasures. We try to show him that there are different pleasures which he can expect to enjoy when he gives up spontaneous, impulsive, uncontrolled expulsion of feces and urine. In other words, we ask him to give up the immediate body-based satisfactions for other rewards that are related to his position in the eyes of the people who have contributed to his pleasures and have satisfied his needs. The most notable new pleasure, of course, will be the attention, love, and commendation he's going to get from his mother and others who care for him.

You'll remember that in the beginning we emphasized the numerous basic bodily processes in which are rooted all behavior. We made the point that all these processes, and particularly those of the gastrointestinal tract, have a great deal of pleasure attached to them. In other words, it is pleasurable to eat, it is pleasurable to feel full rather than empty, and it is pleasurable to exercise those functions having to do with the lower gastrointestinal tract. These last feelings we tend to repress as we get older; we forget them. But children are not forgetful of the fact that the processes of elimination *are* pleasurable activities, and they resist having them regulated by outside "controllers."

Now, I suppose you rightfully can say that it doesn't make very much difference at precisely which month of life you begin to control the child's habits of elimination. Usually the parents' timetable will be in accordance with their own feelings about these bodily functions. If the parents are overly neat and place a high value upon cleanliness, if the child's messing himself and wetting himself disgusts them, they probably will start the training period as soon as they possibly can. If they are more relaxed and do not find the messiness completely repugnant, they will tend to begin training later. The only condition the specialists in pediatrics or child psychology would insist upon, I think, is that one cannot expect this control to appear until the central nervous system has developed to a certain degree. In other words, you cannot expect a very, very young infant to be able to master this task. The nervous system itself, the nerve tracts and their connections, are not sufficiently developed to enable such control to be established and lasting habits to be formed. There is also a relationship between this phase of training and the child's verbal education, that is, his use of words in place of the more primitive grunts, gestures, grimaces, shouts, or cries. Of equal importance, of course, will be his comprehension of his mother's words of request—or demands!—and his willingness to obey them. The time for toilet training will depend upon a number of factors, but from multitudinous case histories I gather that training usually begins when the child is between one and two years old.

What I want to talk about in some detail is the relationship of this training to the formation of traits of character. Very involved here is the pleasurable significance of food to the child, a significance and meaning long forgotten by the time adulthood is reached. By "food" I mean the entire process of food intake and utilization, beginning with food sucked or bitten, taken into the mouth, ingested, moved into the gastro-intestinal tract, and converted to energy sources and to waste products to be expelled from the bowel. All these processes and their child-level "meanings" are aroused in the training, and the regimen inculcated in the child contributes to the formation of certain basic character traits he will exhibit in later life.

First, there is the inherited instinct of sucking and the individual pattern of sucking behavior. There is the biting mechanism when he has his first teeth. After food is digested and assimilated comes the sense of fullness if you have enough to eat or the sense of emptiness if you have not. Finally, there is the expulsion or elimination of the wastes. Now, all the words I have used are related to specific physical processes, processes that are either pleasurable or painful to the child, but I'm sure that you are aware of the other, nonphysiological meanings those same words have for all of us. For instance, we say that we "incorporate" ideas or "assimilate" material and "retain" it in our memory. It is not just happenstance that these words are used for both processes, the physiological ones and the psychological or behavioral ones. The linguist familiar with many different languages will tell you that a majority of the nouns we use, if traced back to their origins, will be found to refer either to functions of the human body or to the houses or structures in which people live. Note that five or six of the words we used to describe getting ideas or information into or out of the organism—incorporation, digestion, assimilation, retention, elimination, and expulsion—are the same words we use in describing the processes of the gastrointestinal tract. Another example is the term "smearing," which describes a messy but pleasurable activity of the child. We also talk of "smearing" the candidate in an election campaign, of "smearing" someone's character.

I don't know if I am drawing this analogy effectively or not, but if I haven't, we'll come back to it again. I find that parents tend to understand these matters much more readily than my students do because parents are involved daily with habit formation and the inculcation of controls. If I talk to students about the Oedipus complex—where the little boy of four to five and a half is in love with his mother, and the little girl of the same age in love with her father—they just don't believe it. They have forgotten all about it in their own lives. But the mothers of this world knew all about this complex long before Freud came on the scene. They weren't the least bit astounded when they heard about it.

When you begin to toilet-train a child, you are really beginning to build into the child a *basic* control mechanism, a mechanism which he will use to control his other instinctual or learned impulses. The *manner* in which this training is effected will have much to do with his later responses to all controls and authority figures—other adults, teachers, recreation leaders, police, bosses—who try to elicit acceptable behavior from him.

We believe that bowel control and certain traits of character are established at the same time. There are close associations having to do with the *meanings* that food has for the infant, but no longer remembered by us as adults. We set up these inevitable associations when we make rules as to what the infant shall or shall not do in respect to his food—intake and the expulsion of his wastes. We know perfectly well that food is necessary to sustain life. So the first meaning is more than symbolic. Food equals life; lack of food equals death. We know, too, that for the young child food becomes equated with love.

But apart from these direct, realistic meanings, food also has symbolic meanings and associations. Just as food constitutes a gift, to the very young child you're trying to train, the fecal material he expels is also a "gift" that he's giving to you, his mother. He puts a very high value on these body products. As far as he's concerned, they seem to be an actual part of his own physical equipment that he is "giving." All of you have had the experience of seeing how proud these young children are once they are able to demonstrate that they can control this process.

Many of you have heard and some will agree that there is a close association in people's minds between money, in short, that which is valuable, and feces. We even have an expression called "filthy lucre," remember? There are other much more crude terms than this that have to do with the association between feces and money. It is quite possible for a person throughout his childhood and possibly into adult life to maintain this high, precious value on both sides of this equation, in regard to feces and in regard to money. He will in some fashion retain or hoard both in order to see to it that nobody gets it away from him. This is what I mean by the formation of a personality trait based on gastrointestinal functions and early training methods as an origin. The training and the method used in training may well determine later attitudes related to cleanliness and neatness.

It is not unusual, as I mentioned, for very young children to consider the fecal material to be a part of themselves to the degree that they just will not go to the bathroom. They will not give up these materials because they consider them not so much as a gift, if you will, or something precious in one sense, but rather as a part of their body itself that is being taken from them and destroyed. Although we promised not to go into abnormal behavior in this series, we do have to jump over to pathology once in a while. We have cases where children have toilet phobias. In these phobias, which usually are transitory, the children basically are afraid of mutilation. They feel something is taken away from them that is a part of their body and that they're being hurt—flushed down the drain, so to speak. A much more common type of toilet phobia is the fear that not just their fecal material but they themselves may go down the drain. In their primitive thinking they can't understand why a loving parent would allow anything like that to happen, that is, would allow a part of their body to be destroyed. That's why they get so upset or terrified when they are placed on the toilet. To you as adults it is just some waste material that you want to send down the sewer but not so to them—it's a real threat of body loss or mutilation.

In our vocabulary the functions at the lower end of the gastrointestinal tract are frequently invoked to express aggression and sadism. If you think of all the expletives, swear words, insults, and condemnations that are hurled against people in the angry conversations of this world, you will see that often they revert to the contents of the lower bowel or to the expulsion of those contents. This is universal in all countries, in all cultures. This is the ultimate symbol when one deprecates other people.

In the light of the foregoing it is interesting to note that there is a stage in early development which professionals call the "anal-aggressive stage." What happens in the training that takes place in this stage will tend to set certain character traits. We all know people who are concerned interminably with their bowels. There is the exacting individual who has to go at precisely the same time, day after day, and gets terribly upset if his schedule is violated. It is our expectation that this "overtrained" person may well be compulsive about everything in his life. This is an obsessive kind of self-regulation. That sort of compulsion we don't want. The obsessive person regulates his life to the degree that all his creative imagination is repressed. His thinking, instead of being free and constructive, becomes rigid. The person who is excessively concerned for neatness and cleanliness in his personal and domestic habits is likely to view anything the least bit out of order as cause for alarm. And there is the associated trait of moral cleanliness. "Cleanliness is next to godliness," we are told. Why have all these dicta on cleanliness entered into our language? They are really a part of the basic "body language" that is associated with physiological processes and their control and inculcated in us so early. Without even thinking, we use body language constantly. People in all cultures do. As we acquire larger vocabularies our earliest associations to words are somewhat modified and repressed. Our pathologies in behavior, however, would indicate that they are never entirely forgotten!

Our image of ourselves—that is, our feelings about the kind of people we are, the value we place on ourselves or feel others place on us—may have its roots in our early training experience. It will depend on whether our response to those demands was a succession of failures attended by punishment or derogation and leaving a sense of loss of prestige or "goodness" in the eyes of our parents.

Whether a person has adequate self-control or not is related to this early experience, too. One person may lack inner control and demonstrate later a great need for firm external controls to make him do the right thing. Many delinquents, for example, are really crying for external controls to keep them from doing things they know are wrong but in respect to which they have weak controls or none at all. There is, of course, also the person who can't wait to give expression to his impulses and needs. This character trait, too, is related to the demand on the child that he delay his impulsive actions, not only in bowel and bladder training, but also in respect to other limitations placed on his behavior. But in the main, the first and basic training that is demanded of the child is related to the control of the processes of the gastrointestinal and genitourinary tracts.

For some people there is built in at this stage a tendency to have to control everything and everybody at all costs. The child may try to control you rather than the other way around, and later we see both those who must always be in control and those who wish to be controlled. These are the two extremes I am giving you. We hope that somewhere along the line the child will end up with strong inner controls but that he also will be able to tolerate the external controls imposed on him by society. People at one extreme want to run everything. Those at the other extreme allow people to control and manipulate them. It is observed repeatedly that when the child feels that the approbation, love, and fond attention he receives for his control of his bowel and bladder functions are more satisfying than the physiological pleasure he gets out of going wherever and whenever he pleases, he will train himself. Until that moment is reached, he's probably still going to choose the instant gratification. Some people go on operating in the very same way. "I want what I want when I want it." Never mind the future or the approbation of others.

Also in this training period comes the first appreciation of rules and regulations. This is extremely important. Learning that things go by rules and are regulated, that we must all learn the habit of regulation, of following the rule, is vital in development. Many children who have learning problems have not assimilated the notion that things go by rules and regulations. Certain things don't change. Involved here in a larger sense is the beginning of respect for authority, as opposed to unrestricted independence and autonomy. Here again people will vary in their response.

The values and traits I have discussed seem to me to be of great significance. My main point is that their background or foundation is related in great measure to those hundreds and hundreds of things that we do in getting the very young child to assume an adult attitude toward bladder and bowel control.

QUESTIONS

Mrs. _____: Could you give us some practical suggestions or ideas on bowel training for children?

Dr. G.: One thing I can say is that I don't think there is much sense in starting before a child is at least a year old. I want to avoid giving you specific rules of timing and procedures, for, as individuals, you must all go through this a little bit differently, each in her own way. All we can tell you is to avoid the extremes. Bladder and bowel training is a very important phase in a mother's life because every mother is anxious to get a child past this messy stage. But as long as you don't begin too early, I would think that you need not worry about following the book exactly. You are trying to do something impossible if you insist on this sort of thing before the child is physiologically capable of response. You would just be running against the barrier of an underdeveloped central nervous system and you would both become frustrated and anxious.

One practical suggestion, however, is that the attitude, the tone of voice, the response of the mother to success or failure are all extremely important aspects of the whole procedure. These items far outweigh in importance any set rules or specific methods. Don't allow the battle lines to be drawn up over this issue. Play it by ear.

Mrs. _____: Sometimes children who have been trained for a while suddenly begin to wet and soil themselves again. Is this usually related to some emotional problem the child is having at that point?

Dr. G.: It is not unusual for children up to the age of five to regress in this manner at a time of crisis. In fact, it is a response that one can almost predict.

The emotionally laden crisis that most often brings on this temporary regression is the birth of a baby brother or sister. His mother has to shift the great bulk of her attention, love, and body contact to the newly arrived infant at that time. Naturally the preschooler feels like a displaced person. This sets the stage for one of the first great losses the child will experience. As if to combat this feeling of loss, the child seems to reason, "If I did become a baby again, if I give up all signs of being independent, then she will have to take care of me the way she does the baby." He then acts out these feelings of loss in an effort to become entirely dependent on his mother and to force her to respond to his dependence.

Other familiar crises that can bring on this regression is illness, hospitalization, or a period of absence from his mother.

Most mothers are somewhat startled when they witness this reaction in their children for the first time. They are concerned lest all the gains in development the child has attained will be lost and the "training" will have to be done all over again. Except in an extremely rare case these fears are not justified. The regression is usually short-lived and the child resumes his previous habits and level of development.

During these periods of stress, a mother should respond with understanding and sympathy. I know this isn't always easy. She should deliberately try to apportion her schedule to include some time alone with the child. She should let him know that she understands his feelings, loves him for himself, and particularly for all the advanced or grown-up things he has learned to do.

Mothers should also try to understand their own feelings that unconsciously may motivate them to exclude the older child. Some mothers who are extremely dedicated and devoted to children in their infancy tend to be alarmed or put off by their children when they reach the age where they are no longer totally dependent on her. This type of mother "loves babies" and often wants one baby after another to satisfy emotional needs of which she is only dimly aware. A mother who realizes she has some of these feelings may need to consciously direct her feelings and activities to the older preschooler in order to overcome whatever tendencies she might have to distance or exclude him or to unknowingly motivate his regression.

Mrs. _____: Girls seem to get trained earlier and easier than boys. Is this because they are more anxious to please or because they are physiologically more mature?

Dr. G.: It is probably due to a subtle combination of both these issues. As you know, preschool girls do develop and mature faster than boys. Their nervous systems show more readiness for developing the inner controls that are required in training. The verbal cues utilized in training also may be understood and acted on by girls at an earlier age.

It is conjectured by many child-development specialists that preschool girls are natively more passive than boys, in that they do seem to accept and follow directions and behavioral controls more readily and agreeably than boys. It is well established that enuresis (day- and bed-time wetting) is far more prevalent in boys than in girls. Any such marked differences in behavior between the sexes always raises the question of a possible inborn tendency or genetic factor that governs these developmental sequences.

Mrs. _____: Most of the emphasis is on too early or too rigid training. Is there apt to be an effect on the personality of the child whose mother lets him go on and on untrained?

Dr. G.: For the past half century there has been an on-going battle between those who would start early and be firm and those who would be totally permissive in the training routine. During that time alternate generations of mothers have been urged to utilize totally differing approaches and timing to achieve the same end result. Probbly neither of these extreme approaches are in the best interests of the child. Though it is usually felt that early and rigid training demands are the more harmful I see no immediate or long-range advantages accruing to the child whose mother allows him to "go on and on untrained." The mother's intuitiveness plus the initial results of trial and error in training usually indicate to her whether or not she should continue in her attempts to train her child.

We are told, of course, by anthropologists that children in primitive societies—i.e., in non-Western, nonliterate societies —are allowed to "train themselves." The one advantage in this scheme of things is that bowel and bladder control does not become a battle ground with mother and child poised as adversaries pitted against one another. Perhaps this system works well in a more "primitive" milieu, but I see little positive data that would support our adherence to their methods. Almost any child who is untrained past the age of three is going to come in for teasing by his older siblings and playmates. This will usually bring even the most recalcitrant diaper wearer into line!

Mrs. _____: Some mothers promise rewards like food or

small gifts when their child "performs" on the toilet. What do you feel about this? Is it a bribe?

Dr. G.: I see no great harm—nor do I see any great advantage—in rewarding a child with gifts for successful performance. I should say, however, that no reward the child receives equals his mother's demonstration of her affection for and pride in the child who responds to her training procedures. Material gifts are and hopefully always will be secondary in importance as the child develops year after year. One does have to be careful about constantly offering rewards, for there seems to be no end—nor any limit—to the "bribe system" once it is instituted with children.

4

Discipline

THE ONLY DISCIPLINE that is of any value either to the individual and his own happiness or to groups of people living together in any society is self-discipline. No externally applied discipline can ever be counted upon to protect the individual, even from himself and his own harmful drives. Unless the great majority of its members is controlled by self-discipline, no society could possibly supply the external protections necessary for its very existence.

Self-discipline depends upon the establishment within the individual of a set of mental processes that will ensure the control of his instinctual drives. You may call this "mechanism of control," what you will, a "conscience," a "soul" or a "superego." Whatever the name, the function, the method of development, and the expression are the same. To establish this mechanism is one of the early major developmental tasks; to maintain it is evidence of good mental health and adjustment.

This instrument or process of control follows a definite course in development that includes a set of tasks or problems to be solved or mastered at various age levels in childhood. There is (1) the control of bodily functions, (2) the control of aggression directed against people, (3) the taking on of a *property* sense, (4) the control of pleasurable drives and fantasies so that *precision* learning may take place, and (5) the control of the multiple infantile or early childhood components of the sexual impulse. It goes almost without saying that the control necessary here is an *inner* control and the discipline a *self*-discipline.

Many parents overlook that these inner controls are established—or fail to be established—by virtue of the life experiences to which the child is subjected, the experiences the child has with his parents and with those who follow his parents in authority. From these experiences he builds his concept of human beings as well as his concept of himself as an individual. Those concepts are his models for the roles he later in life will grow into.

The incorporation of these inner concepts, roles, and controls depends at least in part on his relationship with his parents and others in authority. The first requisite is that in their own behavior the child's models must appear as human beings with whom he can identify without fear and without guilt; the second is that the "emotional climate" of his home and his school shall be one to foster in him a sense of trust in other humans. Only under such circumstances can control and self-discipline emerge, and only under such conditions can one expect it to be maintained.

Corporal punishment can contribute only in a very limited

way to the establishment or maintenance of self-discipline, and if used to excess or as an exclusive method of control it will actually prevent the establishment of inner controls in the child. The reasons are not hard to see. First, corporal punishment exemplifies for the child the "person-directed" aggression that he is himself trying desperately to give up—to curb this aggression, indeed, is one of the major tasks in development we have set for him. Second, it shows him that people when frustrated can be hurtful and not at all the model of humanity that parents and teachers say they wish *him* to be. In store for the corporal punisher is an equally unhealthy fate in that he himself regresses and falls victim to the impulse to personalize his aggressive tendencies and thereby suffers the attendant feelings of guilt. Such an infantile expression also sets up within him a neurotic cycle; he must justify the corporal punishment by noting, even seeking, proof that such was "needed," and, once convinced, he tends to justify further punishment of a like sort. In the relationship of the parent or the teacher and the child, these regressions and cycles in respect to control through physical punishments can block the hoped-for development of the individual child. In the more complex societal relationships of groups of mankind dealing with their fellows, justification of these neurotic needs gives us the gas chamber and the electric chair!

Only discipline or punishment applied in the context of felt and expressed love can lead to *self*-control and *self*-discipline. Even if one wanted to, one could not impose on the child unwavering compliance with the demands of society. One can only construct a setting and arrange sequences of fruitful and pleasurable consequences that eventually will lead the child to *prefer* a disciplined life, a life that conforms to the justified and beneficial demands society makes upon him.

QUESTIONS

Mrs. _____: Have you any set rules as to when spanking is justified?

Dr. G.: I hope I don't have any *set* rules about anything. We must try to see each child as an individual, and that approach is just the opposite of having *set* rules. I will agree that there are times when spanking is indicated. You reason with a child and assure yourself that he has heard and comprehended. Then if he persists in doing something that is going to harm him or somebody else, I think a bit of a spanking may be in order. I think most parents do try to reason with the child up to that point of utter exasperation where as human beings they can take no more. But hurting the child physically cannot be condoned at any time.

Mrs. _____: Doesn't it get to a point where spanking doesn't do any good? I've had occasion to see one boy in our neighborhood who should know very well what he should and shouldn't do, but he does half of these things to attract his mother's attention. She'll tell him, "If you do it again, I will whack you." So he does it immediately. She whacks him, but he doesn't learn a thing.

Dr. G.: What do you mean by "whack"?

Mrs. _____: Well, she slaps him in the face. Sometimes she even knocks him down. He will scream. Maybe he'll be put in his room for five minutes, but then she can't stand the noise of the screaming so he'll come out and do exactly the same thing. This goes on and on and on.

Dr. G.: I think this is an individual case where they have got themselves locked in an aggression-counteraggression bind and neither one is able to give way. Children will attempt all kinds of strategies to bring their parents under their control. This drive for control is an attempt to cling as long as possible to those feelings of omnipotence which are engendered in the child in early infancy. Those were the days, remember, when all of his demands and needs actually were met, and had to be met, by the parents. Some parents allow them to get away with it because they are afraid of hurting them or of damaging their own worth in the mind of the child.

Then there is the child who seems to be asking for punishment. He will set up a situation where almost certainly he is going to get punished and then he will feel better. It takes care of his feelings of guilt. Often nothing will stop a child from harming himself, from disrupting the whole family or actually hurting somebody else unless you make it "sting" a little. Spanking is not the punishment of choice, but I don't think the parent who resorts to it once in a while should be tagged as a poor parent. There are many parents who feel that if they resort to spanking the child they are admitting defeat, because they have not been able to find another means of handling the situation. I don't believe that's true.

Mrs. _____: You mention the child who "asks" for a spanking to relieve his guilt. If the mother complies doesn't this set up a vicious cycle? Shouldn't the child learn to handle these feelings in another way?

Dr. G.: Of course, we would hope so. This guilt, by the way, is often for things the child doesn't tell you about. It is for actions he *feels* were naughty. Sometimes we see this in children we call "accident-prone." The child harms himself unconsciously as a means of self-punishment for undetected acts or unexpressed thoughts and feelings that he has learned are "bad" and deserving of punishment.

Mrs. _____: I recently read an article about the child who misbehaves in order to get attention. It suggested a remedy that I've tried with some success. When a small child does something he's been told not to, a mother is apt to go over and spank him only to see him go right back and do it again. Some go over to him and say, "Mommy really doesn't like you to do that and I wish you wouldn't do it again." Either way, he sees that she is really upset—he's found a way to get to her. If you can manage not to dash in but to call from afar in a calm voice, it seems to take away some of the enjoyment because he hasn't been able to make you drop everything and pay attention to him. I tried this with my three-year-old. It took a while, but when he saw this seeming disinterest, that I really didn't get all hot and bothered chasing around the house after him, he seemed to forget a lot of his mischievousness.

Dr. G.: I think mothers after a while pick up a certain indifference. You cannot follow a child around every minute of the day, spanking his hand hour after hour. I think some indifference is a good thing as long as it is not doing the child any harm. Of course, you cannot be indifferent if they're pulling the plug out of the wall or running their hand along the electric light fixtures and things like that.

Mrs. _____: I heard about a test done at some nursery school. They had two groups of children and a fire engine that everybody was very interested in. They said to one group, "If you play with this fire engine you will be punished —no juice or stories." All sorts of threats. They took the other group aside and said, "If you play with this fire engine it will make all the teachers very unhappy. We really wish you wouldn't do it." They repeated this for several days. The group that had been told they were not allowed to play with it kept going back to the fire engine, picking it up, and playing with it. The group that had the milder sort of approach didn't seem to bother with it. It was really striking.

Dr. G.: You mean the more intense the prohibition, the more they persisted? It's an interesting story. A mild prohibition is often more effective than a strong threat, particularly when the adult states his reason for feeling the way he does. The child then has something to understand and incorporate. A threat can only remain discipline from the outside.

Mrs. _____: Does anyone ever use *that* certain tone of voice anymore? I remember my mother had what you would call her "dangerous voice." When I heard it, I knew without question what it meant!

Mrs. _____: My oldest child is almost four. She plays with a group of older children. I find she holds up very well outdoors, but when she comes in, she seems very tired and very frustrated. The least little thing sets her off and everything seems to be wrong. Either I haven't prepared her a lunch that is attractive or I haven't done this or I haven't done that. I just can't seem to satisfy her in any way. I have wondered whether it is primarily because she works so hard to keep up with these older playmates that she is exhausted and frustrated.

Dr. G.: It's hard for me to relate her behavior to the fact that she plays with older children. I don't know what the relation between those two would be.

Mrs. _____: If I reprimand her for anything, she deliberately picks up something that she shouldn't. I feel that I can't just overlook these things, yet I am not quite sure where to draw the line.

Dr. G.: You should try to get at her underlying feelings. What is she trying to prove?

Mrs. _____: I wonder if she is trying to get my attention. She has been outdoors with her friends, and now maybe when she comes in she wants my undivided attention. This may be the way she goes about getting it.

Dr. G.: As we have said, children will do most anything to get attention. Even if they have to do something naughty, they still want the attention—positive or negative. And I think, too, that this sort of attention getting is something that lasts with some people throughout their lives. All of us are pretty narcissistic in some way or other. We see people who have to keep proving that they are liked by people, and they do it by getting their attention, good or bad. Perhaps you might try seizing the offensive by initiating a pleasant conversation with your daughter as she comes into the house.

She may need and crave some time with you after she's been out on her own with other children.

Mrs. _____: I have just the opposite problem. My daughter gets too much attention! She was born when my husband was fifty years old, his only child. He had no children in a previous marriage. He is very indulgent. Our pediatrician suggested that nursery school would be a fine idea because there are no other children in the household. When she's with me or our housekeeper, she's fine, but the minute he walks in the door her behavior changes.

Dr. G.: How old is she?

Mrs. _____: She's two and a half. When her father is around she starts whining. If she doesn't get her way she starts crying instantly. When she goes to bed it takes her hours to go to sleep. It's a nightmare! She'll call, "Daddy!" and no matter what I say, he'll run right in to her. He has tried sleeping with her for an hour or so. He tries to reason with her, but he says she is so bright that she outreasons him. His constant attention just prolongs the problem. What I want to know is whether I should allow this to go on or should I put my foot down. When I speak to him, he'll say, "See, Judy, if you don't get into bed, Mamma's going to spank you." Now, right away I become the witch!

Dr. G.: How much time does your husband get to spend with her?

Mrs. _____: Not very much. Here's how it all started. When she was an infant he used to get home around 11:00 at night. He would wake her up then. Now he gets home earlier. If he's late, she'll go to sleep. She won't come out of the room or make a big fuss or cry. She'll just lie there and go to sleep. She'll sing but fall asleep easily. When he's home, she cries and carries on. I have always felt that when the husband's home his word should be law and there should be no disputing, but this is too much.

Dr. G.: From what you say I take it that your husband

loves his daughter very much. I think it's tough to shut off the father's expression of affection for his child, but maybe he could keep it within bounds. I should tell you that this situation may get a little worse before it gets better. There comes the time, you know, at four or five when children battle for the affection of the parent of the opposite sex. This is a perfectly normal stage of development. One thing I would say is that no parent should put the other parent in a bad light. "Your mother is going to come in and spank you" shifts all the responsibility to the other parent. What does your pediatrician say about the question of upsetting the child's routine?

Mrs. _____: He told my husband, "Your wife has done a wonderful job so far. But if you don't learn to hold back a little bit and leave the child asleep when she's gone to sleep, she'll begin to be a problem."

Dr. G.: It seems that the pediatrician probably knows more about the family situation than I do, and he seems to be giving sensible advice. So you should continue to encourage your husband to accept what the pediatrician has had to say.

Mrs. _____: One other thing, is it really a good idea to talk about a child in front of her?

Dr. G.: Oh, I think it can be done with moderation. It's best to talk about their good points, although boasting of their wonderful accomplishments in development might be done at another time. You can get just as much enjoyment from talking alone together as you can having the child there. Some people, you know, are very reticent about praising a child in front of the child. No old New England family would praise a child in his presence! They would insist they *expect* these wonderful things of him! Praise should always be kept on a realistic level, of course. Otherwise, the child gets the feeling that you'll be terribly disappointed if he's ever anything less than unusual.

Mrs. _____: My question goes back to an earlier period. From generation to generation, there are usually large swings of opinion on specific matters of child rearing. Do you feed on demand or on schedule, for example, and how soon do you pick up the baby when he cries? Do you spank or don't you spank? How does one learn to strike a good balance without frustrating the baby so much as to shake his basic trust, or lead him to believe someone will always jump the moment he squawks?

Dr. G.: I need not tell mothers that there have been two rather extreme theories in relation to child-rearing practices. At one extreme, there is the suggestion that from the very first there should be a rigid approach, that the child should be put on a fixed schedule, devised and exacted by the mother, and that he should be made to adhere to it. It is held by advocates of this school that only in this way can the child's respect for the parents' rules and controls be established, to leave him with a strong sense of the authority and discipline of others in society, such as the schoolteacher, his boss, and the policeman.

This program of child training was exceedingly popular with psychologists and child-development specialists in the 1920s and 1930s. Most pediatricians will remember that they were expected to pass on this point of view as they endeavored to advise mothers in their private practices and in the rapidly growing well-baby clinics. I should say, too, that many mothers were made to feel unhappy—and perhaps even to feel inadequate as mothers. Their own inner feelings just wouldn't allow them to "demand" of their babies and children such rigid adherence to schedules and rules.

Then came an abrupt change, an about-face, on allegedly scientific grounds. This change came about in the same way women's fashions change, usually going to the extreme opposite. There was no gradualism. Hence, the emphasis in the 1940s and 1950s was on nonscheduled feedings and on minimal attention to rules, regulations, expectations, discipline, and parental demands. As you remember, it was the era of demand feeding, and it was felt that the child could and would "train himself." Many mothers tried religiously to follow these permissive practices, but many had misgivings, even feelings of guilt about such a hands-off and seemingly unconcerned attitude.

Stirrings of revolt among the mothers of those two contradictory periods and among their successors in the 1960s have led to a modification of the extremes. This compromise has come about, I feel, because we have observed the day-after-day successes or failures of the methods and because we have listened to the concerns and feelings of parents as they endeavored to apply either of these two general systems. The result is that we now take a middle-of-the-road position in respect to demands, rules, regulations, and discipline.

It is clear to us all that we wish the child to receive the notion from the mother and father that he is to follow certain routines and practices when his maturity makes it possible for him to do so with understanding. Parental behavior that leads the child to assume that he himself has the freedom to follow or not to follow these reasonable rules or regulations prepares him poorly for the important developmental steps he must take.

I should call to your attention—and I hope your experience will bear me out—that if we, as parents, by our free and unconcerned attitude put a low level of value on the child's achievement or self-regulation, we are really depriving him of the satisfactions of achievement that he has a right to know. An "I don't-care" or "it-doesn't-mean-anything-to-me" attitude in respect to these achievements does not help him to establish within himself that all-important motivation for achievement that we hope will give meaning and zest to his life.

It seems to me that the best course in child rearing lies somewhere between the two extremes outlined, in respect to freedom versus rules, regulations, and discipline. Much of the difference in approach to our own children will be determined by our feelings as parents—feelings determined within us by the social and cultural inheritance we derived from our own past lives. My greatest hope, and my earnest suggestion, is that you follow a course that will leave you, as a parent, with a minimum of concern and guilt, regardless of what we experts may say. I hope that our discussions together will indicate that I am a Jeffersonian in these matters; that is to say, to the extent that Thomas Jefferson urged us forever to "trust the people," so do I as a professional trust mothers and fathers of babies and developing children. It may be that there is an occasional need for advice and counsel, but there is an even greater need to follow day-to-day events with your children and to make your own decisions about how best to guide them. No group of scientists could have a more accurate check on their hypotheses and deductions than do parents who live with their children.

Mrs. _____: In a very young child how do you recognize behavior that points to trouble ahead? Is a particularly stubborn child or a child very hard to train destined for trouble in later years?

Dr. G.: There are some predictive studies. Drs. Eleanor and Sheldon Glueck of Harvard University have made intensive studies in an effort to predict which child will become delinquent. They have worked out a series of predictive scales. They have interested themselves in preschool youngsters and tried to identify the constellation of factors in the family and the child's environment that may predispose him to trouble. They studied the development of children who became delinquents, and on the basis of case histories and the parents' recollections they came up with a number of factors that seemed to occur again and again in the backgrounds of delinquent children. None of them had anything to do with stubbornness, I might add quickly. The broken home, persistent enuresis, early school truancy, a tendency toward hyperactivity, and a short attention span in precision learning were some of the conditions cited. The

Gluecks' study in New York City is still in progress. The initial results seem to indicate that their prediction scales are of great value. They are following children for ten years. All along the line they watch for these factors, and they have made predictions as to whether or not the children in the survey seem to be headed for real trouble. As far as I know, stubbornness, temper tantrums, or behavior like that don't appear in their scale of criteria. Furthermore, it's not the individual child's actions alone that are important but the environment to which he may be responding.

When I was in the Navy in World War II, we were getting large numbers of youngsters in the draft who within two or three months landed in the brig. They just wouldn't obey the rules. The Navy began to get worried about this great wastage. We collected a sample of 700 men who within six months of coming into the Navy had been sent to the brig and had appeared before the Naval courts. We had no family histories except what they gave us. We also studied 200 men who had been in the Navy for two years or more without being charged with even the slightest offense. We, too, came up with some interesting predictive findings, many of which were identical with those found in the Glueck studies.

There are definite traits and behavioral trends to be concerned about if they seem to continue into the middle-school years. One would be a continuation of person directed aggression.

Mrs. _____: You read so much in the papers today about criminals who were recognized as disturbed children but whose families ignored these early childhood signs. Everybody seems to remember them. I don't understand why something wasn't done if there were signs that were noticeable.

Dr. G.: Well, this takes in the whole field of prevention. I suppose that's why we're here. There will be more and more preventive work done in this regard. First, you have to have more and more accurate predictive scales of the kind I just mentioned so you can spot the vulnerable child with a high degree of certainty. Then you must try to surround this vulnerable child with an environment that can give him a decent relationship with people and a good start in life to modify or eliminate this vulnerability. Much more emphasis on early diagnosis and treatment is needed, but the best approach to prevention is to have more parents who are aware of what goes on in a child, who recognize the signs that indicate whether orderly growth and maturation is taking place or not.

No other single problem in child development concerns parents more deeply than the control of aggressive behavior. And it has been so throughout the ages. The task of the parent today in respect to the control of physical aggression is made even more difficult by social factors impinging upon the child. The parent has little or no control over many of these events. I refer here to the day-after-day discussion and depiction of violence by the communications media. That this violence is extant is obvious, and that the communications media must of necessity report upon it is also obvious. But neither the existence of violence nor the reporting of it makes the task of the parent any easier. Models depicting both aggression and methods of expressing it tend to weaken or destroy the best parental models and damage the non-aggressive relationships that we expect between members of the family.

An outbreak of violence in the community holds important lessons for all of us who are interested in child development. We are witnessing the adverse social effects that come from the feelings of insecurity that children have whose homes have been rendered inadequate and unstable or indeed have been broken by harsh economic conditions and inequalities. If you compound these familial insecurities of both the parents and the children by superimposing upon them the additional insecurities arising from the harshness of the world beyond the home and the local community, then you can look for physical violence. When parents and young adults resort to violence, they create the models that much younger children will follow. The results of this unhappy cycle have now become apparent to us all.

If we are to break this cycle, we must find a way to modify the existing insecurities of both the parents and the children and to prevent recurrence of the same feelings of hopeless inadequacy. Since insecurities develop from both influences inside the home and influences outside the home, a program along a broad front of social and economic action is called for.

III. THE AGE OF
MASTERY

5

Developmental Tasks Between Six and Twelve

THE PERIOD of childhood between age six and the beginning of adolescence was best described by Professor Ives Hendrik as the "period of mastery." This description alludes to the child's increasing ability to cope with his physical environment. He is also at this time becoming more aware of his own inner desires and impulses and the fact that they lead him to behave in ways that evoke both very positive and very negative responses in the people around him. In short, it is a period in which he gathers an enormous number of facts with which he can improve his ability to control both his inner and outer worlds.

The mastery of his environment is achieved, in the main, through his everyday experiences and observations, by trial and error, and through the admonitions he hears from the adults in his life. He now begins to have a greater appreciation of the complexities that surround him and is able to respond more appropriately to them.

It is during these years that the child makes his greatest strides forward as a social being. He learns that rules and regulations, now so important in his work at school, also play a large part in his relationship to other people. He comes to know which of his actions will be accepted with praise, which only tolerated or met with indifference, and which are sure to bring immediate punishment. He also learns the more subtle distinctions about the appropriate time and place for certain kinds of behavior. Some actions are fine at home but frowned on in the outside world.

There has been a marked change in his play and in the way he relates to his peers. He wants and needs companionship. Sharing and taking turns can be tolerated more easily. He knows the rules of the game now and wants them adhered to—most of the time—because he feels they guarantee fairness. And through the medium of the game and its rules he begins to get some idea of how he compares with his friends in his ability to play the game. It is here that the competitive spirit in its most constructive sense flourishes.

The road that leads the child away from solitary, ego-centric play to participatory and more organized or rule-governed play is a road fraught with frustrations, partial joys, and momentary miseries. It requires patience on the part of parents, and indeed on the part of companions, and the child himself.

It is at this time that the shift from what we have called "romantic learning" to "precision learning" takes place. As the child progresses in school, this type of learning becomes his "work"—analogous, in terms of fixed demands and expectations, to the work of the adult. In the past century and a quarter, various methods have been instituted to make this "work" less onerous and rigid and more palatable. Most of these successful attempts have tried to conserve and extend the exciting aspects—the creativity and spontaneity—inherent in the "romantic learning" of earlier childhood.

Here, again, the insights the child has gained regarding rules and regulations establish within him ways of approaching and thinking through the problems he will encounter in school. The ability that allows people to look over or supervise the quality of their thinking and to make certain they are indeed thinking "straight" will burgeon in the child during these years.

The years a child spends in elementary school may represent a calm between the somewhat stormy preschool years and the turbulent times we associate with adolescence. He will probably be on a more even keel—more at peace with the world. Important developmental growth *is* taking place, but the changes are more subtle than in other years.

Now, what are some of the problems and stresses of the age group six to twelve? By this time, I suppose, you may be getting the notion that our world is the worst of all possible worlds for children. I am not so sure that is how I feel about it, but I do know, and you do, too, that for them it's not the happiest of all happy worlds. As adults we tend to look back upon childhood as being in the child's view a very happy state of affairs. But to a little fellow, or a little girl, in a great big world with great big people all around telling him what to do, what to eat, when to go to bed, when to get up, telling him this and that, it's not always all that pleasant. Big people are supposed to be omnipotent—so they think.

Everywhere a child turns in our society today there's an agent of death waiting for him. He is warned and warned and warned again. There is always the electric light plug or the high window. When he goes outside, there is always the car that may roar down on him out of control. In actuality, it is a world that is quite terrifying for him, and he not only senses the perils but also hears about them all the time. It is difficult today to picture a situation where there would not be some danger near at hand. You are aware of this reality, and he soon becomes aware, too. He has to learn something about these dangers for his self-protection.

When it comes to dealing with these stresses and dangers, parents are always beset with a conflict. If they spend all their time keeping the child out of danger and never allow him to experiment or follow where his curiosity leads, he probably is not going to develop much independence. More likely, he will become completely dependent upon others for an external type of control.

The other side of the coin brings problems, too. If parents allow him to climb picket fences and trees, rush into the water when he goes to the beach, learn how to work the stop lights in the street, if he enjoys a great deal of freedom of expression without much supervision, then he runs the risk of being hurt. It's a difficult life no matter which way you turn. You need to find some kind of balance between the two extremes. You cannot completely thwart the child. But neither can you allow him to get himself into a position of danger. So, much of the life of a parent, I think, is concerned with this single problem. How much freedom shall I allow this child? How much should I guard him against the possibility of danger?

One way to learn about something is to compare its differences and similarities with other things. These are the years of the great comparison. Children are constantly comparing themselves with someone else. A boy is distressed because the boy next door is one-half inch taller, or has larger muscles, or can run faster, or throw a ball farther. And so it goes, day after day. You can tell from children's talk that they are always comparing their physical habits and appearance, their strength and endurance with others of their peer group. This continuous accounting of physical assets and disabilities is a worrying preoccupation, I think, of all youngsters. In a single group there can be at most only one child of nine who surpasses physically all the other nine-year-olds. And if his travels take him outside this group, even he, sooner or later, will encounter some nine-year-old whose genetic determinants have made him taller or huskier still. Hence, there is always somebody somewhere who will give the child the feeling of physical inferiority.

Just as the child is always comparing himself physically with his siblings and with other children of the same sex and age group, so also does he draw comparisons in regard to his mental abilities. This comparison appears, of course, the very first time children are in competition with other children. It does not take a child in the first or second grade long to know that the boy in the front seat in the first row is always the one who has everything right. He always has the arithmetic problems done first, and most often correctly. Then there's another child in the third row who can draw well or write well, and one somewhere else who not only can answer the teacher's questions, but also can ask the right questions himself, and who manages to demonstrate in every way that he is very, very bright indeed. And, of course, there is the ever-present yardstick, the report card.

The comparison of mental abilities goes on apace year after year, and children begin to have feelings about where they stand alongside other children. They soon learn who is "the stupid one." They learn, too, that there are geniuses in the world. They know that there are children who may not be mentally retarded but who have certain emotional difficulties. We often hear that children are cruel and overly critical of others. Much of the derision that takes place is really an attempt to allay the derider's own anxieties and should so be understood when it comes to disciplining the one who appears to be cruel.

Some children seem to feel deprived, and indeed they are, of certain material or emotional benefits. Here again the individual child compares himself to his siblings or to the boy or girl next door. I am sure you all have heard these complaints from time to time. Within the family, there is always a measuring of this, or a looking at that, comparing it to what they have. This sense of deprivation may not be at all realistic, of course, but children are very sensitive to the fact that they may be quantitatively and perhaps qualitatively less loved than their siblings. They may be concerned that *their* father or mother loves them less than the child down the street is loved. There are many children who fear that something is going to happen within the family group and they will be deprived physically—deprived of food or clothing or warmth. Many of the stories that we have them read or allow them to watch on TV tend to increase this fear, or at least tend to suggest the possibility of this deprivation. Of course, the stories usually come out all right, but even when they do, the child still wonders. What would happen if things didn't turn out right?

The child's continuing comparison of himself and other children of the same age is generated in two ways: First, his own observations lead him to the realization that there are differences, marked or subtle. Second, the urge to excel is soon established as a very important motivation. Within it are the basic ingredients of a constructive competitive spirit.

Many parents tend to use comparisons to motivate excellence in behavior and accomplishment. They are quick to point out to Johnny that Jimmy, the same age, already can tie his own shoes. They may even make the derogatory generalization, "*All* children your age can tie their own shoes. Why can't you?" So the criteria he sees employed to judge adequate behavior, achievements, and even "goodness" become a frame of reference in the child's mind. Thus, when a child takes his place within a new group of children, or indeed becomes acquainted with a new companion, it is not without significance that almost the first question put to or by the newcomer is, "How old are you?" The answer immedi-

ately sets in motion the inevitable comparisons. If he measures up, literally and figuratively, he is content. If he does
not, he tries to close the gap by practice or by demonstrating
other skills that his companion or group has not yet acquired.

There is a positive side to all this comparing. It is of no
small importance in aiding the child to sense his adequacies,
and it also assists him to maintain within himself the very
important concept of self-identity.

Up the scale of stress in the later elementary school years,
the fear of disgrace makes its appearance. If children do
not live up to certain codes set for them by parents and
society, they have a feeling of guilt. They feel disgraced in
the eyes of other people who are significant to them. If the
stress is great enough, they may worry that there will be
nobody left who loves them since they must be defective in
some way.

I cite these stresses because they impinge not only upon
children but upon us all. Their great destructive potential,
I think, is their continuation as threats. They may not be
voiced, except from time to time, but they remain as threats
because they have something to do basically with continued
existence. The way these stresses are interpreted inside us, in
the deeper regions or recesses of the mind, if you will, in
the unconscious, has a definite physiological reference. It
is the reaction of the newborn baby who yells in terror when
he is not fed. He is in genuine panic. It is some kind of instinctive, inborn recognition of danger. It is one of nature's
signals.

I have mentioned that the usual reaction to threats or
stresses is a regressive one. People under threat or in crisis
tend always to revert to a lower level of organization of
behavior. Now in nature's scheme this may be all to the
good, but the fact remains that momentarily at least it can
be disabling. We have mentioned the child who regresses
at the impact of a new child coming into the family. This
same tendency to act more simply, more directly, with much

less reference to the consequences, tends to occur when any crisis arises. Afterward, it may take a few minutes, a few days, or even a few months to resume the progress toward maturity. For example, if someone attacks you or your child physically, your first impulse is to reply with a physical blow. If you are insulted by somebody, there is the same tendency to resort to a much lower level of response than normal for you. Very often you are able to stop short, having regressed momentarily but been able to collect yourself. But if you think, "I'll insult him right back," and proceed to hunt for the most cutting insult, you are operating at a lower level of organization than you had attained before the incident. The regression is not, of course, as far back as a physical response to threat or stress would have been, but there's always this vulnerability, this disposition to be pulled back into infancy, to a lower level of response. The tendency to regress is particularly strong if some of the stages of development have been skipped. There is a tendency to go back to the one point where gratification was absent altogether or was not commensurate with what would have been appropriate to that age level.

Now that we have looked at some of the existent external forces surrounding our school-age child, let's talk about some of the specific tasks in development he faces during this period.

All parents who have observed their children carefully through the various stages of development will agree, I think, that the child's ever-increasing power to control his aggressive tendencies toward his parents, siblings, and playmates is the outstanding feature in his growth. And there is nothing more alarming to the parent than to note that this expected control is not appearing.

In the first place, as the child gets older there must be a modification of the *aim* of his aggression. In the early years, it is aimed primarily at destroying, eliminating, or causing damage to the body or to the possessions of another person. There must be a gradual replacement of these destructive aims by a more socially *acceptable* form of protest. We cannot ask the child to repress his anger but rather to cope with it in a more impersonal manner. The soldiers, cowboys, gangsters, and supermen begin to appear in the play of most boys around age five and are easily recognized as examples of this partial modification of the child's destructive aims through his use of fantasy. It represents the phase, or stage, in the child's life when he is beginning to learn to control his aggression.

Coupled with this change in the direction of increased fantasy and less overtly destructive play, there is an increase in the aim to *master*—not destroy—the people around him. He tries to make them do his bidding—to overcome the frustrations and blocks and limitations they place in his way. In short, a desire for—or aim toward—*mastery* replaces the aim to destroy or damage. Here we see emerging the elements of constructive and worthwhile aggression.

The second and at least equally important change in the character of aggressive behavior in children is the accomplishment of the gradual *impersonalization* of the *object* against which the child is hostile or aggressive. Previously the child directed his aggression against the people in his world about him. They were the *objects* of his hostility that he wished to harm, eliminate, or punish. But just as the *aim* of aggression changes from destruction to mastery, so also does the *object* of these aims change from *persons* to *things*. A frustrating event, a set of circumstances, or inanimate objects gradually replace people as the focus of the child's aggression.

Now, it is important for us to understand how or in what circumstances this orderly and hoped-for development takes place so that we may prevent unfortunate deviations or delays in the development of our children as they endeavor to control and use their aggressive impulses. As I said before, we don't know the detailed *how* of the process, but we have a fairly definite idea of the climate, or milieu, in which the child will best be able to develop along these lines. We recognize in the light of repeated case histories and intensive study of children at all levels of development that primitive, aggressive responses can be modified in the manner we have outlined above *only* when the child senses he is not in danger. If the infant—or even the school child or the adolescent, for that matter—senses a lack of love or interest or a feeling of hostility or rejection on the part of the most important people in his environment, the destructive aspects of aggression are called forth. The actual or implied threat of desertion, bodily harm, or emotional deprivation will not only *block* the development of the child in this area but also tend to undo those advances he has already made. In the latter case, destructive-aggressive acts directed against actual *persons* will continue. It is not at all difficult to observe this reaction in a child whose anxiety or sense of danger is aroused by a feeling of insecurity. I might note in passing that the insecurity we speak of most often results from the aggressive-destructive acts of others—parental hostility, punishment, coldness, or rejection.

Paradoxically enough, this more primitive, destructive, person-directed aggression cannot be given up or changed except in a family environment that makes them feel secure. The danger that negative, hostile feelings may replace positive and warm, loving relations with their parents makes for an anxiety that keeps them tied to their old "defensive" aggressive responses and inhibits attempts to find or develop newer ways of handling their feelings. In short, learning and development tend to cease or slow down in such a milieu.

Those of us who are now adults know that this control of aggression is a continually reappearing task. We ourselves have to work at it each day in our relations with other people.

We continually have to modify our aggressive wishes toward others so that we do not hurt them, and this inhibition requires finding new outlets of a nonpersonal nature for our aggression. Particularly in relation to our own children in their most "pestiferous" moments, we have to keep in constant check our hostile words and actions. It goes without saying that we are, again, the models on which our children pattern their behavior. Every mother is brought up short now and again when she hears her child use a phrase or tone of voice that she knows is her own. I am not encouraging parents to deny or stifle their angry feelings—children always sense when someone is really upset anyway—but rather that they make a real effort to express them in ways that will have a constructive effect on the child.

When he came into this "period of mastery" from the previous phase, the child brought with him, as we have seen, one of his most important developmental tasks. He has yet to find or achieve a satisfactory resolution of the close attachment to his parent of the opposite sex. It is not necessary to emphasize that these Oedipal stirrings cannot ever be fulfilled. A boy cannot own and control his mother, nor can a girl look on her father as the *unshared* object of her love. The parent must reject these impulses, and the child often feels hostile and may behave aggressively toward the parent he sees as his rival.

This drama is played out in each generation, and though the child is fated to lose and must give up his intentions, it is very important that this intrafamily struggle be resolved in a constructive manner, so that it furthers his development. There seem to be at least three aspects of this resolution that constitute a constructive outcome:

First, the child should emerge from the Oedipal stage, albeit a "loser," without a severe sense of loss of prestige. He must feel that his worth in the eyes of both parents and others in the family is firmly established.

Second, the child should make a strong and binding identification with those of his own sex, and this identification must be free from fear and anxiety.

Third, although it is hoped that the post-Oedipal child will identify more and more with his own biological role, it is hoped that thereafter he will continue to have a "healthy bisexuality." By this I mean that the boy child will incorporate the male spirit of competition, or aggression, if you will, but will also retain the female components of tenderness and of compassion for the helpless that he acquired in his primary identification with his mother. The post-Oedipal girl, we hope, will retain the best elements of her identification with both sexes. Her ability to be warm, tender, and caring yet able to act aggressively and purposefully when the need arises is the goal we would like to see her attain. I hasten to add that "healthy bisexuality" as a personality structure has nothing to do with homosexuality! It does have much to do with the eventual satisfactory adjustment each of us must make in our later interpersonal relationships.

In the years immediately following the resolution of this task a sharp division between the sexes takes place. Girls and boys repudiate one another almost completely. This is thought to be an overreaction in the attempt to demonstrate in no uncertain terms that the required or expected sexual-role identification has indeed taken place. Again, it is hoped that beneath this outward demonstration of division, the best personality ingredients of each sex are retained.

Further resolution of this task will take place in adolescence, but it is essential that these beginning struggles occur at this time.

As the child gets older his fantasies don't disappear but their character changes rather markedly. In the school-age child we begin to see what we refer to as the "achievement fantasy." This fantasy can be based in the here and now, as when the child sees himself demonstrating in some current undertaking the great skill that will convince others—

parents, teachers, or friends—of his tremendous competence or strength. The pleasurable feelings that accompany even the thought of performing such feats is exciting in and of itself. Such a fantasy can cover anything from learning the secrets of multiplication to hitting the winning home run in the Little League game.

And then there are the fantasies for the future. These are usually based on the great things he "knows" he will do as an adult. Very often they stem from his admiration for or identification with a certain adult. Now he dreams not just of starring in tomorrow's game but rather of being a famous baseball star—an idol of fathers and sons alike. At four he may have thought of himself as Superman, but by the time he is ten he is more apt to dream of the super *man* he'll be someday. His willingness to stick with the "boring" facts at school may be founded on his fantasies of needing those facts when he is "doctor, lawyer, or merchant chief." This type of fantasy helps him to accept certain realities even though he knows that years separate him from the day when the actual achievement will replace the dream. It is common for these thoughts to change—sometimes every few days —in childhood. All children play many roles, but as time goes on the fantasy becomes more realistic and in keeping with the child's abilities. These dreams of things to come play a powerful part in a child's motivation to learn.

It is important to recognize that the child cannot indulge in either of these fantasies—present or future—if he is beset by anxiety. If he is deeply concerned and anxious about his home situation, his parents' love for him or for each other, their preference for a sibling, illness in the family, fears, guilt, or a host of other worries, he is more likely to take recourse in another fantasy system. He will not dwell on possible achievement but rather on the pleasurable day-dreaming that will reduce his anxieties and remove him from the real world in which he lives. In short, he cannot attend to the tasks at hand because of the inhibiting and distorting elements in his anxiety and cannot, therefore, achieve a happy solution of what needs to be done. The energy generated within him by the achievement fantasy cannot make its way through the overlay of his worry.

The development of a "property sense"—the ability to recognize and respect the difference between "mine and thine"—is consolidated in the early school years, and it raises the old issue of stealing. Even for those of us who have been comparatively lucky in life, it is easy to imagine the longings that rack a severely deprived child when he sees desperately longed-for toys in a store window, on a TV commercial or, perhaps worst of all, in the hands of another his own age. Deprivation of even the simplest pleasures of childhood or of all but the barest essentials for living is undoubtedly the most powerful factor in the failure to acquire a strict sense of ownership. A clear-cut property sense will come late to the child who has been deprived. His grasp of it may be shaky and subject to occasional breakdown throughout his entire life. Though it by no means follows that only those children who suffered marked deprivation steal, it is easily demonstrable that most of the stealing by children and adults is carried out by those who during childhood suffered either material or emotional deprivation. A home where love is in short supply can be as devastating as poverty. To my mind, a child who suffers both forms of deprivation is the most likely candidate to become the juvenile and adult larcenist.

It can certainly be presumed that some of the looting that accompanies many of the episodes of violence in our inner cities occurs as the culmination of years of deep feeling about impoverishment. The final breakdown, in an otherwise and hitherto honest citizen, of that fragile property sense may come when his frustrations over not being able to attain what he has a legal right to have become unbearable.

To look beyond this milieu of deprivation for the failure of a child to develop a strong property sense, one has to look at two other important factors: One is the primitive, but very important, meaning of material objects to an infant and young child—meanings that must undergo a change as he grows older. The other is the unconscious meaning of the impulses associated with the *act* of stealing.

In the primitive thought processes of a small child, objects are felt to be a part of, or indeed an extension of, the person's body and a means of power for action. The stick in his hand, for example, is viewed as an extension of his arm and its power is considered to be his. Stealing the belongings of others may then be seen as an attack upon the person of the owner. Again, unquestionably, a portion of the present-day violence and destruction of property in street and university demonstrations is a conscious or at best an unconscious attack upon the persons of the establishments who control these properties.

We have seen that young children tend to equate love with the number of gifts they are given. If these material objects are missing it is interpreted as a harbinger of the loss or lack of love. In the face of threatened deprivation of parental love and affection, the child may steal as a substitute for the emotional gifts he feels he has been denied. It is in this context that most stealing by children under ten years of age takes place.

When a child psychiatrist is called on to consider the problem of a child who steals, he will need to ask an important question: "Does the child steal solely at home or does he steal from those who are not members of his family group?" If the theft is confined within the family, some attention to the balance and benefits accruing to the child and his siblings is in order. It may be that the shifting of this balance will see an end to the problem. Stealing beyond the home may also have symbolic or emotional roots, particularly if the stolen objects have little or no value to the child or when the object stolen is always the same. Today our more sophisticated juvenile court judges utilize the sound psychological principle that if stealing "just doesn't make sense" the child needs to be evaluated in a clinical setting.

Clinical observations of the child who fails to develop or who shows a marked delay in mastering this developmental task usually suggest three different possible explanations:

First, the act of stealing is a highly charged emotional act. It is charged with feelings of fear not unlike those that accompany acts of a sexual nature which are punishable. The thrill—today we would say "kick"—that either juvenile or adult delinquents claim accompany both the detailed preparations for stealing and the execution of the forbidden act are by no means markedly different from the thrills associated with the preparation, planning, and execution of prohibited sexual activities. Perhaps, then, some stealing at all ages is a thinly disguised substitute for the sexual drive.

A second possibility is that stealing, with its expected consequent punishment, may be the resort of persons who have a need to be punished for their guilt feelings related to other thoughts, impulses, and activities. These people set the stage deliberately—albeit unconsciously!—to elicit punishment. The weight of punishment for guilt is great, and it can be evoked for activities seemingly far removed from those that initially created the guilt. The surest method of provoking punishment for unconscious guilt, the causes of which may not be at all understood, is to use a well-known route to severe censure. Stealing almost always incurs punishment by an outside authority, and very often the person who steals will arrange to be caught.

In the third place, the *act* of stealing may be motivated by the inner cry of "Save me," that is, "Save me from acting out impulses of an even more aggressive or forbidden nature." This individual may be quite depressed and filled with many doubts of his own worth or his ability to "save" himself.

These are some of the complexities involved in establishing within the child an inviolate distinction between "mine and thine"—a property sense that will be firm and not fragile, that will thereafter need no external force in the family or the larger society to elicit proper behavior. This is a tremendous task, and our amazement as adults should not be that boys and girls of this age have solved it slowly or imperfectly but that by adolescence so many of them have solved it forever.

As I explained earlier, the preschool child's conscience is a highly personalized mechanism. In the beginning, his parents served as his conscience. Gradually he began to incorporate their "do's" and "don't's," and it was almost as though he carried with him a picture of them dealing out rewards and punishments for his activities. As he grows older, an unconscious inner mechanism takes over the task of scrutinizing the things he has done or is planning to do. This device becomes stronger as he enjoys the pleasurable feelings associated with the approving response of the people around him. When he feels guilty or is punished for his sins of commission or omission, he feels uneasy and unhappy. In an effort to keep the balance on the positive side, he listens more and more to that small inner voice.

As in so many phases of personality development, he begins to "impersonalize" his view of right or wrong during this period. He learns that many or most of the people he comes into contact with share the same view of what is and is not acceptable, and he is able to react correctly when called upon. This is not to say that it may not be very difficult for him to rise to the occasion, or that he may not slip often or be sorely tempted to avoid what he knows is right. But by and large in these years he will make strides.

As this process continues to expand and consolidate, the child's need for external controls diminishes. It is our hope that this development will avoid two unfortunate extremes: We hope the prohibitions he absorbs will not be so rigid and narrow as to inhibit his spontaneity and doom him to an obsessive, guilt-laden concern about the correctness of his thoughts, impulses, and actions. Neither would we like to see him confused about what is right or wrong as the result of the inconsistency in the behavior of those who serve as his role models.

Closely associated with this development of the child's conscience is the gradual growth of his own value system— his personal estimate of the correctness and worth of things. He will also be deciding what he feels about the worth of those around him. Usually a child goes through three phases in learning about the importance of people: In infancy, there is primarily one person of value, his mother. She is, for the most part, all good and all powerful. Later, the same or very similar attributes are ascribed to the father or others close to the child. Then, through broadening experience, these feelings are generalized to include other human beings outside the home. Unfortunately, however, the difficulties that exist in some homes stifle the positive feelings about parents, and it is then particularly difficult for the child to generalize positive feelings to others outside the home. Nevertheless, it is safe to say that most children begin with the assumption that all people are good. Experience in the larger world soon indicates that all people are not worthy of this respect and a "healthy mistrust" of *some* people is as valuable as the child's initial trust for *all* people. A flexible, realistic balance should keep the person, on the one hand, from being taken advantage of, and, on the other, from growing to suspect the motives of everyone else.

Sometimes it seems that the education of the child follows a rather curious route in developing these insights about people. We tend to present to them the extremes in human nature through fairy tales, stories, and television programs. People are heroes or villains— honest, reliable, and strong, or evil, irresponsible, and weak. By the time a child is in school he can point out the "good guy" and the "bad guy" in the first chapter of a book or the early scenes of a television show. Fortunately, their experience in the real world gradually indicates to him that people are usually not all good nor all bad but for the most part a little of both.

The end of the "period of mastery" really marks the end of childhood. The child's readiness to cope with the problems of adolescence is determined in no small degree by his success in solving the problems of this stage of his development. Some of his developmental tasks will have been solved easily and fully by this time; others will have unfinished or faulty solutions and will require a better or more complete solution in the coming years. I must continue to remind you that all children do not develop at the same rate nor do individual children develop all their capacities and potentials at the same pace. Certain attributes of maturity, however, should have been acquired in this period. Among these we should look for appreciation of, and a firm hold on, some of the major realities of the world. For example, this child should appreciate himself as an individual distinct and different from other individuals and should have a reasonably realistic notion of his own worth. We want him to have developed a practical set of values for his assessments of other human beings and a relatively stable moral code for his personal and social behavior.

From literally thousands of diverse experiences during these early years he should have carried away the lesson that this world of ours is basically a "problem-solving" world, and he should have learned some of the basic rules that regulate our encounters with these problems.

QUESTIONS

Mrs. _____: How do you help an emotionally immature child to grow, and what bearing does having an immature nervous system at birth have to do with this problem?

Dr. G.: That's a very complex question and requires some definition of the child's trouble. You say he is an immature child?

Mrs. _____: Emotionally immature, yes.

Dr. G.: This is a rather general statement. I think we would have to cut it down a bit. How old is the child? What form does his immaturity take?

Mrs. _____: He is six years old now. He's in the first grade, but his kindergarten teacher, last year, told me he is a little young. She called it "emotionally young."

Dr. G.: How is he doing in the first grade?

Mrs. _____: Rather shakily, I would say. He doesn't seem to handle his emotions as well as other children in the first grade.

Dr. G.: What are some of the acts that you find immature?

Mrs. _____: Well, if something displeases him, instead of just saying, "I don't like the way you do that," he will rant and rave. He doesn't seem to be able to control his emotions.

Dr. G.: Do you have other children?

Mrs. _____: Two others.

Dr. G.: How old are they?

Mrs. _____: One older and one younger. He's the second child.

Dr. G.: I gather you are also saying that this child seems to have less control over his feelings than the other two.

Mrs. _____: Yes. By the way, one of the things the teacher said to me this year was, "Well, he is the middle child." She didn't go any further, so apparently she feels this might have some relevance.

Dr. G.: There are a lot of notions about the way children should be brought up and about the danger signals they are supposed to show because of their ordinal position in the sibling group. Many of these beliefs come from the folklore. Either they are handed down from one generation to the next without much basis in fact, or they represent a current fad. One of the reasons I myself decided to study problems alleged to be those of the middle child was a personal one—being a middle child—but I was also hoping to explode this notion. There are middle children who don't do so well and there are middle children who are far more successful than either their older or younger brothers or sisters. I don't believe that their position has very much to do with it. Each position in the family—oldest, youngest, or middle—has some problems of adjustment that are specific for that position. And each position has some positive values that the other positions do not have. My impression is that these positive and negative aspects of each position tend to balance out and that generalizations about them are of very little value. It depends entirely on the constellation of the family, the child's sense of worth, his sense of his prestige in the family. You can't expect all the children in the family to have the same attitude toward their own worth or the same assessment of how their parents feel about them in comparison with their brothers and sisters. The child's original position in the family is important *to him*. He's always comparing what he wants or is allowed to do with the sibling ahead of him. And the one behind wants to crowd in and compete with him.

Mrs. _____: In general, this child of mine is more sensitive, I would say, than the other children.

Dr. G.: He is more sensitive to what you think about him or to what other people think about him?

Mrs. _____: Both. The teacher says she'll give him something to do and he'll immediately say, "Oh, I can't do it." She says you can see the tears beginning to come right at that point.

Dr. G.: We see this sort of response in children quite frequently. Because of previous failures in competition with other children in the family or outside, some children will become convinced of the inevitability of failure before the fact. In other words, the child says, "I am not going to be able to do it," because every time he encounters something new, something different, he is afraid that he'll fail and be thought even less of. He knows that the older sibling can do the task easily and he is not going to run the risk of finding out that his younger sibling can also do it. I think teachers all recognize this kind of child. This is a defensive technique and is used to save one's feelings about one's own shortcomings. There is always the student who tells you ahead of time that he is going to fail an examination. He posits this kind of a "failure before the fact." Often students like this are the ones who do very well on examinations. It's as though they needed to warn you not to be disappointed in their performance. If the failure should happen, they think that the blow won't be so great to them or to you if they have already alerted you to the possibility that such is going to happen.

Some children just can't stand to be criticized in any way. They assume that their total worth is in question if they err or fail ever so slightly. They are highly sensitive to what's going on and to what they suppose to be the positive and negative feelings of others toward them. Some of the most creative people are also the most sensitive. As a matter of fact, we hammer out—to our loss—some kinds of sensitivity in children because we put them through such rigid training and education. Creativity is often stamped out along with sensitivity.

I would assume that this youngster whom you're talking about may be battling for a position in the family in respect to your, and his father's, feelings. It may be difficult for him in a way because he cannot challenge the prestige of the older youngster nor win the attention the baby commands. So he resorts to the more infantile tactics that will get him immediate attention in the center of the stage. I think this is essentially the only difference that comes with being the child in the middle. He may, therefore, be a little slower in arriving at the notion that he doesn't have to use this primitive behavior to gain what he wants to gain. How old is the youngest child?

Mrs. _____: He's four, and a little devil. He can do everything the six-year-old does!

Dr. G.: I thought probably he could, but sometimes I can make some very wrong guesses. I guessed that the little one was pressing on his heels. Everything he does, the little one wants to do, right?

Mrs. _____: And probably can even do it better.

Dr. G.: This is momentarily disastrous for the feelings of the older of the two children. He feels the rivalry deeply. "I am just learning to do something new. I should get a lot of acclaim for this because I am now six years old, but here's this four-year-old doing it, too." It's an awful blow. You have to be sympathetic and understanding and be very careful to give him praise for what he does. Also, you are reluctant to hold back the development of the younger one so the older one can get some glory. You are in a tough spot to see to it that both children get full credit for their accomplishments and achievements. Do they spend much time playing together?

Mrs. _____: Yes, except when the six-year-old is in school.

Dr. G.: There should be some prestige for this boy by virtue of the fact that he goes to school where the younger one does not. See, the point is you can't discourage the younger one for wanting to grow and develop, too. This competition has meaning for him.

Mrs. _____: I come from a large family where everyone tries to give the six-year-old an extra boost to his self-confidence. When he brings home a good paper, we try to praise it, but apparently this isn't enough at this stage of the game.

Dr. G.: Perhaps not, but I don't think it's doing him any harm to give him this extra attention and a little extra love. Some children are insatiable for love and attention because of their inner needs, but that doesn't mean that they are unusual or atypical or abnormal. They will find their own niche in the family eventually and know that they are prized for themselves and for their competence and achievements. It sounds to me as if you are doing a lot to help this child. Additional help of considerable importance to this middle child would ensue if you could but enlist the acceptance of—and help from—the child next older. If the latter offered more companionship and participation in a few of his games and activities to the middle child, both would be urging the child toward growth and progression. The tendency toward defensive immaturity and regression would be minimized.

Mrs. _____: How does a mother help develop a child's personality without getting a carbon copy of herself as the result?

Dr. G.: Am I to assume from this question that you have some concern about your daughter's becoming a carbon copy of yourself?

Mrs. _____: I'd rather that they just be themselves, especially my oldest one. She is very similar to me.

Dr. G.: In the first place, that the child is similar to one or the other parent may not be a problem at all. Second, I think it's inevitable that the child will tend to copy certain of the parent's traits and mannerisms, certain ways of thinking and feeling, because obviously the child does identify with his parents. You seem to imply that you have a little concern about whether she's copying the right model! Perhaps you would like to have her be different from you? I don't see why you are worried. You think she's not enough of an individual?

Mrs. _____: I think she picks up the *wrong* things from me! She likes the things that I wish she wouldn't like. I'm flip and she's very flip, but I'd just as soon she'd not be. She came home the other day when I happened to have pigtails, and she said, "Oh, Mother, what do you think you are, a college girl?"

Dr. G.: Yes?

Mrs. _____: Well, I might say that to someone, but I don't want a child her age saying it.

Dr. G.: Isn't it all right if she says it to you as long as she doesn't say it in the same manner and tone to people outside? In other words, there's a certain camaraderie, it seems to me, between the two of you. How old is this child?

Mrs. _____: Eight.

Dr. G.: I would assume that she probably identifies with a lot of your good qualities, too. But most parents are rather gratified by some sort of imitation, you see. They like the idea of their children's having a sense of humor or being fast with an answer, as your child seems to be, just as they want the child to be a person of good manners or good presence. You want them to pick up the very best attributes that you have. You have to take a chance on their picking some of your "bad" ones, too. I don't think her individuality is being destroyed because she's like her mother.

Mrs. _____: That is my main concern. I just want her to be herself.

Dr. G.: I agree with you; she should be herself. But I wouldn't worry. There is a tendency in all parents to hope that their child will be unique at least in some small way, a little exceptional, in a positive sense a little different. Unless our children are unique, we sometimes are disappointed and even discouraged. But the time to worry is when parents identify the child with some person and then behave as if the child were in fact exactly like that person. We don't often hear a mother saying, "My daughter is like me and I don't like it." More often it is, "She is like Aunt Susie and I don't like it." In these cases Aunt Susie is usually not the best friend or favorite relative.

Ordinarily, parents are concerned when their children aren't the least bit like them. You say to yourself, "I don't know where she gets this trait or that trait. I am not like this. My husband isn't like this. What's the matter with her, because she isn't like us." So, I guess, this child of yours will probably show her individuality. If she has the characteristic of being a little flip, then she probably will have all the more tendency to be a little individual as she goes along. When she gets to be an adolescent, maybe you'll wish she were *more* like you! Then you'll come back to me complaining, "How can I make her into my model?"

Mrs. _____: It seems to be during this period when children spend more time in the outside world that they begin to take on ideas and values that are different from those they've learned at home. I think this threatens many parents. How can they best handle it?

Dr. G.: It is inevitable that children will encounter standards and modes of behavior that are quite different from those acceptable in their own homes. Unfortunately, these standards are usually those of a lower order of excellence than those expected by the child's own parents. Usually, too, they are directed at more freedom of action for the child than his parents want to go along with.

Most often the child brings these new ideas home as a basis for explaining and justifying something he has done or wants to do. Parents *are* threatened when they see their own standards dismissed as old-fashioned or too rigid. Frequently they explode angrily, and then it's hard to solve the conflict constructively.

The only effective response, if they feel they are right, is to quietly outline again what they expect in this regard and then hold firm to see that the child meets their standards. This, of course, implies that care has been taken to be certain the family's views are reasonable, that they have proved themselves to be worthwhile and that adhering to them will not, in fact, make the child appear ridiculous in the outside world.

Mrs. _____: Most children around eight or nine seem to have lots of friends. How about "the loner"? Should he be encouraged to join a group or should he be left alone to establish his own friendships?

Dr. G.: Most children eight or nine are very gregarious

and like nothing better than association and activities with children of their own age. They can stand being with adults for only a relatively brief period of time before they complain "there's nothing to do." This phrase usually indicates that they are bored with the present company and long for the companionship of other children.

One occasionally encounters a child who seems, by nature, to prefer to spend an inordinate amount of time by himself or in relatively close association with adult relatives. Solitary play or adult-associated play should not be condemned out of hand. Any child should be encouraged to develop skills and enjoyable activities that involve only his own participation.

The genuine "loner" is a child who through fear, often due to an unfortunate past experience, or shyness prefers to be alone. He may lack the basic social skills to reach out to others. He should be encouraged to do so, and it may be that companions have to be sought for him until his anxiety is reduced to the degree that he can do this on his own. Parents should remember that some aspects of the child's personality growth and socialization can go forward only through satisfactory and satisfying relationships with other children.

Mrs. _____: I agree children can be cruel to other children. Is there any way to teach kindness and compassion, or does it develop from the child's *own* experiences?

Dr. G.: Children often do learn the sad effects of cruelty at the hands of other children. They learn the physical discomfort dealt them by the bully—and they experience feelings of depression and frustration generated by the derogatory remarks of their companions who taunt them over a million things. I'm afraid the pain and anxiety resulting from these physical and verbal abuses go far to strengthen their own impulses to be cruel. Whenever an episode of this kind occurs to them, it is helpful if the parents underline the ill effects that cruelty has. When a child is cruel he should be reminded how he felt in a similar circumstance. His behavior should not be allowed to go unchallenged. One of the best opportunities that a parent has, of course, to teach kindness is by his own conduct. Children are very aware of the way their parents behave not only toward them but also toward those around them.

6

School

IN WHAT we have called the "age of mastery," those years from six to twelve, one of the child's most important tasks in development is to become aware that his world is ordered by cause and effect, by rules and regulations. He comes to learn that there are eternal natural laws and inexorable rhythms which no inner wish can change. This knowledge lends an orderliness and a stability to the universe and strengthens the child's growing confidence in his ability to understand and handle the situations he encounters. A child is not ready for school until he has made this awareness a part of himself. At school, one of his most important tasks is to grasp the methods by which he will acquire precision learning. He will "learn how to learn." By "precision learning" I mean the accurate use of symbols for things and for the relations between things. These symbols, of course, are words and numbers.

Words, you must remember, can have two different meanings for us. The first, which we all recognize, is the literal definition, of which the word is the accurate symbol. This enables us to communicate with others. The second is the psychological connotation of the word, which may be different for each of us and which expresses the positive or negative, the good or bad relationships between ourselves and the people around us. This second meaning, largely unconscious, may reflect a child's success or failure in solving some of the many preschool problems of development.

With the exceptions of "No!" "Good boy!" "Naughty!" and various other constantly applied admonitions, all words probably have more or less the same psychological values to children in their earliest years. But later—that is, after the fourth or fifth grade—the situation has changed. It is quite possible that people after this age can be separated into two classes: those who love words and use them well and easily, and those who tend to fear words and use them sparingly, haltingly, and without much discrimination as to exact meanings. These different attitudes toward words can often be traced back to a child's positive or negative relationships with his parents or others in authority.

Volumes and volumes have been written by educational specialists in an attempt to prevent or to overcome the problems and disabilities that may arise in learning to read. Every psychologist at some time in his professional career has become interested in the learning process. The results of all this research occupy whole shelves in university libraries. Here, to keep within our main theme of personality development, we must restrict ourselves to the factors that have a bearing, for good or ill, both upon personality development and learning in the classroom. In short, we will consider some psychological—or better, emotional—factors that seem to us to be important.

Because of the psychological implications in word usage, we search for emotional blocks in children who have trouble learning to read. This whole problem of learning difficulty is an exceedingly complex one. The children so afflicted range from those with evident troubles in the central nervous system to those whose problems can only be suspected from the histories given by their mothers. Whether the difficulty is organic or emotional, those of us who see children with problems have only potential causes for clues. It is our job to find the actual source of the difficulty, and this calls for sorting out the clues. We will limit our concern here to the emotional factors involved—factors relating to the positive and negative interpersonal relationships that the child has experienced.

For a child, the first words that have a profound psychological significance may be those having to do with his control of bodily functions. The child notes that his mother uses certain words in the positive, happy situations and certain other words in the negative situations. It does not escape him that the words his mother uses in these situations carry strong emotional overtones, and these early emotional experiences will have an influence on his subsequent attitude toward not only specific words but also the use of words in general.

So, while we may be born vulnerable or, if you will, predisposed to disabilities affecting our use of words, we also can acquire disabilities from the environmental influences of our early years. Clinical cases of emotionally based reading disabilities bear out this theory. For example, we find a greater-than-expected incidence of learning difficulties among children whose early injuries and illnesses have left them with a high level of anxiety. It is hard to quantify degrees of anxiety, but certainly anxiety levels do vary from child to child, depending on the circumstances of their early lives.

It is significant that learning difficulties occur far more frequently in boys than in girls. The proportion is seven or eight to one. On the basis of present knowledge, we cannot say that boys are born with a different kind of nervous system that affects their abilities to use words and numbers. In an effort to explain the statistically significant difference between boys and girls who have mild to severe learning disabilities, we at the Judge Baker Guidance Center have searched for "negative experience factors" in the lives of these children. We begin by looking for possible psychological causes of their "nonlearning." I think it might be well for you to hear some of the impressions we have received from our studies. Keep in mind that all the boys with learning disabilities whom we studied have normal, even superior, intelligence. Remember, too, that our particular concept is but one of several responsible and respectable theories advanced by professionals working in this field. All these theories, including ours, seem to have merit in respect to *some* but not *all* nonlearners. The more we study learning disabilities, the more we become aware of their complexity. One should be wary of any theory that is alleged to "explain" all such cases. No single theory that I know of explains adequately all the diverse types of learning disabilities that we encounter in day by day clinical experience. Let me acquaint you with at least some of the many psychological factors we feel have been significant in the creation and persistence of the "nonlearning roles" our boy patients play.

First of all, a higher level of anxiety, a greater feeling of insecurity, often appears to beset the nonlearning boy than the adequate learner. Though the nonlearner may be boisterously talkative in school, actively disruptive, or even given to atrocious bullying, he reveals himself in intensive psychotherapeutic interviews to be struggling with strong feelings of insecurity and fear. His insecurities, fears, and distrust relate to people in general, both in and out of the home, and to his own sense of worth. Our explorations into the origins of these extreme feelings led us to look for threatening or actually traumatic or harmful experiences to which the boy had been subjected. Traumatic experiences, we find, are far more prevalent and severe among boys with learning disabilities than among children of the same intellectual potential who get along adequately or well in school.

These negative experiences tend to have a general effect on the child's development rather than being specific to the development of a learning disability. Some of the traumatic events were death of a member of the family, a life-threatening illness in the child himself or in a member of the immediate family, divorce or separation of his parents, hospitalization or emergency surgery, or an experience of violence or grave danger. Often the child's very environment is traumatic: members of his family are mentally or physically ill, violent, alcoholic, or there is severe marital discord or financial deprivation.

In emphasizing that these boys show high levels of insecurity and anxiety, I am not placing blame on their parents or anyone else. Many of the traumas occurred in incidents or in circumstances quite beyond the parents' control. In addition, our research tends to support the notion that these children may have a basic vulnerability that modifies or delays their preschool maturation and hence their later precision learning. As the research progresses, we see emerging a preschool pattern of response in many that indicates this vulnerability. If this is proved to be so, early detection and prevention of later disabilities may well become possible.

At this point a question naturally arises. We know that feelings of insecurity can carry children into emotional and behavioral problems other than learning disabilities. Why, then, in a certain proportion of these boys should it be a learning disability that appears? Why should they select this as their neurosis—if it can be called a neurosis—to defend themselves against their feelings of insecurity? Why not one of the other emotional or behavioral problems? The inevitable conclusion, it seems to me, is that these learning disabilities relate to, or stem from, something *specific* in the demands and methods of precision learning itself or in the way in which those demands and methods are presented in our classrooms. For these boys this specific something makes learning in school very difficult, if not altogether impossible.

As I said before, we usually find anxiety at the core of the problem. What is the essence of this state of anxiety? What does the school child do to lower the intensity of his anxiety in order to be able to live with it? There seem to be two basic psychological mechanisms of defense:

One response is to resort to wishful daydreaming or fantasy. In his mind the child dwells in another world, a world in which he is never threatened or injured, a pleasant world that allows him freedom from fear and consoles him with dreams of being loved and wanted for his imagined achievements. In this world he is safe from injury and punishment, from the hated words of derogation and condemnation, and is given the power to overcome them.

The other type of defense for the anxious and fearful is movement, hyperactivity, an eternal busyness in countless abruptly chosen and quickly disposed of activities, each of which calls for only short-lived attention, shallow investment, and fleeting involvement.

If fantasy and hyperactivity are the defensive maneuvers employed most frequently by children when they are burdened with feelings of insecurity and anxiety, feelings of helplessness and hopelessness, then it is not difficult to see how these psychological mechanisms bring all efforts to learn to a temporary or total halt. The child's primary and major task in the precision-learning process is to attend, without inner or outer distraction, to the material presented to him. His attention must be immediate and it must be sustained.

His "attention span," as we say, must be long enough for him to be able to appreciate and assimilate the bit of learning or skills presented to him, to attain the solution of the task set for him. Every other requirement of the learning process is secondary in importance to this ability to pay attention to what is going on.

It necessarily follows that the child who is anxiety ridden and resorts to daydreaming or hyperactivity in defense against his feelings will not be able to satisfy the first requisite of precision learning: He will not be able to pay attention. Defensive hyperactivity or daydreaming makes sustained attention impossible. Either defensive maneuver has the power to distort or to cut off the child's perception. Learning the basic facts and skills in the classroom becomes largely or totally impossible, and the child develops a severe learning disability. This disability may be mild and only partially disabling or so severe that the child retains almost nothing of what is taught.

All the boys we see in our remedial classes fall into these two main behavioral categories. On the one hand there is the quiet, withdrawn, inattentive daydreamer, whose thoughts are anywhere but in the classroom, and on the other hand there is the hyperactive child who cannot sit still but is in perpetual motion.

Other psychological factors also figure in the problem of the nonlearning boy. These factors may operate alone or are allied to those I have discussed. But whether primary or secondary or mere accompaniments in the disability, they, like the others, are based on certain strong anxieties.

Much of the anxiety these boys feel comes from the aggression and hostility that grown-ups have visited upon them. They become even more anxious when, in their deep resentments, they contemplate the aggressive reprisals they would like to make. They know and fear not only the aggression of others but also their own. As a child recites these fears to us, it is easy to detect that any type of hostility is a threat to life or body integrity. Aggression, in short, is death dealing.

How does this emotional "set" of the boy enter into the learning process and make it difficult for him to learn? If one thinks for a moment about the process of learning, it is not difficult to see that the *mastery* of fact requires some minimum of aggression—in this case a constructive, not destructive, type of sustained *attack* upon the problem presented. Learning—and indeed the curiosity that motivates learning—contains within itself as a driving factor a free expression of this type of aggression. That we *master* the learning material, *dig* it out, *digest* it or *eat* it up, and *throw* it all back at examinations indicates that learning is by no means a passive process of quiet drinking in or absorbing. On the contrary, it requires aggression. But the boy with the learning problem just isn't able to allow himself the expression of this so necessary aggression. In his anxiety, any expression of aggression contains the threat of person-directed hostility of a fearful type. To him no aggression is allowable, and hence for him no approach to learning is possible.

At the other end of the stick, the nonlearner is a belligerent, suspicious, antisocial, disruptive, bullying youngster who insists and is adamantly certain that the whole world is hostile. He, too, believes that any expression of aggression is hostility, and his basic impulse is to strike first, to hit hardest, and to maintain the integrity of his body by a sustained attack upon others. He is incapable of modifying this total hostility and thus is unable to differentiate between his senseless aggression and the controlled expression of aggressiveness that he needs in order to learn.

Another pattern of response that results in an inhibition to learn is one we describe as an "arrest of maturation." This mechanism is, in short, a refusal, as a defense, to grow up and assume the role of adult. In the mind of these boys, to allow oneself to learn, and particularly to allow oneself to demonstrate through schoolwork that one has learned, is to identify oneself with the masculine role. And it is precisely this eventuality, that is, of having to become a grown-up man, that the nonlearner fears. Once again, the fear of self-directed or other-directed aggression seems to initiate this defense. Such boys assume that any expression of aggression will lead to hostility and violence. The masculine models in their lives have exhibited violent acts, and so they have assumed that males, when adult, are expected to act in the same way. Masculinity for them is inexorably associated with aggressive competition. Inasmuch as learning requires these expressions, even though in a modified and constructive sense, they avoid it. Their best and surest defense is to demonstrate that they are not mature and that they intend not to take any steps toward maturity.

This discussion has covered briefly and by no means exhaustively some of the psychological factors that our learning research team has observed to be at work in a sizable number of boys who are in our care. I should emphasize again that no single theory or combination of theories exists today that "explains" all the different *types* of learning disabilities that one sees. What I have tried to do here is to expose the psychological links which we think exist between nonlearners' fears and feelings of aggression and their response to the expectations of our society in regard to maleness. Obviously, these expectations differ markedly from our expectations for girls, and the differences should offer us some hints as to why learning disabilities are far more prevalent among boys than girls. Note that in trying to account for this sex difference, I cautiously restrict myself to the word "hint." But any theory advanced to explain the "cause" of learning disabilities must account for this pronounced difference in the performance of boys and girls.

All the emphasis we have put here on the psychological disabilities of nonlearners might lead you to infer that all adequate learners and superior learners have carefree, happy childhoods. This, of course, is not always so. The compulsive learner, perhaps no less than the nonlearner, may have his psychological disabilities, but they are far more acceptable to society and, in fact, may bring him society's greatest rewards.

But to get back to the early encounter with precision learning, let me call to your attention that the discipline of the classroom requires us to appreciate and accept the fact that certain things in this life go by specific and precise rules and regulations. It is important to the child's development to be able to appreciate the concept of rules and regulations and to be able to acquire some understanding of their effects. In examining the way in which this concept is acquired, once again we have to go back to infancy, particularly to the age when the child is first expected to use words. This is the same age—and the chronology is very important—at which he is introduced to control of bodily functions, the control of bladder and bowels. The parental activities relative to this introduction to rules and regulations can leave lasting impressions, and we must remember that words figure in most of the mother's responses. It would be difficult to separate here the insistence on control of bodily functions and the emotional implications in the use of words.

There are other rules and regulations that the child will encounter as he prepares himself to enter the world of precise symbols. First, of course, come those that govern his social conduct. He hears these primarily from his parents and secondarily from his classroom teacher. If he has troubles with the rules and regulations at home, he may carry his problems with him to the classroom where they will reflect on his performance. His attitude toward authority is the basic issue here.

Then there are the rules and regulations concerning property and the sharing of material possessions with other children. There is his gradual acceptance of the rules and regulations governing play and games. The child's response to all these different sets of rules will be reflected in his response to the classroom and to the precision learning that goes on there. For in precision learning all progress goes according to rule. The letter *A* precedes the letter *B*. *C-a-t* spells cat. We read from left to right. At least in the "old" math, two times two always equals four. Our picture of the entire universe is drawn by rule. The child must acquire this concept, must come to realize that the haphazard approach or the guess does not lead to success in precision learning.

Factors within the family itself may condition the child positively or negatively for his encounter with precision learning. It is notable that many of the children we see with emotional, not organic, learning disabilities have been regarded by their parents as inferior learners in comparison with siblings or other children of the same age. These children seem to hold at best a marginal position within the family. Then there is the child who is the victim of what we might call a family policy of "selective silence." They have a family secret, a skeleton in the cupboard. The child is aware that certain matters are not to be talked about, certain questions never to be asked. If they are, punishment will follow swift and sure. When information is hoarded and children are cut off from it under threat of punishment, they become anxious about exhibiting curiosity in any direction. The lid has been clamped on the most essential activity of the learning process. The child fears to follow where curiosity should lead. Learning comes fastest when the child is gathering it in to satisfy his own curiosity.

Consciously or unconsciously, the family may encourage a "favorite" child in aggression against a sibling with learning disabilities. By making a display of their favoritism, they call attention to the sibling's lack of development. He responds by withdrawing further and further from the risk of having to compete and again fail. Here, within the family, at the critical point when the child is taking on his identification as an individual human being, he is tagged as the "slow learner." From the conversations he hears every day, he puts together the picture of himself as the stupid one in the family, the child who can't learn and will never get anywhere in school.

There is also a more subtle process by which the family can aggravate learning disabilities. Learning itself, rather than the learner, is derogated. When parents set a very low value on education, the child may never come to see himself as one who is expected to learn, because in this life it is essential to *know*. He misses all motivation toward achievement and competence. It is this motivation that we regard as one of the most valuable products of the early school years.

QUESTIONS

Mrs. _____: We all seem to have some ideas about the differences in development between boys and girls. Girls seem to have a little easier time learning to control their bowels and bladders. They seem to talk earlier than boys do, and you said that they don't seem to have as much trouble with learning disabilities. Now, is this really because they don't have the same fear of having to be aggressive and competitive? Is it also because in our culture they are expected to be passive?

Dr. G.: I would think that your answers and conjectures are as near to the fact as any of us know. It is well known that girls develop faster than boys; in other words, an eighteen-month-old girl will be more developed than an eighteen-month-old boy, although both of them presumably could have the same native intelligence, or native potential. In regard to the girls' earlier word usage and their relative lack of trouble later from learning disabilities, I think that your suggestion may be largely correct. Girls are expected to be more compliant. It is the role of the little girl to be a more compliant and conforming individual, quieter and less mobile. The boy, however, does not live long within the family group before he gathers the notion that he as a boy is expected to be much more active, much more mobile, much more aggressive and competitive, that is, if in the eyes of his father he's going to be a "real boy!" This motivation and the role that results will be all to the good unless, as I have explained, it is carried to the extreme. But if, due to traumatic happenings within the family, he notes or thinks he notes that the masculine role is necessarily accompanied by excessive firmness, punishment, or even brutality, if an excessively aggressive or condemnatory father is held up to him as the model for emulation, he will have a tendency to turn away in fear of masculinity and fear of competition.

A girl is not subjected to expectations of this sort and need not develop this fear of hostility. As I said before, she is inclined or held or expected to be more compliant. This difference can be of great significance when she goes into the schoolroom where the confining aspects, the rules and regulations with regard to behavior and the expectation in regard to acquisition of knowledge, do not threaten her as they threaten the boy.

Mrs. _____: From your experience with children who seem to have learning difficulties, does it seem to you, in looking at the family history, that any characteristic pattern or disturbance appears in the roles that the parents play? That is, are you likely to find unusually aggressive fathers and very passive mothers or aggressive mothers and unusually passive fathers? Does a pattern like this seem to play a part in setting the stage for later learning difficulties?

Dr. G.: I think it would be very difficult to say that the mothers and fathers were of any specific type. I thought you were going to ask whether there is a tendency for learning difficulties to run in families. There is considerable evidence that this disability does run in families, which leads to the theory of predisposition or vulnerability that I mentioned. I don't think one could type the parents of these children, but if there is any trend I would say that probably the fathers tend to be more passive but given to intermittent outbursts of harsh tempers. I think that this unpredictable inconsistency in behavior, particularly in regard to aggressive outbursts, is the marked difference in such fathers. The mother tends to be the disciplinarian and the ruler of the family. Here again there are no universal patterns.

Mrs. _____: Is it a predisposition in families, or could it be the continuing constellation of relationships contained in a given family that disturbs learning ability? That is, if the triangle relationship of parents and child sets the stage, then is it not perhaps equally likely for two children or three to respond in the same way?

Dr. G.: There again you raise the problem of "nature versus nurture," inherited versus environmental factors. How one regards the issue depends a good bit on one's orientation. If you're an out-and-out advocate of organismic theory, you think all trends in development are due to cells and their behavior. Then you will cling to the belief that this tendency is built in. If you are more of an environmentalist, you probably will look for a cultural repetition of some kind within the family, a passing of the same emotional factors, good and bad, from one generation to the next under environmental pressures. In many instances a process very like that seems to be the cause of certain types of emotional disabilities emerging in family groups.

Then we have all seen families which include both excellent learners and children who have difficulty in learning. Sometimes three children in a family may exhibit the same kind of aversion to learning. Remember, we are talking here about the disabilities in which emotional factors seem to cause the learning block. We do not argue even for a moment that there are not other types of learning disabilities. One of the big problems in the whole field is in diagnosis, determining the relative importance of organic factors versus environmental factors. As I said, regardless of the cause, we have to work out ways of reducing anxiety in children and increasing their learning potential. The method may vary from one aimed at overcoming neurological difficulties to one aimed at ameliorating emotional factors. In my own particular group we have confined ourselves to what we call the "fear of learning," but we hope that other people will work on all the other factors in different types of patients. What we try to emphasize is that the attitude of the parents toward learning, their attitude toward the specific learner in the family, is of extreme importance.

Mrs. _____: Does the child who is prone to have a problem in learning usually demonstrate this problem very early?

Dr. G.: I touched upon this before in my general remarks. It is our feeling that the child does demonstrate his problem, or potential problem, from the very beginning of his schoolwork and often even as a preschooler. His earlier successes or failures in using words to communicate will be of central importance here. We are now at the point of working on some type of prediction scale which would indicate at the preschool level the child's learning ability or his potential for disability. This takes us back immediately to the beginnings, to the use of words. You must remember that the children I'm talking about are always children of normal or superior intelligence. Nevertheless, there has been a delay in the use of words or a delay in sentence formation or partial sentence formation which we would look for at eighteen months or twenty-four months. Not only may there be a delay in the use of words, but also there may be a persistence of stuttering or stammering of some kind. Or, idiosyncratic speech—that is, baby talk which none but the mother or other members of the family can interpret—may persist. When the child goes to school the teacher cannot understand this idiosyncratic language the child is using. Only with great difficulty can the child be induced to give up this highly personalized and circumscribed word usage for the usage of the schoolroom and of the world beyond the family.

We also see in these youngsters a tendency to be hyperactive from a very early age. There may also be a delay in the acquisition of bowel and bladder control. All these factors may be present, or at least suggestions of them. So, whether or not one can accurately tell whether a three- or three-and-a-half-year-old child has a potential language disability we don't know, but we can have a legitimate hope that this is not an unobtainable goal. If it does come to pass, then intervention in the nursery-school or kindergarten levels may avert some of the difficulties. In this society of ours the most important task of all seems to be the development of language abilities. All learning is based upon use of language. The progress of the child, in school and out, depends on a free and full realization of his potential ability to master the letters, words, and numbers of precision learning. Success in this sphere, plus an acquired attitude of friendliness toward other human beings, argues well for his later adjustment.

Mrs. _____: I felt very upset when you spoke about rules as being the necessary precondition for learning. I thought, "Well, my child simply is not going to master the ABC's!" She's only two, and I feel that there is so much that we must do on schedule that I have always tried going in the opposite direction in order not to impose unnecessary routines.

Dr. G.: She is apparently going along very well, so she must be following some kind of orderly development. You can't tell me there are no rules in the house or expectations regarding her behavior!

Mrs. _____: Of course, there are rules regarding regularity of basic functions, but I have observed families where even very young children have every hour of their existence planned out. This hour you play in this room and this hour you do such and such in preparation for something else. This really goes against my grain, and I was wondering if this is what you were suggesting.

Dr. G.: You see, what you're doing here is setting up a straw man for me to knock over. Or else you're setting *me* up as the straw man to knock over! You bring up an extreme example. Of course, I couldn't approve of such a system. As we have said from the beginning, I think a mother's intuition and her common sense are worth an awful lot more sometimes than professional rules and advice. Now let's get back to this rule business.

It is true that we get much of our data from children who are not learning although their intellectual potential is adequate. As we look at the households of these children, we seem to find a great lack of orderliness. I don't mean cleanliness but rather a more or less completely unscheduled atmosphere. If the children want their lunch at 10:00 in the morning, they'll get their lunch at 10:00 in the morning. There is no set time for this, there is no set time for that. There is a glaring lack of rules and regulations, not only personal rules and regulations but also social rules and regulations. These children tend to play that way, too. A familiar refrain is, "You can't make me do it this way because I am going to do it that way." They want to make up their own rules in a game as they go along—rules that will twist the fairness of the game in their favor. These youngsters we see tend to have a background of this sort. We have great difficulty getting them to assume that anything goes by rule or regulation. Whether we like it or not, if there is any activity that is governed to the nth degree by rules, it is precision learning. If a child is not ready to accept that certain things do go by rules, and not in accordance with the child's wish for a continuing infantile omnipotence, he will have great difficulty at school. I won't say it is the only factor involved, but it seems to us that it is a very common and a very important one.

Mrs. _____: I must say that my temptation to break the routine for a preschooler is very strong. First of all, you don't want to impose too much upon them when they are being toilet-trained because there can be too much discipline there.

There is also a lot we insist on having to do with their physical safety. I'd rather let them feel unpressured in the rest of their existence.

Dr. G.: I think you are resisting my *generalizations* about this, and I am happy that you are! Well, all I know is that an appreciation of the inflexibility of certain rules and regulations has something to do with learning! We don't want to have them so regulated they'll never be able to do anything creative. In all these affairs you have to run a sensible course between certain extremes. A completely unregulated child is in the same boat as an overcontrolled one as far as the ultimate outcome is concerned. At some point in education, of course, the child has got to learn—and we want him to learn—that there may be a new combination, a new slant for looking at things he's being taught. If he is too rigid, he'll just take everything he is taught at face value and fail to think it through for himself. But in the middle grades, when he is faced with the traditional facts of precision learning, he just cannot avoid appreciating and following basic rules that have systematized learning.

In this connection most professional educators imply or explicitly state that this ability to follow the reasonable directions of the teacher is an important indicator of the child's readiness to go to school. In the nursery schools there is a traditional insistence that the beginning child must have attained a self-regulation of bladder and bowels. In addition, of course, it is stated, or assumed, that a child is not ready for the kindergarten or first grade until he can "control" his impulses and "regulate" his demands in respect to integrating with the group and being ready to share, in turn, with the other children not only the teacher's attention but also the positions of power and preference in the group. That the child is intellectually "ready" for school is not the only readiness required. There is the important social readiness also.

Mrs. _____: My oldest son is four. He goes to nursery

school, and recently it seems that every time he tries something new he gets very upset if he doesn't do it just right. Several weeks ago, for instance, he was sick. His teacher brought him something to cut out which the other children had done in school, and I was trying to help him. I cut on one side of the line and he was supposed to cut on the other side of it. He went into an absolute rage about how stupid I was and how it was all spoiled. He was really upset. Why should it be so *important* to him? I also noticed that he learns much better outside the home, where I have nothing to do with it and when he just comes back and shows me what he has done.

Dr. G.: That's been noted by lots of parents. This, of course, gets us into the homework situation. Perhaps you wonder how a teacher can handle twenty-five youngsters? One reason is that she is more objective than you can be. She can divide her emotional investment from one child to the next. If teachers were as heavily invested in every child as every parent is in her own child, they wouldn't be able to do the good job that they do. The mother-child emotional involvement puts a totally different emphasis on the effort to teach a child anything. Your investment is far greater than that of any teacher, and your child's investment in you—as the most significant person to please—is also far greater than is his allegiance to his teacher.

Mrs. _____: He was angry at me because I didn't know how to do it exactly the way that he thought he was supposed to do it.

Dr. G.: I think you have to get used to the fact that after a while anybody outside of the home can do things better than mother and father can! But your child is rather young to have arrived at this type of devaluation. This is the kind of devaluation seen in adolescence, but it can appear at a much earlier age.

Mrs. _____: I have just about given up trying to teach him things. I used to teach him his numbers and letters, but he didn't seem interested. So I just stopped. He has learned amazingly well in school, though. I find that whenever he asks me anything he doesn't like my answer.

Dr. G.: Well, his motivation is maybe not so simple as you think. It may be very complex. He may need to put you on the spot, so to speak. He may need to demonstrate that he doesn't need you, although he desperately does. "I can do it myself," is what they often say. The same thing occurs when people try to help with homework. You get in a terrible jam. Because of your close relationship with him, this whole issue of learning or not learning becomes emotionally loaded. Many children feel that their prestige and your continuing value of them are involved. They can make the mistake of saying that four and four are nine, and it's corrected by the teacher in a very objective way. But that mistake in front of Mother may pose the feeling of terrible defeat and loss of face. That a person of such great significance should find that they are inefficient or incorrect may trigger the whole complex of feelings about their wish to be perfect in the eyes of the parent. I think this is where the efforts of mothers, and fathers, too, never turn out very well. But Uncle Joe, who may be an old slob, can come along and teach the boy anything! It is quite devastating to a parent's sense of worth—but we have to learn to live with it!

Mrs. _____: Is it better to leave them alone?

Dr. G.: Yes, I would say leave them alone, at least in areas where someone else is designated to teach them and where a really technical approach is called for. But I wouldn't let them alone to the degree that you do not show an interest in their schoolwork or that you omit complimenting them on their achievements and increasing competence.

Mrs. _____: What do you do when he asks a question and then fights your answer?

Dr. G.: You might just say, "Look, I can help you, but if you feel at any time that you can do it better, then don't be afraid to do it yourself. I'll help if you want me to." As for fighting your answer, the very most important tactic in this area is to avoid, always, the setting up of a fighting situation.

Mrs. _____: In school he helps everybody else! I found that out the day I went to school. He zippers everyone's zipper. A little girl lost her blanket and he knew where it was and ran to get it.

Dr. G.: I think what is happening here is another interesting thing that we note in children. You'll find this in children at about the age of four. They go to nursery school and kindergarten and then they come home and try to reverse the roles that they and their mother have had. They may do this directly or they do it as a game, but they're really reversing the teacher-pupil role and mother-child role and making you into the pupil. They are identifying with the teacher, and the teacher is one who is the great authority—sometimes with no questions asked. They may get a little fed up with that after two or three hours in school, so they identify with the aggressor, as we put it. If a person in authority is being aggressive toward you, you may tend to mimic that toughness. This is a defensive and protective kind of mechanism that we all have. Now that you have told us this other story, we can see that this may be what the boy is doing. He may be making you into the learner. He is the teacher and you are the learner—and maybe you can be classed as "stupid." This is a passing phase, I am sure, but he is probably getting a tremendous amount of satisfaction out of this game of role reversal. For the first time, he is able to tell you what to do, just as his controlling and exacting teacher tells him what he must do. "You are stupid, my teacher is much smarter—even I know how to do this better than you do!" We see this frequently in youngsters. I know it can be a shock or downright exasperating, but it will pass. Something else will take its place!

Mrs. _____: I think this homework question is very big, and I am dreading the day it comes up at our house. My oldest is only two, but I'm dreading it already! I see and hear about things happening in my friends' homes, and I don't know how I am going to cope later on. I see these families wanting to raise very independent children who will think for themselves, and yet every night they check all of their children's homework. They even compose part of it! I have questioned this. The rationale is that helping with homework is standard procedure—all parents do it. One friend lives in a very aggressive educational community, and another comes from an ordinary town, but it seems that this is the custom in both places. I would refrain from helping with homework on principle, and yet this stand would put my child in a position where she would seem to have less to offer than everybody else. Can you sacrifice your child's happiness for something that you believe is right? I really believe that it is the *child's* responsibility. It's his project—his learning. If somebody else comes in to do it or to help him with it, it defeats the purpose.

Dr. G.: Yes, I am sure that assuming responsibility for his own work is a very important issue. This task is a prime one in adolescence.

Mrs. _____: But these children are eight, nine, ten!

Dr. G.: I thought you were talking about much older children. I think there are several principles to enunciate. Sometimes, however, you have to modify the rigidity of a principle like that. If you don't help the child when he really needs this kind of help and you are able to give it, you really are abandoning him. He needs that help.

Mrs. _____: But the children I am talking about are not asking for it. It is being imposed upon them because the parents feel that they must live up to very high standards.

Dr. G.: Of course, if the child is doing all right the parents shouldn't be looking over his shoulder to make sure his work is correct, but when a child asks for help, it is very difficult to deny it.

Mrs. _____: I went to boarding school and *we* did homework every night alone. I mean, if you are at home, why should your parents help you? It is your homework and you are supposed to do it. It's not the parent who needs the practice.

Dr. G.: I am the president of the board of trustees of a boarding school. They have an evening study period where they all get together to prepare the next day's lessons. There is a preceptor in the room who is there not primarily to keep order but to give help to those who need help. In the boarding schools in this country the school stands *in loco parentis;* that is, they are in the position of parents. I assume that they expect parents should behave in the same way.

Mrs. _____: But the teacher explains the lesson the next day. The purpose of homework is to see what you can do by yourself, so that when she marks the paper she can see where you went wrong and need help.

Dr. G.: That, of course, is the best way of doing it, to get the child to assume this responsibility. Then, if he doesn't do it correctly, you pitch in and help by making suggestions, but, in doing so, you do not actually do his work.

Mrs. _____: Isn't there a difference if the child has asked for help? Here the parent is imposing it. Supposedly, when a child is doing homework, he will ask you if he needs help. If he doesn't, then don't impose your knowledge on him.

Mrs. _____: Supposing when you inspect your child's work, you see that there are certain things wrong. Now, are you going to correct these things so that he can hand it in to the teacher perfect?

Mrs. _____: Can't you point out that there is an error and let the child find it himself? Just the fact that you raise a question will make him look again and perhaps he'll see what's wrong.

Dr. G.: If he's made an earnest effort to do the work himself and is falling in error over some technique, I certainly think you can suggest corrections to his faulty technique. I agree, however, that his work should be a matter between himself and his teacher.

Mrs. _____: As a former teacher, I feel parents just shouldn't be involved. If a child makes a mistake and his mother explains it to him, she'll do it in the way she learned it when she went to school years ago. Chances are there's an entirely different way of going about it now. The child will come to school with his homework correct, but he really won't know what he's doing. He doesn't know how he got the answer. His mother explained it to him. "O.K., Mom, that's right," he says, "I really understand it and I'm all done for the night." Then the child takes a test and shows he has no idea what he's doing, and the teacher asks, "Well, how come you didn't know it when you had it all right on your homework paper?"

Dr. G.: Now you are raising another issue. You are now talking about the fact that parents these days may not be competent to follow the right methods. The basic question is: How do you feel about parents helping children and in what way should they help them? This is the basic question that you are asking. There seem to be two schools of thought here. Maybe three. One seems to be that you should let the child make his errors, stumble along with them and hope that he'll eventually work them out himself, but you make him completely responsible for everything he does, and without any help whatsoever. The other school of thought seems to be that parents should be a little more charitable and sympathetic. They give the child some help when he is foundering to see if they can show him where the errors are, but he himself must correct them. Some others feel it's all right to be helpful so long as the child understands what he's done. I gather your attitude, Mrs. _____, is that you'll have none of this business whatsoever!

Mrs. _____: Yes, the child will go to school and get his education there. He and they will be responsible for it. I'm his mother, not his teacher.

Dr. G.: What will happen if some night he is stuck in his homework and he comes out and says to you, "I cannot get this question." What are you going to do?

Mrs. _____: Fine. Then we will discuss whether he has the correct resources to turn to. That much direction I'll give him. But I will not impose my help because I will think then he's not living up to his potential. And I won't do it for him. The other night when I walked into my neighbor's house, her little third grader had written a paper about Thanksgiving and had all the periods and capitals completely wrong. Now, when I walked in the father was saying, "Put a capital letter here and put a period there. Put a capital letter here and a period there and then it will be right." He was actually doing the work for the child. Now, it seems to me that the child has also learned something else from this experience which is going to get in the way. He has learned that Mother is going to be willing to take the responsibility for doing something that he himself ought to be doing. That, it seems to me, is going to be a long-lasting lesson.

Dr. G.: I guess we've arrived at a position in which we can say you should take a common-sense attitude toward helping the child with his homework!

Mrs. _____: May I change the subject? What happens to a child who because of his advanced verbal ability is treated very much as an older child? When his behavior is average for his age, people tend to become impatient. What is the effect on this child likely to be?

Dr. G.: How old is he?

Mrs. _____: He's four. This is a child who talked in sentences when he was a year old. Because of this precocity, he has always been taken at his verbal rather than his physical age.

Dr. G.: I think that "verbal age" is a good expression. I think I'll appropriate that, if you don't mind. Are you worried about encouraging his precocity?

Mrs. _____: No. I'm just worried about the pressure

put on him when he does act like a four-year-old—when he has a typical four-year-old tantrum, for instance.

Dr. G.: You forget he's four years old?

Mrs. _____: That's right. I wonder why this six-year-old child is acting like a baby!

Dr. G.: Well, you do have to make sure that you allow him, or have allowed him, to have the joys of early childhood. However, this is not an unusual situation. It comes about because his intellectual and behavioral development is accelerated. His emotional development is probably more in line with his chronological age. You are often surprised when there are these sudden changes. One minute he's using full sentences with adverbs in proper syntax and then he suddenly seems much younger. I think you have to be careful not to be surprised, to keep in mind that these ladders of development, as I called them earlier, are not always synchronized. It is hard for children to have great expectations put upon them. They like it if they succeed in meeting them, but if they don't succeed, then they feel badly—as though they have failed. You always have to watch a child who is accelerated for whatever reason. He must be allowed periods of nonacceleration or even an occasional satisfying regression.

Mrs. _____: I would like to talk on this point from personal experience. I have an eighteen-year-old, whose precocious development was obvious very early. It was very difficult though, as Mrs. _____ tells us, to remember how young he really was. It isn't only what happens at home. It's what happens when they get out into the world, too. Our son was pushed ahead in school. Things seemed to go along very, very well when he was small and through elementary school, but around the time of puberty things became difficult. He had been young when he began school, and then because of skipping a grade he was two years younger than many of the other boys and girls at school. They all grew. He hadn't begun to grow. They were all interested in the other sex. He still didn't have these interests, but felt he had to assume them because this was what the peer group was doing. So it made a very false kind of situation for him. He has had a difficult adolescence. He was quite resentful that he always had felt pushed. And yet you couldn't talk to him the way you talk to a little child.

Dr. G.: Especially if he is the first child. If the others are precocious, I don't think you ever invest quite as much in them. You just don't have the time. Well, I think that is a very good case history.

Mrs. _____: What else can you do? If the child is bright and is ahead of himself, you can't keep him back.

Dr. G.: I think there is a tendency on the part of parents who have very bright children to assume that intellectual companionship is what the child needs from them. Intellectual companionship, of course, is not enough. Furthermore, although I am all for aiding and abetting the development of the bright and creative youngster, I think that the precocious child can get a rather distorted view of reality. This is why I think public schools are so important in one way, if they're well run. The child has a chance to see various and different kinds of people—the good and the bad and the bright and the not so bright. They get a much more realistic picture of what the population is, with whom they have to live. When you take them out and put them with only those who are intellectually superior, then you are always inviting a continued emphasis on the intellectual side of their being. You stratify their scheme of living among children who are very gifted and very talented. There is a lot to be said in favor of that, of course, as educators will tell you, but there are a lot of shortcomings, too, I think. There is no doubt that the advanced child presents very special problems for his parents.

Mrs. _____: When you speak of gifted children, you touch a point I'm curious about. The IQ a child is given when he is four or five years old—is he going to have the same IQ all his life?

Dr. G.: It has been noted and emphasized by psychologists that the IQ arrived at in psychological testing may or may not be truly representative of the child's intellectual potential. The factors surrounding the child before and during the testing may alter the results. It is for this reason, among others, that clinical psychologists today are very reluctant to ascribe to a child a definitive IQ, but rather to talk more about his general range of intelligence as demonstrated by testing.

Repeated observations of thousands of children have unearthed the fact that a given child just may not have had the family milieu and the experiences that could have enabled him to pick up the information asked for on the test. In such families, the child's general store of knowledge and his ability to know how to approach the testing situation is grossly inadequate. His vocabulary may be far below the level expected for a child of his age. But these are "cultural" lacks. The IQ scored by a child from such a home will not reflect at all his real abilities or potential.

Mrs. _____: Up until this point you've concentrated on psychological learning difficulties. Have you any comments to make on the emotional problems of the child who suffers from mixed dominance? Two of my children are said to have this disorder, and I'm aware that there is much disagreement about the theory.

Dr. G.: The theory of mixed dominance in regard to reading disability is a respectable theory, but it's not by any means an all-encompassing theory. There are many children who have mixed dominance and yet read quite well. There are many children who don't read who don't have any sign of mixed dominance.

Mrs. _____: Could you tell me what mixed dominance is? Does it have to do with people who are left-handed?

Dr. G.: It's a condition in which the child has an eye-hand incoordination. They are right-eyed and left-handed or the opposite. It is obviously clear that the factor of left-handedness in and of itself is no problem, because we have millions of left-handed people who have never had any trouble at all learning to read. The left-handed people who have no trouble must be left-eyed, too. There's no conflict. But the condition where the eyedness doesn't go together with the handedness is supposed to create difficulty in the communication system in the cortex of the brain. I wish it were as simple as that. Actually, it's a rather complex theory to explain, and, I might add, one that itself by no means explains or establishes the single cause of reading disabilities.

Mrs. _____: My children are now eleven and twelve, and this condition turned up rather early in their school careers. They read beautifully, but they can't spell anything, and they're both underachievers according to the testing of their intelligence. They should be doing a lot better. I wonder if we've done everything we should along this line. They are in a school system that handles such things up to a point but. . . . They never had to be tutored every afternoon like so many of these other children who really can't read at all, but I know they have the feeling they aren't doing very well in school and I don't think this is very good for them.

Dr. G.: You say they read very well but you're concerned about their spelling, is that it?

Mrs. _____: I'm not as concerned about it as the school is. It's a very competitive system we have. Now, for instance, I've got a third one coming along, and I have no idea about her since she's just four. The others started off well and then in about the second or third grade started displaying many of the classic symptoms. They would have a spelling lesson and seem to know it, but the next day the words were all written backward.

Dr. G.: I live with those cases every day at our psycho-educational laboratory school. Do you actually have data that shows mixed dominance in both of them?

Mrs. _____: The preliminary tests were done at the clinic at the Massachusetts General Hospital. On the basis of this information the answer is "Yes," but the general theory now seems to be not to do too much about it if they're getting along reasonably well. The question is that today "reasonably well" isn't enough. The school feels I haven't been pushing them enough. So you see how these two opinions conflict.

Dr. G.: Are you talking about pushing them or having some special remedial tutoring?

Mrs. _____: Well, it's all part of the same situation, isn't it? Every year the teacher sends back a report that this child is not working up to his ability, and the children are told this, too. What effect does this have on the child? The older one is very conscientious, so she does better, but it seems much harder for my son. His general attitude is that he's just not terribly interested. Everybody says, "Oh, he's such a nice boy—maybe he'll be a late bloomer."

Dr. G.: He may well be. If you're anxious about it, I would have a thorough study made of the child to see if there is any particular reason why he should be having difficulty using symbols, such as words and numbers. Obviously, there is no set conclusion to arrive at here, no absolute answer.

As to the suggestion that he may be a "late bloomer," I can say that my observations indicate that this type of child does exist. It is true that many people who have later become famous through their contributions to science and scholarship, including literary production, were observed in the early grades at school to be poor or moderately slow learners. Then at adolescence—usually when they have made a solid and enthusiastic, possibly all-consuming, commitment and dedication to one field of learning or scholarship—their innate potential for intellectual greatness is activated. Not unusually this activation comes about through their strong positive identification in adolescence with some great teacher, actual or in history, and from that point on their devotion to a field of study or action is complete. Albert Einstein and Winston Churchill are good examples of the late-bloomer phenomena. Neither of them was regarded as an outstanding learner in the early years at school. It may be that with development and maturation this type of child suddenly and by some subtle process becomes freed from some disabling neurotic block that directly or indirectly is related to learning. With the resolution of his conflicts he is then free to utilize his real capacities. We just do not know with any accuracy what does happen in such children or adolescents, but we do know that delayed or late utilization of one's potentials does occur, and once that has happened the individual performs at an extremely high level.

Mrs. _____: How do you differentiate between a child who has a neurological problem and one who has emotional problems that interfere with learning?

Dr. G.: There are two main ways: First, the history you take from the parents helps to document any injury that might have occurred at birth or any trauma to the head or infectious disease that supervened after birth. Second, there are very precise neurological examinations that can be made. If the child is found to have a completely clean bill of health in both respects, historically and on examination, we have to look then for some reasonable psychological explanation. Of course, during these examinations it may become obvious that the child is emotionally upset. Every child has anxieties. When he isn't able to handle them very well or when they are continuous, they are bound to get in the way of his ability to learn. Often this type of child is tagged as mentally retarded and he ends up in a special school or institution. These children are educational retardates, if you will, but they are not mental retardates. It is the serious business of the medical and paramedical specialists to determine with the greatest possible accuracy whether the nonlearning child is or is not a mentally retarded child. All proper planning and care for the child depends on the accuracy of this differential diagnosis. And you must believe me when I state that in such cases the pediatricians, child psychiatrists, and child clinical psychologists are fully aware of their obligation to arrive at a correct appraisal of the situation.

Mrs. _____: I was wondering if you have an opinion regarding the Montessori nursery-school system as opposed to regular nursery schools.

Dr. G.: I have always thought that many aspects of the Montessori method are very good for preschool children. It is very important to get the child to pay attention in the relation of his sensations to his conceptions of the world about him. In Denver recently, I observed at a school in which they were trying to get the children who were nonreaders or poor readers to pay attention to what they were hearing. It was called "auditory enrichment." I'll get back to your question in a moment, but this bears on it somewhat. The psychologist took a recording machine and went to various public places, restaurants, the airport, a bus station. He made tapes of the sounds in each place and had the children listen to them. He would start the tape and ask them to tell him what clues they heard. He wouldn't accept any outright guesses that this was a gas station, for instance, but he would accept the clue which led them to think it might be a gas station. A teacher at the other end of the room wrote the clues on the blackboard. The whole class was jumping with excitement until they finally decided what the place was. This in a sense illustrates what the Montessori method relies on. Of course, Madame Montessori's view of psychology is rather antiquated now. Her ideas were based on the psychology of the late-19th century. She was a physician and relied heavily on neurological aspects of the child's development. But I think for youngsters in the preschool age the approach I've described is wonderful. They like it, and it is an ingenious way of getting children to develop and sharpen their sensory systems.

Mrs. _____: Don't you think that her method is rather rigid for such young children? I read in her book about the thirteen steps to be taken in washing the hands. When I visited a Montessori-method school to observe the method, I saw that the child could take only one thing out at a time and play with it. Then he had to put it back. The whole routine just seemed so rigid for such young children.

Dr. G.: But the value, I think, is along the line I mentioned. Getting them to know the differences in shapes, sizes, sounds, textures has a great deal of importance. Just recently I had occasion to review Montessori and her works, and my interest was reactivated. I do agree with you, however, about the rigidity.

Mrs. _____: My three-year-old was a Montessori dropout! She just hated it. The entire first three days they spent trying to show her how to push a chair into the table. If they could dispense with this type of rigidity, it would be great.

Mrs. _____: I was watching these kids wash their hands. If I ever had to wait that long for my children to wash up I'd never get anything done!

Mrs. _____: I have a good Montessori story. Recently, I was at an ice-cream parlor with a friend and our six children. My three-year-old spilled his ice-cream soda. A five-year-old who is a Montessori child grabbed a napkin, and in a very, very determined and systematic way she began to clean it up. She wiped only in a counterclockwise direction. She would take the napkin, soak up the liquid, and then squeeze it into my son's glass. We all just sat and marveled at her efficiency. My three-year-old wanted to drink what went back into the glass, but she even took care of that by moving it away from him.

Dr. G.: Madame Montessori did make a great contribution. If she did nothing else, she at least got the teaching profession to stop looking upon the child as a "little adult." She stressed that it was a *child* they were dealing with. She was an expert teacher herself, and it has been very difficult for any teacher since to utilize her methods with the excellence, thoroughness, and understanding that Madame Montessori herself could.

IV. THE LEAP INTO ADULTHOOD

7

Developmental Tasks Between Twelve and Twenty-One

IN EACH GENERATION adults devote a great deal of talk and much head shaking to the alleged shortcomings of the young. "The adolescents of *today,* they proclaim, "will never be able to meet the rigors of adult responsibility *tomorrow.*" You can find these direful predictions throughout the long written record of history, even as far back as the ancient Greeks, but it is hard to believe that the complaints have ever been as insistent as they are now. And as we approach the close of our tumultuous century, another development adds to the discomfort of adults. The long-cherished adage "children are to be seen and not heard" has gone by the board. Today's young are coming through to us loud and clear!

Too often we discuss the problems of adolescence without putting them into a relevant framework. We have trouble recognizing that much of the so-called "generation gap" comes from our reactions to youthful reactions that are quite normal for this particular individual at his particular stage of development. The task of maintaining good mental health is a continuing and ever-changing one. It is never completed.

Through the teen-age years these changes come at a faster pace and are often more dramatic than at any other time in our lives. Perhaps as we discuss the kinds of developmental tasks these no-longer-children, not-yet-adults grapple with, we'll come to see the real issues involved in their behavior and not give all our attention to the merely superficial manifestations.

First, I would like to emphasize that the new pressures appearing in adolescence are, of course, superimposed on the old concerns which have been present since infancy and which we already have discussed. The adolescent has a continuing need for the security that comes when he senses that he is wanted, loved, and respected as an individual, when he can accept that he is being treated fairly in relation to his brothers and sisters and others of his age, and when he realizes that his parents love not only their children but also each other.

One problem that antedates his adolescence but has a tremendous effect on his adjustment in this trying period is the continuing chore of dealing with his own aggressive instincts. From his earliest days the child learns to cope with frustrations and to work out ways of handling his "angry feelings," and in the years after puberty and into adolescence, these old methods will receive some very severe testing. But the child who is comfortable with his own controls will not find it so difficult to handle these feelings and drives that are appearing with a new insistence and with a new demand for expression in action.

We will talk later about sexual adjustment and sexual identification, but, again, this task is not solved during these years alone. The foundation in truthful fact and trusting reference that his parents—we hope—have established for him in earlier years will largely determine how smooth or how upsetting his sexual maturation will be. The elaborate and intensive studies of the psychoanalytic school certainly show us that sexual instincts and body pleasures are present in a diffuse form in infancy and childhood and that their meanings and the control of them are part of the child's early education. My point in bringing up again early tasks that have required adequate interim solutions is to show how they inevitably represent themselves for resolution in adolescence.

Now let's turn to some of the particular or peculiar concerns and problems which set this age off from the other stages within the developmental scheme which we have followed while tracing the growth of personality.

How to express the seemingly innate drive for emancipation and independence from his parents is at the very core of the teen-ager's problems, and it requires a solution at once satisfying to him and satisfactory to his environment. His own internal forces and the external pressures of society as a whole insist that he find a solution to his dependency problems. Suddenly, so it seems, he must be self-sufficient and independent. This drive for "instant independence" cannot help but set up serious conflicts. He *must* believe himself capable of standing alone, yet at the same time he has to decide whether or not he wants to and, more importantly, whether he is able to. There has always been the fear of losing the help and guidance of his parents. Now, though fearing that total independence may present added problems he cannot solve, he must *choose* to separate himself from them. The indecision of normal boys and girls at this age is one of their most noted characteristics. Never is this indecision or ambivalence so apparent as in the question of when and how and under what circumstances adolescents will stand apart from those upon whom they have leaned so heavily. Is it any wonder that they hesitate before making the decisions that will irrevocably determine not only their social and vocational futures but also their future emotional health?

Even for the adolescent who has great self-confidence there is always the question of whether he is really up to meeting the demands of the many new situations he is to face. His limited experience in complex human affairs can only raise fears that he may not be able to do for himself what others have so long done for him. From early childhood, he has carried the image of his parents as all-knowing and all-powerful. Even though a child may be aware of some of the limitations of his parents, he still has drawn from their store of knowledge and opinion a good part of what he knows and believes. How then can he decide to rely solely on his own untested resources? The most natural and satisfying way, of course, is to cut these all-knowing and all-powerful parents down to size—to decide that their way is not the only way or even the best way. As a matter of fact, he is inclined to dismiss their way as the least likely to do well what needs to be done! And so begins that great devaluation of the parents he has loved so much and trusted so completely. But is it the best way? Is it any wonder this child is in such a state of conflict?

The adolescent's belittlement and derogation of his parents may come early or late, but come it must if the child is to grow emotionally and become an "independent" adult. This is the age of overreaction in respect to all issues, and certainly the tendency to devalue unduly everything a parent says or does or stands for is a good example of this overreaction. We would hope that adolescents won't have to question *all* the values they've learned, but sometimes they do. It may be they have to do this in order to figure out where they stand themselves as separated individauls—even if they end up coming reluctantly, and much later, to some of the same conclusions their mothers and fathers have held. No one can mature if he believes that some other person holds all the solutions to all the questions. He must feel he can come up with some of the answers himself.

As painful as this stage may be, it has to come and it is best to have it come on schedule. If the teen-ager does not throw off this abject total dependence on his parents, their ideas and their ideals, two things may happen. He may never emerge from childlike dependency on his parents, or he may carry over the same relationship of dependency to the other persons who come into his life—perhaps the one he marries. The rebellion necessarily will come out in later life. Perhaps you all know a perennial adolescent who either hasn't done anything at all about the solution of this basic developmental problem or even as an adult seems to be in constant revolt. Some wives and husbands will recognize this type of delayed adolescent rebellion, or the total absence of it, in their spouses. There is an optimal time for this step to be taken, a "critical developmental moment" in respect to the whole sequence of steps in personality development.

If you look at the parents' side of the picture, you find that they, too, are caught somewhere in the conflicts of their adolescent child. They are gratified that the child is able to make sensible decisions for himself, that he is able to think through problems and come up with answers that may be unique and quite workable. If the child is not allowed to be independent, or if he shows no urge to be independent or is afraid of being independent, then the mother and father worry that they have not allowed this child to grow up. Their success as parents seems to be threatened. So they, like the adolescent himself, are pushed and pressured from all sides.

There is on the parental side the drive to steer children toward independence, and, as you and I know, sometimes parents urge or require their children to assume adult behavior too early. When they fail in these efforts everyone is disappointed. I suppose there are some parents who have an urge to push the child out of the nest, but more parents probably have an excessive need to be needed. It's often a severe blow to parents to discover that they're no longer wanted or needed by their children to the extent and with the intensity they were wanted and needed only yesterday. Hence, we find some mothers who can do an excellent job when their children are young and completely dependent but who cannot tolerate the independence of adolescents. There are other parents who do not like the utter dependency of the little child and who tend always to urge forward the growth and development of the child into the self-sufficiency of adolescence. These parents get on quite well as the children reach their teens. Sometimes these parents can achieve companionship with the child only after he reaches a stage where they can talk together and share more or less adult activities. The point I'm making is that there are conflicts on both sides—i.e., in the adolescents and in their parents—and the ramifications of these dual conflicts in the feelings of the two generations can lead to troublesome battles between them. At any rate, both sides have a great stake in this drive of the adolescent for independent thought and action, and it is well not to overlook the fact that your own involvement in this drive, whether positive or negative, may determine some of your responses to this young person.

Before I move on, I must give a word of practical advice. It is true that some youngsters are quite aggressive in their devaluation of their parents, but for the parents to meet this aggression with equal aggression is only to compound the difficulty. If the adolescent can provoke you and involve you in counteraggression, then you have played into his hands. The real issue under discussion at the moment gets lost or clouded, and your reaction becomes the focal point for struggle. Having had a couple of children go through this stage of adolescence, I know how trying they can be! It's not easy to choke back that hostile retort, but every time you manage to control it, you're ahead of the game. And I say this in full awareness that the provocation can be very intense and painful.

In most adolescents the behavior so exasperating to parents follows fairly consistent patterns. Take, for example, the disheveled phase of adolescence, which in recent years has been dirty as well as disheveled. We will all remember what tremendous energy we expended in teaching our children to be clean. Some families more than others have put great emphasis on early toilet training, table manners, tidy rooms, and regular baths. Our children, too, remember! What more natural choice could there be for the opening assault on parental standards? So they begin to chip away. As a weapon, the resulting "new look" has another point in its favor—it almost always brings strong parental reaction. We worked hard to get them clean, and after all the effort we're not about to settle for less.

Some years back this disheveled phase seemed to confine itself to boys, and we consoled ourselves with the notion that our young man would shape up as soon as he began to notice the opposite sex. How naïve this simple faith seems today! And how out of place a washed and starched young man would feel among today's disheveled maidens!

On the current adolescent scene the comparatively minor parental "expectancies" regarding dress and cleanliness have been seized upon by the adolescent for special derision within his more general strategy for total devaluation of the older generation's values and standards and its hitherto unchallengeable authority. We might have expected the tangled locks, the scraggly beard and the filthy jeans as symbols of the drive for total devaluation and we should treat them as such. To the adolescent, of course, they have the added value of visibility and therefore obvious provocation, almost certain to arouse anger and bring counteraggressive acts from the parental generation. Although neither group has given voice to the inner meaning of these symbols, I am sure that the adolescents and their parents both know the true significance. My suggestion to parents would be that they refrain from joining battle over these minor items, for while they conceivably could win the battle, they might lose the far more important war, if we may so designate the outcome of the adolescent's personality development. What really counts here is not the appearance of the moment but whether and how soon the adolescent will come to view his present in the true perspective of his future, whether he will choose the education and make the occupational or professional identification that will free his innate abilities for the most constructive and satisfying applications. And all this to the end that he will be a happy and contributing member of his own adult society to come.

In almost no other aspect of their relationship is the adolescent so able to thwart his parents' ideas and values as in their expectations for his performance at school and in his vocational plans for the future. Even if he isn't protesting loudly that he "hates school," you can depend that at least one course he is taking at his parent's direction is boring, too hard, and, according to him, of no possible use for later life. While this particular protest is far from new, it is couched today in terms that make it much more difficult to deal with.

It is my impression that the significant concern of many, perhaps most, of today's parents is not for the momentarily "deviant" behavior of the adolescent or even for his ruthless attack on parental standards. Deep down in the parents' system of values lies a genuine fear that lapse of time alone will cost the adolescent his educational opportunity and thus his hope of realizing worthwhile ambitions. From their own experience and observation of the realities of life, parents know only too well that certain of the classroom doors *do* close on the high-school dropout, on the leave-of-absence college undergraduate, and, in general, on the roaming adolescent whose lust for devaluation seems never to attain satisfaction. There is a ray of hope to be found in recent studies showing that seventy percent or so of college dropouts do eventually return and get the bachelor's degree, but not necessarily at the colleges of their choice. Nevertheless, similar studies indicate that high school dropouts, including those of demonstrably high potential, do not go back to school in appreciable numbers.

And so it is not the superficial appearance of dress or hair that really concerns today's parents. Fundamental to their anxiety is a dim but sensible realization that these are *symptoms* signaling a potential for the destruction of the educational and occupational futures of their children. As a clinician dealing with such problems, I have to agree. Professional research would indicate that these parental anxieties are not unrealistic; they do not arise merely from the intractable need and determination of parents to make adolescent children conform to every traditional standard of conduct and behavior.

Another change in adolescent or preadolescent behavior is noticeable today. The "I-hate-girls-and-I'm-never-going-to-get-married" stage seems to be fading. More infrequently we see girls who wish to extend the "tomboy" phase (eleven to fifteen), with its passion for strenuous athletics, into mid- or late-adolescence. On the contrary, there is more "companionship" than ever before between adolescent boys and girls of both high-school and college age. There is a stronger alliance between them, by no means reserved to social and education affairs. In all the student movements and civil-rights demonstrations even to the manning of the barricades in the streets and the "seizure" of college buildings, the sexes band together in "causes" and programs for the betterment of society. While we may quarrel sometimes with their methods or worry that they will fall prey to the false and self-seeking leader, we must nonetheless concede that they are more involved in and committed to sociopolitical ideals than were their predecessors. But the item for emphasis here is the fact that the adolescents so involved and so committed comprise both sexes.

Needless to say, all this joining of forces leads to a "new conformity." It is not a conformity to the Establishment that has been forced upon them, but it is no less a group conformity and quite anti-individualistic in its nature. The basic tenet of their philosophy is the conviction that betterment of society is of much greater importance than enhancement or advancement of the individual.

In the past, young people formed attachments to, and identification with, older men or older women and developed strong desires to identify with these older people and to emulate them. Often these were schoolteachers, club leaders, or friends of the father or mother. I need not tell you that it took a strong, tolerant, and secure parent to watch this switch of allegiance to another adult without a sense of hurt. Today, we hear, "Don't trust anyone over thirty." It would seem that youth is rejecting these valuable role models. The models of today are creations of youth itself—they are to be found in the members of the contemporary group.

I have described adolescence as the age of indecision. It is hard to keep up with the changes of mood and mind. One moment our children seem set on a certain path, only to reverse themselves in the next breath. These constant changes become really important, sometimes crucial, when they involve decisions about school. The trouble is, we are calling on the adolescent to make long-range plans at a time when to him nothing past tomorrow or this weekend seems very real.

Adolescents are constantly confronted with what we want and expect of them. Our feelings are conveyed not just by words but by the tone of voice, or the look of shock or gratification. Sometimes our children cannot meet our expectations. Sometimes they choose not to comply.

Today, because of the numbers of young people and the structure of our educational system, it is possible for the individual to become locked into a certain tract that may not be right for him. The faulty evaluation may not be exposed until too late. If a child decides as early as the ninth or tenth grade that he doesn't want to go along with this plan, if he begins then to defect, his opportunities may start to diminish. Parents see this and in their terror often come down on the child very hard. This sort of discipline rarely works. In the past there was a more compliant attitude. There were more choices open, particularly for the late bloomer. Now, however, what you do at fourteen may have real importance not just for college but for graduate school and thus for the rest of life.

You all know someone who was a good student until high school and who then fell apart academically. It's very sad to see bright young people who, because of their need to revolt against parental pressure, cut off their own potential. It is no less sad to watch the struggles of the not-so-bright under the burden of parents' unrealistic expectations.

Vocational choices will rarely be sound when they are arrived at before the individual has any sense of his own identity. They may change from week to week or they may be clung to in an effort to avoid the confusion of making other decisions. The best we can do is to help our children hold on to as many possibilities as they can, not to close doors they can't reopen.

Through many discussions with adolescents, I have learned that a considerable part of their frustration and dissatisfaction in respect to academic and vocational planning is due to the seeming endlessness of the road that leads to an acceptable future. For example, in the days of their fathers and grandfathers a college education—I was going to say a "mere" college education—was held to be quite sufficient for almost any position outside the law and medicine. Today, however, a college education, with perhaps even a master's degree, is no longer adequate if one is aiming for the higher levels in management, administration, research, teaching, or scholarship. The enormous increase in the amount and diversity of knowledge in the past half century just cannot be assimilated in four years of college education. The old four-year road to acceptable proficiency now stretches out to a seemingly interminable grind of the seven or eight years required for a doctorate. At mere thought of the ordeal and of the mountains of material to be mastered many of our brightest adolescents tend to quail. Responsible and self-sufficient adulthood seems to fade further and further into the future.

More and more, fortunately, the psychological implications of this long travail are on the minds of sensible college deans when they have to deal with the dropout or the potential dropout. Not all the cries for curricular reform come from members of Students for a Democratic Society. In medicine and the law new curricula, with a minimum of "core studies" and a broadened choice of electives for finer and finer specialization, seek to cover more ground in the same time and spare the student from "education expansion shock." The other hard subjects, such as the sciences and mathematics, seem destined, sooner or later, to take similar paths.

It seems a little pointless to dwell here on the "generation gap" and the "failure of communication" between teen-agers and their parents. We hear too much about them now. Families who are communicating well know it; if they aren't they know that, too. Of course, it is extremely important to keep dialogue open between the generations, but much of the adolescent's withdrawn, quiet demeanor is again of developmental origins. This is the age of short answers, or no answers at all. The disdainful look or the attitude of resigned tolerance greets most of the genuine concerns of their elders. But here again, exterior appearance belies much of what these young ones really feel. They would be happier if they were as certain of everything as they would lead you to believe, if they were in as firm control of their own feelings as they pretend.

To separate from those you've depended upon, to have to learn to think and decide for yourself, isn't easy and can't always be accomplished in a nice or even a polite way. Parents must respect and understand this struggle, their child's need for time alone, his choice of an afternoon doing "nothing" with a friend in preference to a family expedition. Parents must be ready to listen when an adolescent does want to talk, and must accept without too much resentment his failure to respond when they themselves have something to say.

I do not want to imply that it's easy for a mother or father to see a child make decisions that can't work out. I certainly do not believe in the "anything-goes" way of life. We all need rules and guidelines for our behavior, but we also need understanding and some flexibility to fit our specific circumstances. One of the most difficult lessons to learn is that individual actions have consequences. No one can or should be shielded from this truth, and home is the easiest place for it to be learned. Though it may be difficult for the parent, youth's cry, "I'll make my own mistakes," can lead to further development and greater maturity as often as it leads to failure and unhappiness.

Events all through this particular stage of development show that the need for independence and the need for dependence alternate. Children of this age do not quite dare give up their childhood altogether, nor can they quite bring themselves to refuse to grow up. The parents' role in all this, it seems to me, is to recognize that such conflicts are inherent in these wild swings of attitude and behavior but that beneath the indifference and devaluation there is a strong need for parental empathy and guidance.

The adolescent does not actually *believe* he is capable of

controlling all his inner wishes and demands; he is not quite sure to what lengths he can allow himself to go. He must be helped to see that there are few "either-or" situations in life—it doesn't have to be "my way" or "your way" if we are both interested in the "best way." With some patience and effort a negotiated peace usually can be found.

Obviously, one of the biggest problems this growing person faces, and one which perhaps more than any other fills many parents with fear and trembling is the control and sublimation of his sexual instincts.

It is in this period, we must recognize, that boys and girls must take the definitive step to firmly establish their identity with their own sex. This is not an easy task. More is involved than sexual aspirations and activities. Two possibilities commonly are seen. The phase of sexual identification may be accelerated with the child throwing himself into the social swim, taking on all the latest fads and showing an endless concern in the other sex. At the other extreme is the tendency to extend the rather neutral boy-girl stage. Adolescents in the latter phase often stay somewhat apart from the group and hang on to their childish interests. It is important to realize that either approach can be motivated by anxiety about growing up and coping with these new feelings. By anticipating some of the inevitable questions and confusions, an alert parent can do much to make this transition easier. It is helpful to know that some of these concerns are universal and that the basic questions come up generation after generation.

Out of all the differences of opinion, ideas, ideals, and moral codes that hit him from all sides, the adolescent must formulate a satisfactory and satisfying code of conduct for himself. He has to find some code of conduct that is satisfactory just for him. This is not only a moral code in regard to right or wrong but also a social code that has to do with his total attitude toward the other members of the human race. A code of social behavior which he can follow without guilt or self-incrimination is as essential to him as the code of moral behavior. Unfortunately, attainment of these goals is a much more difficult task for today's adolescents than it was a generation ago. Today's communications networks and today's jet-powered mobility confront him with more sets of conflicting values. Our affluence puts off the day when he must earn his own living, and this postponement of the world's work afflicts him with conflicts, which can be severe, of frustration and guilt. It is not surprising that all this inner discord should lead to flight or, worse, to recourse to harmful but for the moment anxiety-alleviating drugs. Has any previous generation ever had its normal and expected tasks of maturation so compounded by the world's ills? When adolescents insist that the "over-thirty" generations "just don't understand," it is to these compounded complexities in their lives they are referring. And, indeed, can we over thirty really understand?

I hope three points have come across. The first is perhaps best called the "genetic point of view," in which current behavior can be understood only in the light of the individual's past experience. The second point of emphasis has been that the establishment of good mental health has to be "worked at" and is a continuing, day-after-day, never-ending process. And, finally, we stress that although adolescents do share common concerns with all other ages, they are beset by a special and perilous task—the taking of that final, long leap into adulthood. Their unpredictable, inconsistent behavior is a normal by-product of this most difficult time of life.

But, contrary to what you might expect, I am an incurable optimist as to the eventual outcome of our children, particularly those who worry us. On my side always are the potentially beneficial effects of genetics and irresistible maturation. The effects of these processes may be hard to discern in an individual case under brief scrutiny, but in my experience the eventual expression will be salutary and write an end to our anxieties.

QUESTIONS

Mrs. _____: One of my friends is very worried about her adolescent daughter. As the girl was growing up, she appeared to be mastering all the developmental tasks you have discussed. There seemed to be very few problems. There has never been a feeding or sleeping problem, never undue problems over separation. She seemed to resolve each stage very well as she went along. She did good work in school. There was certainly every reason to believe that she would continue in good shape. But when she hit adolescence, things just seemed to go completely wild. Her schoolwork collapsed. She became promiscuous. She lost interest in her appearance. She has seemed to go through a period in which she has developed not only the usual problems that all adolescents have but also each of them in exaggerated form. Is it common for things to go so wrong after such a good beginning?

Dr. G.: Well, I don't know how common it is, but it can happen. From what you say, she was a model of the very best behavior. One wonders whether or not there was always a certain rigidity there, whether her natural resentments ever came out. She conformed very well; maybe she conformed too well. But when you get to adolescence, you go through a whole restructuring of situations, partly because of the impact of physiology. Getting away from home and learning from your peer group that other kinds of behavior exist in the world are important, too. In other words, what is challenged in adolescence is both the omnipotence and the omniscience of the parent. In a child who has been too restricted, I mean in the sense of "this is it and you do it," the task of breaking away from the power and all-knowingness of the parent may be more of an issue. Perhaps a child like this has never questioned what she's been taught, has never had many ideas of her own, has never stood on her own feet. Now, out of the clear sky, comes a period of very thorough and serious thinking. She may be questioning her parents and everything they stand for. I would assume this questioning comes just as easily to children who up to this point have seemed to be stereotypes of good behavior. Perhaps they have to go to excess in order to demonstrate that they are no longer thinking like a child in regard to their mothers and fathers.

Mrs. _____: We've talked about the importance of the first five or seven years. Are children like this likely then to come out on the other end by resuming the values they have been taught in the early years?

Dr. G.: Yes. Usually when they reach their twenties, they will come back gradually to those values. As they reach their forties most of them will be back where they started. Didn't I tell you the story of the man who said of his father, "Look how much he has learned since I was sixteen"? This revelation tends to come to many youngsters about the time they have graduated from college, but not when they are entering college. I think it continues as they go along. What we're referring to here is not the specific attitude of some particular parent but to the moral and social standards which have come down to all us parents through the centuries. They were written on tablets somewhere. Unfortunately, they broke the tablet, but the tenets still remain. In other words, the injunction "You shall not" in respect to a lot of things begins to make much more sense to the individual as he matures. While parents are waiting for the arrival of this day, it seems to take forever, but it does come.

Mrs. _____: I have a fourteen-year-old who has found herself a constant companion, a boy, and my husband is very upset. She doesn't ignore her girlfriends and she has many of them. What is your feeling about this in a youngster this age? She wants to date, but we won't let her. We told her he is welcome at the house, and if there are any boy-girl parties she is allowed to go to them.

Dr. G.: It seems to me you gave her the right answer. You haven't excluded her from having a male companion under the right auspices, and I think that in the absence of the right auspices at this age they may get into trouble.

Mrs. _____: What is your feeling about a fourteen-year-old's seeing just one boy constantly rather than "playing the field"?

Dr. G.: I think they ought to have some variation. That early adolescent crushes are a reality we all know, but I think where they exist there must be some rules about how much time the boy and girl are to have together by themselves. You don't have to hang around every second, but I think there ought to be someone in the house. You can't say, "You must have four boyfriends," but you can suggest that it's probably better for her to know as many different boys as she can. Point out that boys differ, and that it would be well for her to look over quite a few before she gets too involved with one.

Mrs. _____: Most of the kids feel that if they don't have one person to depend on they are left out of things. They all pair up, which means that there really are no free fields to play.

Dr. G.: This "going steady" to the exclusion of all other companionship is still a relatively new affair. And it's sometimes being fostered, unfortunately, by parents who take great delight in the premature social life of their children.

Mrs. _____: I wonder if it comes more from the insecurity of the boy, and not so much from the girl. I think this is a sort of a switch from what it used to be.

Dr. G.: He wants to be sure that he has a date he can count on, that she's not going to go to the dance with somebody else.

Mrs. _____: As I say, our daughter has not been allowed to go out on dates. This boy does come to the house and at his curfew hour he leaves. He seems like a reliable, good boy, but I have told her that I think she still ought to play the field.

Dr. G.: Oh, I think this is important, because she may find many youngsters far more fascinating than this one. There is a sense of security in always knowing you have somebody to go out with you, and I think you're right that boys tend to feel this much more than girls. Perhaps it's the business of ownership.

Mrs. _____: I am twenty-eight. When I was a freshman in high school, I was over in Japan with my family. Because of the circumstances, I went to an Army dependents' school. I don't know if other people my age, back here in this country, had a similar situation, but over there from the time you were a freshman you dated one particular fellow. After you went out with him once or twice, he gave you a little ID ring or bracelet or something. Then you would go out with just this one person. It was a security, but I think I might have gone steady with about eight different fellows in less than a year!

Dr. G.: That's a good record—a good record of steadiness!

Mrs. _____: The point that I want to make is that my parents were really wonderful in that they accepted this perhaps because I was in special circumstances.

Dr. G.: I think they must have done much better than I did. I can still hear myself saying, "That fellow, is he here again? Hasn't he got a home?"

Mrs. _____: That was another good thing about my parents—they never really chopped away at any fellow that I dated, and when I think back, some of them were just awful! They never—until after I had stopped dating a boy—said anything against him. Many times since then my mother has said that her skin just crawled at the sight of some of those fellows, but she realized that I was an individual and that I should have an opportunity to make decisions about my friends without interference from her. It's amazing, but even after I stopped dating certain fellows, they would come back to visit my parents because they enjoyed them.

Dr. G.: They were remarkable parents. This was obviously a happy household for these people to visit. It's difficult for a parent when a slob comes around. I feel for parents in that situation. Of course, some feel that no one is ever good enough for their child.

Mrs. _____: My mother was certainly never so understanding. There was a lot of pressure in my high school because there were cliques and everybody dated just one fellow. My mother was terrible! She wouldn't let me go out until I was a sophomore, and then not very often, and the boys were deathly afraid of her. When I became a cheerleader in my junior year, I was "somebody" in the school, but even then she was very strict. I suffered a great deal. I feel that it could have been handled a lot more gently. I cried many a night!

Dr. G.: I'm afraid many girls have. It's a pity that more parents don't realize these situations they disapprove of or fear would take care of themselves more quickly if they didn't resist them so vigorously. Making your child's friends feel comfortable in your home has several benefits—aside from demonstrating a pleasant hospitality. It allows you to get to know them, and it also allows your child to see them in the context in which he or she has been raised. The undesirable traits you may notice will probably become more obvious to her in this setting.

Mrs. _____: We have another situation with our oldest girl. What do you do when your daughter decides that she wants to see just one person and this person is Black? We have told our kids, we will do anything in our power to help the Blacks work out their problems, but we frankly don't like this going steady. In this case it might lead to marriage.

Dr. G.: This is a problem, of course, that is highly charged emotionally in the minds of all of us. It's one that parents are facing frequently these days.

Mrs. _____: We've pointed out that if this boy were an intelligent person and had something to offer intellectually we could understand it, but it seems to us that they have no common interests.

Dr. G.: This is a sad thing. You can be all against racism, but you know if there should be a marriage of these two, they would be faced with terrific problems. You can't easily jump out of your heritage even though you think you should if you are really a liberal person. But when there aren't common interests, the relationship seems doomed from the beginning, whether or not there is a difference in color.

Mrs. _____: Maybe this is just my own foolish philosophy, but I think what's more important to teenagers is the experience children have when they feel betrayed by their parents. One of my friends was even disowned because she abandoned her religion. The thing that I remember so vividly was the tremendous satisfaction and happiness I felt when my parents said, "All right, you know what's right and what's wrong. You've lived with us, and we realize that this is something that is extremely important to you, so we will trust you to handle this situation." It seems to me that if you don't give teen-agers a red flag to wave, they're probably going to stay right where you want them nine times out of ten. If all the time you are saying, "No, no, you can't do this or that," you've had it. I went to college with a girl whose father hated Catholics. This was the only issue that would make him absolutely livid. They were Protestants, but this girl, who loved her parents very much, became a Catholic. I am convinced that she had only one reason for doing this. She saw his bigotry as a real weakness or hypocrisy, and it made her seek out this particular means to prove to him that he was wrong. So many teen-agers do the same sort of thing, and this girl discovered what she thought was right for her. I think she would have been a very happy Episcopalian for the rest of her life if her father hadn't hated Catholics so violently.

Dr. G.: Your point about "waving the red flag" is certainly a good one. We've talked about why parents, out of their broader experience, do sometimes overreact when their children embark on what appears to be a dangerous course of action. They see only the threatening long-range consequences. Often, the overreaction—and not the issue at hand—becomes the child's focus of action. He may push *on* really because he now has something to push *at*. The parent thus helps confirm the very reality he has feared. He might have fared better if—to borrow a phrase—he had "kept his cool."

Adolescents, and particularly the present-day adolescents, are against the Establishment. Now, the Establishment may be the family, the church, the political, economic, or educational system. If the Establishment gets its hair cut once every three weeks, they won't. They are disgruntled with the Establishment. Today, they give more open expression to their disgruntlement on all fronts. More than any generation of adolescents I have read about in history, they are totally disenchanted with the Establishment of the family, with its rules and regulations, its concern over wealth and status, and its racial prejudices. They see the injustices of the world—how we mistreat the Blacks or the awful things we did to the American Indians. (I saw a TV program the other night about the American Indians. How can we keep it up year after year for three centuries? It is just unbelievable, this casual cruelty.) It is this kind of Establishment that our children are opposed to, and we must not discourage them. I think this is a good step in a way. Sure, it's rebellion, but it is part of the maturing process and it has a constructive effect. I try to make the point with adolescents that it is possible to carry on a neurotic kind of anti-Establishment activity to a point where you defeat yourself. If you don't study when you're a sophomore in high school, you can commit educational suicide. (There are no two ways about it any more. Either you do or you don't go on to college or if you go you may have to settle for one you don't want. You can revolt against the established school and you can rebel against your father and mother's ideals and ideas, but if you are alone, carrying out your rebellion neurotically for your own internal satisfaction, there is many times a point of no return. There is that point where idealism must meet with realism, and reality has been with us for a long time!

Mrs. _____: Getting back to interracial dating—isn't this a part of evolution? Isn't it going to happen whether or not we want it to? We're just this way because of the age we live in. The simple truth of it is that a person meets a person and if he is of the right character and just as worthy, it isn't wrong. We have as individuals got to make ourselves have the courage to live with this and not to make this distinction if our children bring home a boy of another color who is just as nice as anybody else.

Mrs. _____: My objection is that we don't want an intermarriage because of the many problems that come of it in our society at the present time.

Mrs. _____: If your daughter of marriageable age has been brought up without prejudice, how can you now insist that if she does take the step she wants to take you will not support her?

Mrs. _____: We have never said, "You can't." We have just tried to discuss the possible outcome of such a step.

Dr. G.: As I emphasized before, this problem is becoming increasingly important and significant for adolescents and their parents. We also agree that it is a problem highly charged with emotion and involves a reexamination of some of the deeply ingrained values to which our society has adhered for generations. We sometimes forget that this is as serious a problem in the hearts and minds of the Blacks as it is in those of the Whites. The Blacks rightfully cherish their identity also, and I believe they will do so even more strongly in the years ahead. Who knows what will happen in the way of modification of our present values, and prejudices, when the Blacks, through equitable opportunities in all spheres of life, will be able to demonstrate and realize their human potentials?

It is my feeling that the *youth* of today in America, far more clearly than adults, recognize that these potentials are there, and they recognize, too, that it is they—and the coming generations—who will have to face and solve the problems. Youth, both Black and White, is trying desparately to *tell* us this, and they are also telling us that they view these tasks unafraid.

It is obvious to you that I have no general answer for this problem of interracial marriage that you present. However, as the situation becomes more common, one hopes that those involved will be aware of the reality and mature enough to face it.

Mrs. _____: I have a completely different kind of question. We have a child who is in the process of going for college admission interviews. She is one who pressures herself about her schoolwork to the point where she's exhausted. I am wondering what attitude we should take. As I have told her, if need be, I don't care if she doesn't get into *any* college, and if she wants a year off from school she can have it. She's been an excellent student, but she is pushing herself so that she is driving all of us mad. What can we do?

Dr. G.: Well, you've done your best to make your position clear. If she doesn't get into college *A* it's all right; if she doesn't get into college *B* or college *C* that's all right, too. However, I don't think your saying this is going to have much effect on her, because along the line somewhere she has incorporated the notion that these are the standards that she should live up to academically. She is afraid, of course, of failing not only the standards you and your husband have set for her but also those she has set for herself. She is running against her own standards now, not just yours. I would continue to try to help her by saying, "Please, don't put such a tremendous investment in this business of college admission. We'll be happy with whatever choice you make." I think that all you can do is tell her you are perfectly satisfied with her accomplishments and gratified that her expectations are high but that they must not be so high that she is going to feel let down if a certain college doesn't admit her. I am sure you've done your best, but this is a difficult year for her. The pressure comes from all sides—the peer group and the whole school hierarchy. The schools often feel, "This girl should get into Radcliffe because it will be for the good of our high school, etc." Just try to relieve any additional pressures that she may have on her.

Mrs. _____: Would it be helpful if you worried along with her so that she felt that she had somebody who could understand her problem and would feel as badly as she if she failed? Usually when the parent says, "Don't worry," it doesn't really conteract the pressure. Somehow in the mind of the young person it means that either they don't care or they don't understand. What the young person really feels is a sense of being very alone with this monster concern.

Dr. G.: I certainly don't think a parent should go along and indicate that he or she is going to be disappointed if a child doesn't get into college *A*, for example. I think that would be very sad. I think that the course you are taking in trying to modify these great expectations is the better tactic. We can hope your daughter will recognize that you are not so heavily invested in this that you are going to feel she has failed if she doesn't get in. I am sure you have made this quite plain to her, but I certainly would not identify with her in the sense of sharing her anxiety. That, I think, would be very upsetting for her. This is done once in a while, but I don't think it ever helps very much. Certainly this is not a situation where I'd suggest trying it out.

Mrs. _____: We hear so much today about "finding one's identity." Much of what is written seems to suggest that unless the adolescent breaks away violently from his parents, he hasn't really made the break and found himself. Isn't it possible to do it rather more gently and yet still take all the essential developmental steps? Are all the fireworks necessary?

Dr. G.: It is not necessary for an adolescent to break away "violently" to assure either himself or his parents that he has established his identity and independence. All one has to do to substantiate this fact is to note the millions of adolescents who are solving the various problems involved in growing up without resorting to the extremes of antiparental behavior that we see in a minority of this group. The "few" get all of the attention and publicity through the news media and, indeed, in social science and clinical research studies. Research relative to deviant behavior is extremely important, but the reports that reach the public press are sometimes interpreted to mean that all adolescents, or a great majority of them, are exhibiting behavior bordering on the bizarre. The adolescent turmoil state, with its complete repudiation and derogation of all parental and establishment codes of control, is seen relatively infrequently. For the majority of adolescents such outbursts of violent defiance are seen only rarely and do not involve the young person's total personality. Nor do they make for a complete dissolution of the positive, previously established relationship between themselves and their parents. In short, the fireworks aren't necessary!

Mrs. _____: I can't think of anything that threatens a parent more than finding out that his child is promiscuous. Is this so-called sexual revolution just another way of rebelling against parents?

Dr. G.: I don't see how anyone can expect the parents of an adolescent to accept his sexual promiscuity. The sexual code of ethics that has been instilled in parents has placed this behavioral breech at the very top of the list of unacceptable sexual behavior. In the past, everything from "hellfire and damnation" to social ostracism has been promised these offenders. Young people are questioning—and rightly so— many of our established values, but nowhere do they show a greater lack of reasoning than in their apparent tacit or defiant assumption that their parents should be able to accept this particular aspect of their revolution. Few parents will ever consider alteration of their ethical code. Parents just cannot make such a radical change in their own deeply rooted feelings in respect to sexual expression in a single generation. Adolescents who embark on this path must do it with the knowledge that they cannot expect acceptance or approbation from their parents. It just won't be forthcoming.

Mrs. _____: No one has asked about teen-agers who use drugs. Could you say something about this as it relates to the development of personality?

Dr. G.: Much has been said elsewhere, and I'm certain you know that adolescents resort to taking drugs for various reasons.

In the majority of cases, drugs are tried once or twice so that the individual will be able to say that he's "with it." He cannot then be accused of being a "square," bound to the Establishment. It is not entirely unlike the high-school or college student of earlier years who had to get drunk at least once. These are issues that are among the tests for membership in the adolescent society. One complies once or twice as a token of belonging. And it is antiparent.

However, the increasing seriousness of drug taking is seen in a second group of adolescents who use drugs to allay a temporary anxiety. In the face of a specific severe conflict or some intense frustration or loss, these young people use drugs to blot out the anxiety and depression they feel. This is akin to adults who use alcohol for the very same purpose. These adolescents are not addicts any more than the latter are alcoholics.

And then there is the group of adolescents, or, indeed,

adults, whose conflicts are so widespread and severe and whose attendant anxieties so generalized that no aspect of their reality is conflict-free enough for them to face. They are unable to arrive at reasoned solutions to their problems. They must resort to drugs continuously, day after day and usually in ever-increasing doses in order to blot out their reality. Depending on the specific nature of the drug used they may be classified clinically as addicts or chronic drug users. Such adolescents feel they need and must have drugs to live. They are victims of an underlying, disabling personality disorder, and though they almost invariably resent and refuse intensive psychotherapy, it is just such treatment that is indicated.

Finally, there is a fourth group of adolescent drug users. They are students—members of an academic community who have a deep sense of failure or impending failure as creative scholars. Their motivation for using drugs is not directed primarily at blotting out a severe external world or the repression of conflicts. Rather it is directed at the attempt to create a new *inner* world, an existing, untapped, unconscious world, they believe will be accessible to them through the use of drugs. Once accessible, they feel their creative productivity will be assured and never-ending. Unfortunately this seductive line leads not to significant creativity; rather it leads to a continuing and deepening sense of alienation.

In respect to this whole problem it is important for parents and professionals alike to determine "diagnostically" which of the above classes an individual adolescent falls into. Treatment, if any treatment is necessary, will be determined by this classification. Beyond this it is the duty of society at large to offer preventive programs and therapeutic facilities in an attempt to handle the drug problem. All measures should be based on, and buttressed by, sensible and workable legal measures. This drug problem that is with us is, like the alcohol problem, going to be with us forever and it's going to take the concerted effort of everyone in this society to keep it under adequate control.

Mrs. _____: When a child is small it isn't difficult to find an appropriate punishment for something wrong he has done. It's not so easy as he grows up. A case in point: An older adolescent asks for permission to do something. After careful consideration, his mother says "No" and states her reasons. He goes ahead anyway. How can they pick up their old relationship after a serious break of discipline of this nature?

Dr. G.: The only sensible punishment available to a parent in respect to the deliberate misbehavior of the older adolescent is disapproval. A firm declaration of this disapproval accompanied by an expression of genuine disappointment is about all we have available. Corporal punishment is out; so, too, are the threats of withdrawal of privileges or exclusion from family group activities. The latter usually makes little difference to the adolescent even if his parent has the courage to execute it!

Complicating the reconciliation of an adolescent and his parents after doing what he has been forbidden to do is the parent's loss of face and the adolescent's sense of guilt. And the guilt is there even though he attempts to mask it with nonchalance and bravado. Occasionally there is, too, the martyred stance of the parent who appears to be the abused victim of the adolescent's thoughtlessness, lack of respect and love. Such martyrdoms are usually ineffective because they are so patently and obviously contrived. Only patience, understanding, and the lapse of time usually reestablishes the former good relationship.

In the face of deliberate misbehavior, the one thing that should be avoided on both sides is the tendency to voice condemning generalizations. When a parent feels hurt or has lost face, he may accuse the child of *total* disrespect, irresponsibility, and misconduct on a host of fronts. The adolescent, with his feelings of defiance and guilt may accuse the parent of *never* giving him any freedom of action. Such tempting generalizations always make eventual reconciliation all the more difficult and they should be avoided. Otherwise, the gap becomes harder and harder to bridge.

V. CONTINUING DEVELOPMENTAL TASKS

8

Fantasy, Belief, and Reality

As WE DISCUSSED EARLIER, it is usually held that fantasizing and daydreaming have at least two major useful functions in childhood: They can be generated and utilized as protective devices or as expressions of creativity.

The utilization of fantasy as a protective device is generated by the harshness in the child's environment—his real world—that has created some anxiety or fear. An adult in this situation has at least two recourses open to him. He can flee or he can fight. The child is not so fortunate in his

choices. If he should attempt to flee, he knows he will probably be unsuccessful. If he did manage to escape he would
be alone and, for him, separation is probably even more unbearable and anxiety laden than the frustration he faces.
Because he is small and lacks real strength he is aware that
fighting will end in defeat, perhaps even punishment. But
there is one arena to which he can flee with alacrity and in
which he can fight with impunity—the world of fantasy.

In his world of make-believe he is loved, his strength
knows no bounds, and his achievements are whatever he
wishes them to be. The real value to the child of protective
fantasy is that it serves admirably to reduce his anxiety. It
follows then that the higher the level of anxiety the more
he will resort to fantasy to modify his participation in the
events that are frightening. However, the shortcomings of
this mechanism reside in the child's withdrawal and isolation
from social contacts. Unlike the adult who either flees or
fights a harsh reality, the child faces both alternatives when
he seeks out the protective fantasy. When used to excess, this
method also seems to retard the child's ability to cope with
reality by reason and controlled actions.

Conversely, creative fantasy is the form of make-believe
that children seek not as a protection from anxiety but for
the sheer joy involved. No one has really come up with a
theory that completely explains creative fantasy. But the
explanations of behaviorial theorists as to why children love
to play and why they play as they do also apply to fantasy.
Fantasy is an activity, as is play, that is sought for itself.
Its value resides in the explorative practice of unlimited
role playing and in the utilization of words, manners, and
actions which children have encountered in the world of
adults. Creative fantasy is active. It seeks out the presence
and involvement of other human beings and utilizes the
romantic learning of the preschool child.

QUESTIONS

Dr. G.: Since this is the holiday season, you have all probably been living to a certain degree in the midst of various expressions of fantasy. It's also quite possible that some of these expressions raised a few difficulties. Did Christmas bring any special problems related to child development?

Mrs. _____: In a way it did. My older son is four years old, and I found the adjustment of a Jewish child to the Christmas holidays was a painful thing in our house. At one point he announced, "When I get bigger, my children are going to have Christmas. You and Daddy don't love me, but I'm going to love my children and give them a Christmas tree." I tried to explain that we give Hanukkah presents, but I can see his point. I enjoy things about Christmas. I love the lights and we go to look at them, but in our family, as a tradition, we celebrate Hanukkah. We have certain songs we sing, other rituals we observe, and, of course, there are presents. How can children be helped to understand? They have so many adjustments to make as they grow up, but they must realize that certain things are *so* just because they are *so*. How do you tell a four-year-old that it's *so* just because it is?

Dr. G.: Children always have a hard time being on the outside looking in at any situation. It's difficult to watch others enjoying themselves and not be able to understand why they can't join in the fun. Will he go to Hebrew school? Perhaps the explanations there will help this particular problem.

Mrs. _____: He's been to Hebrew school and he knows that our family celebrates this holiday. He just wants to know why all his friends celebrate something else. He'd like both, I'm sure. I have tried to explain to him that this celebration is of the birth of Christ and that Jewish people do not have the same faith in Christ as Christians do; so we celebrate other holidays. But this doesn't mean anything to him. He's really just interested in the presents and Santa Claus and the tree. I feel badly, though, when he feels deprived and unloved.

Mrs. _____: But children often say they're deprived if you disagree with them or don't give them just what they want.

Mrs. _____: Love isn't a thing—not in my house it isn't—and I want him to learn that.

Mrs. _____: I remember Dr. Gardner mentioned at an earlier session something about the relationship of love and presents when a child is around three. The connotation was that this is sort of a necessary part of development, and I firmly said to myself, "This won't happen to my children!"

Dr. G.: There is a developmental stage when gifts do symbolize love, just as the food that you give them is equated with love, but those feelings gradually fade away.

Mrs. _____: Well, he's going to visit his grandmother because he thinks she's going to give him presents.

Dr. G.: You can't be hurt or surprised when it looks as though they love you for the presents that you give. This is a stage that all children go through. But pretty soon, I think you'll find a differentiation emerging between the joy of getting a gift and the joy of being loved for one's own worth. To get back to your problem, I think we have this situation under control at the Judge Baker. We have a nursery, an intermediate, and an upper school, and we have a total of about fifty youngsters with us. I would say they are about evenly divided, half Jewish children and half Christian. Over the years, we have evolved a pretty good system. We have both Hanukkah candles and a Christmas tree.

The last day before the holidays they put on their Christmas skit. At the beginning, they have a Menorah in the middle of the table, and all the youngsters are lined up. Three boys come out, and they light the candles in the proper ritualistic way. They sing both types of songs. One teacher who's awfully good on the guitar has them sing some wonderful old Hebrew songs. Then, they sing the usual Jingle Bells and all the others associated with Christmas. To avoid pointed issues concerning the fact that Christ was Jewish but not considered a prophet by the Jewish people but rather by a group called Christians, we have tended to upgrade the "pagan" aspects of Christmas, mainly the Christmas tree! As you know, the Christmas tree has nothing whatsoever to do with religion, so we emphasize it. We upgrade the partridges in the pear trees, too! As for gifts, to be sure we give them, but gift giving, at least in this part of the world, is a relatively recent business, you know. When this country was founded they didn't celebrate Christmas at all. They were forbidden to do so right up until the middle of the 18th century. A great-grandfather of one of my social workers was born about 1820. His family was Christian, but the family records indicate that at the time they didn't have Christmas celebrations of any kind or gift giving. There is a lot that has been added on to this thing as time has passed. Chris Kringle was a Dutchman, wasn't he? In our clinical work, both in the out-patient and the in-patient divisions, we emphasize these aspects of the Christmas holiday season and not the religious aspects. Needless to say, this method of approach is easier in the setting of a school or institution. We hope, however, that within the family itself the emphasis will be placed upon the religious aspect of the occasion.

Mrs. _____: I feel you're covering it up that way. In my opinion, Christmas is supposed to be the celebration of the birth of the child of God, and I just cannot see how I can let my son, a Jewish child, celebrate this. This was how I was brought up, and I would like to bring up my son the same way. Of course, I was brought up in a much more closely knit Jewish community. But I would like to retain some of these rituals. How can you make a child understand? If I gave in and celebrated a "little bit of Christmas" just to make him feel good, then that little bit is going to grow up with him.

Dr. G.: Then you should make no compromise with what

you believe, and probably my school example isn't relevant here. It does seem to me, however, that the whole Christian community recognizes Hanukkah far more than it did some years ago, and I sense that it pleases Christians to know that the Jewish people, adults and children, have comparable celebrations at Christmas time.

Mrs. _____: Part of that is because people are fighting to have their own culture acknowledged.

Dr. G.: To continue my observation of recent changes, I myself never heard of Hanukkah as a child because I don't think there was a single Jewish family in the village where I was born and brought up. However, my lack of knowledge of this important event in another religion is not peculiar to me, because I'm sure thousands of others have had the same experience. I guess it was only three years ago that we first tried this type of joint program at Judge Baker, and everything has gone extremely well. I think there is a general tendency, at least in the public demonstrations, to recognize Hanukkah more and more and to emphasize both these religious celebrations as constituting important holidays.

Mrs. _____: Last year my son went to Hebrew nursery school, where they celebrated Hanukkah only. We told him that there was another festivity going on—Christmas. This year he went to a public-sponsored school, and they mainly celebrated Christmas. When Hanukkah time came around, the teacher did not mention it to the class. I had been at the school that week and discussed it with her. When it came Christmas time, she had the children learn a Hanukkah song. She said she hadn't realized that the Jewish parents felt like this.

Mrs. _____: I think, though, that the issue you brought up earlier is a larger one than it suggests. These are decisions that we all make for our own families. It's impossible, even if we wanted to, to protect children from all the hurts or longings or wishes that they might have. As long as you are consistent, I think the child grows up in a stable environment. Now, it's perfectly true that he may decide when he grows up to handle things differently, but that will be his decision. There's no end to this issue. I have a whole houseful of adolescents, and the constant cry is, "But so and so does it some other way." And my reply is always the same—"That's their privilege, but that is not the way we are going to do it here." I understand your feeling because one always hates to see a child feeling as though he's missing something, but I still think that the answer is to hold to your own position once you've decided what it should be.

Mrs. _____: There is an aspect of Hanukkah that you may have overlooked. It lasts for eight days! We used to go to the five-and-ten and buy presents for each day!

Mrs. _____: But the five-and-ten-cent-store toys aren't advertised on television!

Mrs. _____: How about one great big toy and seven of the smaller variety?

Dr. G.: Well, I think that this problem of religious holidays is not a trivial one for young children. Conflicts of culture and of religion are questions of importance to youngsters as they get older, and these differences come into sharp focus, for this country contains many cultures and many ethnic groups. We have greatly differing socioeconomic groups, too. These problems come up in our psychotherapy with children quite frequently. All these difficulties do loom large for them. I still think it can be handled well with some thought. Of course, part of this has to do with the points we made at another of our meetings. Children do tend to compare their lot in life with others who are around them. It takes a long while for them to see themselves as individuals and to realize they are treated as individuals of equal worth.

Mrs. _____: At home, we've been talking about Christmas and about whether to tell a child that Santa Claus isn't real. I thought believing in Santa Claus was one of the greatest experiences I had when I was a little kid. Recently I've spoken to several people who felt that one of the real traumas of their lives was discovering that their parents had lied to them about Santa Claus. There are many other examples—fairy tales, for instance. Some people believe you shouldn't let a child indulge in fantasies like this but should tell him stories about things that are real. How about you, Dr. Gardner, are you opposed to fairy godmothers?

Dr. G.: There are really two parts to your question. In regard to Santa Claus, I tend to agree that many children feel they have been duped once the myth is exposed. Anybody who has been brought up to believe that Santa Claus is actually a person who comes down the chimney inevitably has to learn—usually when he's five or six years old—that someone has been putting him on. This can be a terrific blow, particularly if they find out from someone outside the family. People will argue that it's a lot of fun, that it goes along with the child's belief in magic, and that he'll recover easily enough. We have to weigh then whether the joy children get out of this mythical character is greater than the blow they receive when they hear he's a fraud. My experience has been that almost everybody can remember exactly in what circumstances they learned there wasn't any Santa Claus. It's surprising. It's like people who used to be able—in the old, old days—to remember exactly the spot where they were standing when they heard that President Lincoln was shot. The same sort of thing occurs in regard to Santa Claus. So we must acknowledge that the feelings associated with the myth do have a tremendous hold on people. The loss of that myth probably doesn't wreck them, but it certainly makes them sad for a while. It's like losing a person as well as the fellow who is going to bring you a lot of gifts. These attitudes tend to be modified over the generations.

You have also asked about fairy tales. I believe I've mentioned that I think these, like other fantasies, have a value. They can help the child as a defense against the, to him, harsh, cruel world. You may not think it's particularly harsh or cruel for him, but he sometimes does. There are denials he has to face, the ordinary disappointments of childhood. What he can do to modify his disappointments is to resort to fantasy. A little fellow may say, "I have an automobile. I have an automobile that will reach the sky. I know how to fly on wings and visit everywhere. I have a friend who can fly, too, and we can play all kinds of games." This kind of fantasy gives him an out. It's a defense mechanism. You may make him do things your way, but it's easier if he can "fly." The only trouble is that, after a while, these stories have to go because you can't go on through life believing in fantasies. We hope by that time he will find reality easier to cope with.

Mrs. _____: We watched *Jack and the Beanstalk* on TV the other night. Even I was a little terrified in certain parts.

Dr. G.: I was watching it with a four-year-old. I didn't think she was very amused by some aspects of it. Of course, when they began sliding down the stalk it was amusing, but she found the giant "scary." There is in all drama a building up and then a release of tension. They get to expect it. They begin to know there is going to be a new crisis and then everything will come back to normal. Like every dramatic narrative, the fairy tale depends on the building up of tension. We measure its success by the amount of tension created. Children may deliberately build up tension themselves in order to have the fun of the relief of it. It seems to be a universal habit.

All I can say is that fairy tales have stood the test of many, many centuries. These magical events and characters have been used by people to communicate their deepest feelings, their hopes, their despairs. All cultures seem to contain variations on these same tales, but some societies, more practical-minded or realistic, seem to have fewer fantasies than others. I think there are always some people who eliminate fairy tales from the lives of their children. These people ought to think twice, for they may be taking away one of the best defenses to which the child can resort.

Mrs. _____: My thought is that I can't always censor or

select the things that are good or not good because one can't always predict their effect ahead of time. There was a horrible Western drama on TV recently. I didn't realize the program had changed, and my two-year-old was still there watching it. She woke up with a nightmare that night, and I was sure the TV program was the source of it. I held her on my lap while she cried and then she said, "Did you see the muffin man?" You know there's a song "Do You Know the Muffin Man Who Lives in Drury Lane?" It's the most innocuous song you can think of, but the muffin man conjured up something that was terribly frightening for her.

I also have a precocious eight-year-old nephew who takes the world very, very seriously. He reads the papers now, and his question to his mother is, "Why are there so many horrible things happenings?" My first instinct is to say that there are so many wonderful things happening that you can't count them, but they don't make news. Of course, the realistic answer is that these stories sell newspapers. How do you approach it from there with a child? Why is there such an appetite for violence among people?

Dr. G.: I don't think you can explain to an eight-year-old child why there is such an appetite for violence, anymore than you can explain it adequately to me. This is one of the great mysteries. There is no doubt in my mind that the stable inculcation of effective controls and sublimation of the expression of the aggressive drives of man—particularly controls over destructive aggressive drives directed at the person of another—is the most important single step in personality development in childhood and adolescence. Without such controls, development in respect to other items of individual growth will be modified or halted. And without such controls in its individual members society itself could not exist for long.

There isn't much of anything on the front page except war, violence, and death, destruction, fires, explosions, planes crashing, men getting killed, and what not. Possibly these all have positive effects in the direction of sublimation, but it's difficult to ascertain any such beneficial result. People's passion for hearing about violence is very interesting. As you may know, there has been a study project instituted at Brandeis University on various aspects of violence. Maybe they can come up with some of the meanings of it, but this whole business of death dealing, death receiving, mutilation dealing, and mutilation receiving seems to be a tremendous preoccupation for people.

Mrs. _____: No two authorities seem to agree about whether violence on TV does have an effect on young children. Some seem to feel it helps a child to sublimate his *own* feelings of aggression. What do you feel about this?

Dr. G.: You are quite right. No two authorities seem to agree on the effects of violence depicted on television on children. For every "authoritative" statement on one side of the argument, there's another to counterbalance it. Opinion is certainly polarized.

Some insist that a depiction of violence leads children to express aggression with impunity, that children will learn and utilize these methods of violence and be hardened to man's inhumanity to man. They will become hostile and crafty, with little or no respect for people or their property. Others insist that violence is a demonstrable fact of everyday reality and that children should be aware of this all-pervasive tendency. They may insist also that man is by nature and endowment an aggressive organism, that this aggression cannot be eradicated but only sublimated, and that violence observed on television and in the movies acts as vicarious sublimation. They contend that even the young child knows the depiction is not "real" and that in the end, all will come out well—the good and nonviolent characters will be vindicated.

Neither argument has been adequately studied. It is difficult to design a reliable research project that would allow for validation of the results. We have no solid proof either way, but I can tell you what I feel I observe.

First, I do feel there has been a change in what we see on television. They have added to the nature and content of the violence to be viewed. In the earlier days of the media, the violence shown was essentially "unreal." Both adults and children could easily comprehend the fictional aspects of it. Now actual scenes of terrifying violence are shown, killing on the battlefield and in Vietnamese villages is our after-dinner and before-bedtime fare. We see the killing and mutilation of men, women, and children before our very eyes. They are "real" people and the effective distance associated with fictional violence has disappeared. I, too, have no way of proving my hypothesis, but I do feel this portrayal of naked and real violence causes anxiety and guilt in both the children and adults who view it. Many parents have told me of their own feelings of horror and revulsion and of those voiced by their children. We can only guess at the long-term effects of these feelings.

As I have said over and over again, I feel that all parents have a sacred and inescapable obligation to instill in their growing children an unmodified reverence for life and for the integrity of the body of every human being. Repeatedly, and by every means possible, they must emphasize that person-directed hostility and aggression constitutes the primary evil in this world today. It must be decried wherever it occurs whether it is within or beyond the family. I see no reason why, then, its appearance on a television screen should be treated in any other way.

Mrs. _____: What do you think about the effect of television on a child's sense of reality? I wondered about this in connection with something that happened at our house the other day. We have a student who lives with us who is not Jewish. She has a crucifix above her bed. When my four-year-old asked her about it, she gave him a very detailed explanation which ended with Christ's death and resurrection. It didn't surprise him at all. When he told me the story, I said, "Well weren't you surprised that He came alive again?" He wasn't surprised at all. He explained that somebody gets run over by a steamroller on TV and just pops right back up! Somebody else goes through a glass door and turns into a weird shape and two seconds later he is running around doing whatever he was supposed to do before!

Dr. G.: You mean in the TV cartoons?

Mrs. _____: Right. Why don't these things lead him to think that he could get hit by a car and then two minutes later get up and continue on to what he's doing? I just wonder how distorted children's reality will be when they suddenly realize that *this* is life and *that* is a cartoon?

Mrs. _____: It's not only in cartoons. Batman isn't a cartoon character.

Dr. G.: I don't think it's going to cloud their reality to the degree that they will think they can walk out in front of a car without injury. Everything we teach them is to the contrary. I do think it's a good idea to laughingly emphasize that some of what they see is make-believe. This is done for the fun of it. "Wouldn't it be fun if you could fly around like that? But, of course, you know that people can't, even though it's fun to think about." Children have all kinds of fantasies that are fun to think about, but most of the time they keep them quite separate from their real life. They have a quite good sense of what is not possible. We'd like to know more about just how this sense becomes so well defined. The trouble comes when they begin to become anxious about the not-quite-so-fantastic things becoming possible. Then it's important to correct their concerns by reassuring them about what reality is.

Mrs. _____: You're right. That does somehow come out. "Giants are only on television," they'll say. But I still worry about some child suddenly taking off from a roof because he sees Batman do it on television.

Dr. G.: I can remember very well when a nephew of mine was in the Superman stage. He came down to our beach place, traveled 150 miles, with this secret box. He was about eight or nine. Well, it turned out that the secret in the box was a maternity dress that his mother had packed away in the attic. He had fashioned this into a Superman's cape. I'm not certain what particular power that maternity garment symbolized or what its symbolic power had to do with the power of the cape in his fantasy, but I presume there was some relation. He would get up on rocks and jump off. He didn't try the roof, however. Believe me, if we had seen him go up on the roof or up high in a tree, we would have let him know that his mother's maternity dress, with all its magic power, wasn't going to save him from any fractures. Incidentally, this business you mentioned about getting up and being alive again—did I tell you the story about the little girl in the first grade who was being tested by the school psychologist? They got to the Binet test. Now, there are some quite unusual questions on the Binet—particularly on the original test. There was one which was a nonsense question, and the little girl was supposed to say what was "funny" about this or "crazy" about that. This question read, "The police found the body of a girl cut into 18 pieces. They took her to the hospital and they do not think that she will get up again." The psychologist asked, "What's crazy about that?" She said, "The girl couldn't get up again if she was dead." Then suddenly something new dawned on her and she added, "Unless it was Easter." (Using this item did not secure any extra points on the Binet!)

But to return to your basic problem, has this culture conflict in your household raised other problems?

Mrs. _____: Not really. I think he had been asking her about the crucifix for a long time before she finally decided to tell him. She went into a little bit more detail than I would have, but he really didn't seem very confused or anxious.

Dr. G.: He's going to have a great education in comparative religion! I can see that.

Mrs. _____: Well, you know, I think this hinges on a more general question. How much can you shield a child? How much can you temper what goes on around him or what he hears?

Dr. G.: In being a parent you walk, and sometimes run, along a very, very narrow line. It's almost a knife edge, you know. How much experimentation will you allow the child in order for him to grow, to learn, to become accustomed and acclimated to his world without allowing him so much freedom of activity that he is going to get hurt? It is a tough world for children and it gets tougher all the time. I suppose you could say it was tougher in the Stone Age when everybody was out with hatchets and clubs, but this is a different kind of toughness. You could shield a child from all possible harm, but then he would never develop. You can also neglect children or propel them into situations that have a dangerous element, and then they get into trouble. So you always say, "I want them to grow and develop and I don't want them to get hurt. I don't want them to do the wrong things that may destroy or handicap their future." This always has been the parent's dilemma, I suppose. We know perfectly well, however, that without any frustration or without this chance to experiment and learn for themselves, their development will be stunted. So it is certainly not true that you should take away all frustrations from a child. Conflict is essential to development. In the simplest experiments related to learning, it has been noted again and again that there is always a moderate rise in the anxiety level when the person faces a partly known and partly unknown situation. We call some of this "anxiety curiosity" because it does motivate the individual toward a solution. When a child faces a new situation it's only natural for his parents also to experience an element of anxiety. Maybe it's a mild, constructive anxiety that makes the world go round! It's when this anxiety becomes disabling or holds back development that we must be concerned. But it's not easy for parents to spot these moments.

Mrs. _____: Moving back to TV, what happens to the child's sense of reality when he sees these horrible science-fiction programs? Most children are exposed to them in some degree. How do they juggle what they see with what happens in their world? Even before they go to school, they learn about war and violence. They learn men really do these inhuman things to each other. Without any rationalization or understanding, it's amazing they don't live in constant fear. Is it similar to our other double standards? We grow up and we try to teach them what is right and what is wrong. You must be honest and turn the other cheek—all the things that have been taught and handed down to us, but they learn very early that life doesn't bear out some of these lessons. I don't mean to get off the subject, but what I liked so much about President Kennedy, Senator Kennedy, and Martin Luther King was that they gave children such an idealistic view of life, and look what happened to them! How can we help with the confusion they must feel? I'm not saying this the way I want to but maybe you'll understand what I'm driving at.

Dr. G.: You're not only wording it correctly but also you sound as though you're reciting an excerpt from a paper I wrote not many months ago. This is one of the real problems the adolescent faces. There is at every age the necessity of coming to grips with the opposites in the world. Trying to reconcile these divergent attitudes and come out with a satisfactory, commendable, and also satisfying code of ethics of one's own is a real task. I always have tried to emphasize the very thing that you're emphasizing here. It has to do with creating a code of ethics in regard to the other human beings in your society. How should one react to them when there seem to be great differences? When you come to the subject of war—and that's certainly an issue for every one of us now—you have to keep saying, "We hate war and so do the millions and billions of people around the world, regardless of where they live or what they believe. They don't want anything to do with war either, but the people who run our governments are not wise enough or they don't want to be wise enough to work out ways to ensure that human beings can live together in large groups without trying to destroy each other. There may be different codes of ethics, but we must learn to look for and stress our similarities." I wouldn't make any bones about the war business though. There are those who glamorize or glorify it, but there is nothing heroic about war. There's no fun in it—only devastation. I once saw a gun on which was written, proudly, the inscription, "The last argument of the King." As if guns were the only and the best argument of whatever "kings" we have! There ought to be a lot of argument before we seek this solution. People, we hope, will somehow learn to live together. War, with the weapons we now possess, is unthinkable.

Mrs. _____: I think that what has come up today is fascinating. We've gone from Santa Claus to nuclear destruction, and yet all the questions have had to do with finding real and honest answers and keeping them consistent with our daily actions and reactions to the realities we face. Children learn very early to see hypocrisy. They pick up the differences between what we say and what we do. I have a story which I guess I'll always remember. I was raised in a parsonage in a small town. Shortly after the depression started, the ladies auxiliary of the church—

Dr. G.: They called it the Ladies' Aid Society in those days, didn't they?

Mrs. _____: Yes. You obviously have the right denomination, too! At any rate, they were called together at the parsonage to mend clothes to be given to poor children in the community. I was always very much a part of these groups because I spent most of my time with adults. After they went home, I said, "I know these are nice Christian ladies because they were here fixing clothes for poor children, but if they're nice Christian ladies then why did they talk about other ladies all afternoon?" I was sent off to bed without dinner that night for my impertinence, and although I was only seven at the time, the message never escaped me.

Dr. G.: You were given no answer, I gather.

Mrs. _____: I wasn't given an answer, but I'm afraid I learned something rather sad. The whole question of hypocrisy—and I think children see it in us much earlier than we think they do—must create a lot of confusion for children. It comes up in all sorts of little ways, too. On the one hand we encourage children to grow up, but on the other hand they hear their parents tell the streetcar man or the movie cashier that the child is only eleven—"He's just big for his age"—so as to avoid the extra cost! There are many, many such evidences of hypocrisy and even dishonesty that they see in us.

Dr. G.: You very correctly emphasize consistency and honesty, and I'd like also to emphasize the fact that these direct questions must not be avoided because children also learn something from your unwillingness to take a stand on things.

Mrs. _____: I think that applies to parents, too. You can't play the role that you are omniscient, that you know everything, but without modifying a child's faith in you and your knowledge, you can try to answer his questions. Sometimes you have to say, "I don't know," or "Let me think about that," but don't give him the idea you are trying to duck the question.

Mrs. _____: Sometimes, too, you may feel quite differently about a subject than other people do, but I think it's important to hold the line even though you let your children know that your view is a minority one. After all, we are all responsible for our own children and we have to do what we think is best under the circumstances, even when other people don't agree.

Dr. G.: Yes, you should give them a sense that this is the way it's done in your particular family. You have lots of reasons to think this is the best way. Others may disagree, and that's their right, but in this house it *is* done this way. This is not, as some might tell you, rigidity. It's just sensible. You are giving them guidelines at least as to how you feel about these things. We can't ask that children always be happy about our decisions, but we must try not to confuse them.

Mrs. _____: How do you explain to a young child, who doesn't know anything about tact, that he must not be rude to people who feel or say things that don't agree with what he's heard at home? Let me give you an example. Someone came into our house a few months ago and used a very derogatory term for black people. My four-year-old son heard it and thought it was a great-sounding word and said it a few times. We had a discussion about this, and I told him that he must never use it again. The other day he went to someone's house on the street and he came home after a very short time. I said, "How come you came home?" He said, "Well, I was fresh to Mrs. _____. She said that terrible word you told me not to say, and I told her my mommy said that anybody who said that was stupid." When I saw the woman the next day, I told her that I understood that he had been fresh and I was sorry, but that I had just recently told him we didn't permit this kind of talk. But the thing is, how do you draw the line? He was rude.

Dr. G.: He was rude in good cause.

Mrs. _____: That's right, but being rude in a good cause doesn't excuse it.

Dr. G.: May I think she probably needed a lesson?

Mrs. _____: But I can't excuse this rudeness and then insist that he respect his elders on other occasions.

Dr. G.: Tact comes later, after a child begins to have a clearer sense of other people's feelings. It's not always easy to tell the truth and, in addition, to tell it in a pleasant way.

By setting a good example and sometimes showing him a better way to say something, he'll gradually pick it up. There's a real difference between a remark like this and a thoughtless or angry retort. Also, an occasional comment must not be regarded the same way you regard an often-repeated rudeness.

9

Understanding Sexuality

THE OBSERVANT PARENT soon becomes aware of what an astounding amount of information a child, even a very young child, must gather unto himself in order to make the simplest adjustment with his environment. And this early adaptation is no more than the beginning of what the child must learn before he can feel secure in his world.

Every possible question, ranging from the sources of wood and metals to the intricate movements of the celestial constellations, demands a satisfactory answer. There seems to be no end to a child's curiosity—or his questions!—and there is no way to predict how much information or what

kind he will absorb from the adult conversations he over-
hears.

Of primary importance, of course, is the child's curiosity
about himself, principally the functioning of his own body.
It probably would be proper to say that the child's total
world view begins with his contemplation of, and his concern
for, his bodily functions. His perspective extends from these
functions to all matters external to his body. As a matter of
fact, it is true that *all* the very complex explanations of things
in the material world take on meaning for him in the light of
his observations and knowledge of the structure and functioning of his own body. How unfortunate it is, then, that
the instruction concerning bodily function in general and
the functioning of the sexual organs in particular is usually
the most inadequate and unsuccessful of the lessons taught
by parents.

One reason for this inadequacy is that parents have a difficult time answering children's questions about sex. Whenever the child asks a question even remotely related to sex,
there seems to be an instantaneous flash of fear that he or
she is going to ask for full explanation of *all* the facts. Parents
feel that they will now have to disclose everything they
know about heterosexual adjustment, sexual intercourse, and
the aim of the sexual drive. The truth of the matter, of course,
is that the facts about sexual intercourse are not only those
least needed by young children but also those which the
child is least interested in knowing. The great majority of
preschool-age children ask other, much more important questions long before they inquire about the specific role of the
father in the creation of a baby. It is the fear that this question is about to be asked that keeps even a very alert and
understanding mother from hearing and correctly assessing
what the small child really is asking.

Equally important as a deterrent to satisfactory performance of the parent's role as educator in sexual matters is that
this type of knowledge has been transmitted in the folklore

from one generation to the next clouded with taboos and dogmatic don't's. Parents are often the victims of their own inadequate training, which has left them with feelings of shame.

This shame has come in part from the close association of things sexual with those functions of the body that have to do with the elimination of waste products. It is an unfortunate physiological accident that the two excretory systems have so close an anatomical relationship to the system which has to do with intercourse and the birth of the young. The training for control of bowels and bladder constitutes one of the first and most stringent sets of prohibitions inculcated in each individual. Therefore, it is not strange that the "dirtiness" associated with these functions, the prohibitions demanding "cleanliness," and the taboo against speaking of these functions in polite company should extend to the more external portions of the genital tracts: the penis and the vagina. Many children, long before they have questions of a sexual nature, have been imbued with a feeling of disgust for the "messiness" and "naughtiness" of all things having to do with the area of these body structures. Because these associations are riveted so early in life, it is difficult to shed them. We will hope that the coming generations will realize that these feelings of disgust are not innate, not inborn, not instinctive, and hence are subject to change in children and adults alike.

Children's questions will come in many different forms, but a few general rules can be applied to parental responses. First of all, it is exceedingly important that a child be taught the correct scientific terms for the organs of the body. Children, even very young children, can learn the proper words for the sex organs and the parts of the gastrointestinal and urinary systems just as easily as they can learn any of the silly substitute words that have come down through the generations. This nomenclature is important for a number of reasons, apart from the fact that its names for these organs and functions are the correct ones. These scientific words are, to a large extent, free of the naughtiness that certain other "bad" words may connote. They also will allow the parent to talk in a more objective fashion and will give the child words he may use without fear of embarrassment. Acquaintance with these correct terms will serve as the basis for the later sex education he may encounter in school or through reading.

Here, as is so often the case in talking to children, *how* you impart this information is almost as important as *what* you tell them. Children are very good at sensing how you feel about things. Every mother knows that eventually these questions are going to come up, and it is important that she be able to answer them in a straightforward, matter-of-fact way. In sensing that his parents, but usually his mother at this early stage, are comfortable with these questions, the child learns that he may feel free to continue his inquiries as the years go by.

Perhaps it should seem unnecessary as a general policy to emphasize that what *is* told the child about sex should be the truth and nothing but the truth. Nevertheless, I must stress this point because many parents are unable to answer children's questions truthfully. They resort to some subterfuge—usually in the form of childhood fantasies or fairy-tale expressions—and this deception often is more to cover their own embarrassment than to help the child. These tales in themselves may not be harmful, but they do make it necessary later for the child to relearn the facts. The greatest harm that may result is a loss of trust. The misinformed child may question the validity of other things which his parents tell him.

It has always been a truism in the field of professional education that learning the proper method of doing something in the first instance, even though it may seem initially more complex, is important and easier in the long run. This principle seems to be valid here, too, for we have often seen a child, in spite of repeated instruction to the contrary, revert to the erroneous beliefs of his earlier years. Thus, it would seem unnecessary and educationally expensive to load children down with stories of storks and fairies and heaven-sent brothers and sisters. The "big blooming confusion," which the philosopher William James used to say is the world of the very young child, is certainly not clarified by such teachings about sex. Obviously, you have to tell your child enough about the stork so that when he is older he'll understand some cartoon he sees in *The New Yorker*, but that can wait until later.

Now, even though I emphasize strict adherence to truth and nothing but the truth, I do not mean that the *whole* truth should be given at any one time. Before you answer, it is important to listen to the question and to try to decide what the *limits* of the question are. Other questions may stem from this question, but often you will find that some time will elapse before another question comes up. If you extend your answer beyond the child's question, he may fail to grasp the answer to the actual question he has asked. In the process of learning, the child never grasps the total meaning of all the related bits of information he collects at one time. It is only as he hears things over and over again that he begins to put the pieces together in a related fashion. So it is with what he learns about sex.

It is safe to assume that the first question about sex will come from some observation of the moment or possibly from some anxiety aroused by such an observation. Therefore, the primary object of the mother should be to satisfy the curiosity and to allay the anxiety or eliminate the fear, if fear seems to be an ingredient of the situation that has promoted the question.

We know that playmates in the neighborhood or at school will provide many children with some answers to their questions. Just as we should not assume that our child will pick up all the necessary information outside the home, so we should not feel that it is altogether bad that he does learn some things in this way. Nor should we assume that everything he learns from this source will be evil or untrue. It is not unusual to find that there has been some mutual investigation among children and that their observations have led to correct conclusions! Children do look at each other's bodies, and the focus of interest, of course, will be the unfamiliar. Boys will want to see how girls are made; girls may be less forward but no less interested in the male anatomy. This curiosity is quite normal. Again, it is important for the mothers not to assume immediately that these explorations have come about as the result of sexual impulses in the adult sense, or that now there will be an excess of interest in the whole subject. A matter-of-fact attitude is called for, and if this matter-of-factness is apparent, the child is more likely to feel that he can look to his parents for answers.

A final general rule concerns the citing of the sex life of animals and plants to convey information regarding human physiology. The "birds and bees" are not nearly as valuable for conveying information to children as we once supposed! I say this because the anatomical differences in the physiology of sex and birth are such that these analogies can lead the child to many false conclusions and fantasies. As associated learning, or "enrichment," to use the current jargon, these facts may be useful, but it is really about human beings that the child wants to hear. If children are old enough to understand plant and animal procreation, they are old enough to understand procreation in human beings. Furthermore, if you get to the other aspects of this whole question—and one has to—you must emphasize the personal, social, and cultural values that adhere to sex. Here it is a bit difficult to go from animal life to human life. If one talks about mama cow and papa cow, it will not be easy for a child to understand where papa cow has gone—why he isn't there helping to care for the little ones. It's even more difficult to use the plant example. One can deal with holly trees and point out the differences between the male and female holly, but there the plot tends to come to a dead end. If these are the only explanations a child is to get, he will have a great many facts to relearn. The analogies just do not hold up.

I have been told that some people in sex-education programs in the public schools have gone so far recently as to show motion pictures of dogs copulating. I am quite convinced that this is not an effective way to teach the facts of human sexual life. On the contrary, this approach can confuse the child or adolescent and may impede his search for real knowledge. The picture conjured up by a presentation of this sort leaves out all the human ingredients of sex—love, respect, and mutual fulfillment.

In speaking about the exclusively human ingredients of sex, I am not referring to the significance of the sex act to the prevailing morality as it has been variously drawn from the age-old mores of the different societies on this planet. Nor will I have anything to say about the significance of sex in the organization of our society in accordance with the ties of family and kinship, although this organization does stem from sexual relationships. You are well aware of this significance and recognize its paramount importance in the structure of society. My comments will be confined to the human *values*, and specifically the individual human values, that accrue to the sexual act. None of these values is emphasized or even depicted in the kind of sex instruction that relies for its illustrations on animal activities.

Somewhere along the evolutionary chain from Protozoa to man, nature differentiated the sexes. Since that time, sex has not been unique to any one species, but man, as best we can judge, has been unique in his approach to sex. Obviously, all we can know about the sex lives of other species is what we can infer from observation, but I feel quite safe in saying that, with exceedingly rare exceptions, and those only surmise, the sexual behavior of other mammals does not suggest the existence of a scale of psychological values in any way resembling the values with which we invest the sex act and its consequences. To cover myself, I will note in passing that wolves are said to be monogamous and devoted spouses, but I am reluctant to draw any further romantic conclusions from this fact.

Neither the male nor the female of the human species can feel complete by himself or herself, physiologically or biologically or, indeed, as a psychological unit. An innate drive for completeness, to be realized only in sexual union, motivates them both. It is the psychological components of this drive, which are no less real than the biological components, that should be emphasized in the sex instructions of children. So you see, the goal we should be aiming at is not to stress the similarities in the sexual behavior of dogs and human beings but to point up the differences.

When we listen to the many questions asked by children, we will see that they vary greatly according to the age of the child. The first questions come when the child is anywhere between two and a half and five years old, and they usually concern the anatomical differences between boys and girls. Earlier, I said not to go much beyond the question the child asks, but here it is probably not enough to say, "That's the way he is because he's a boy (or she's a girl)." It should be emphasized that girls and boys have always been different in these ways—that she was always that way and he was always this way. Little boys, for instance, often fear that they may lose their penis and be changed into little girls. Little girls may feel that they have been deprived and are consequently somewhat inferior. Every precaution should be taken to make sure a little girl understands that this difference in no way threatens her importance as a person. That these worries exist is not merely a conjecture of the psychiatrist. The trained worker often finds them to be the basis of a child's anxieties. Often the little boy will try to relocate his concern about being emasculated. He cannot say, "I'm afraid something is going to happen to my penis." He finds it easier to complain that his finger hurts and maybe will fall off. If you hear this type of talk, you can be suspicious that it has something to do with more basic fears.

An anatomical question of perhaps less importance, but always asked by both sexes, concerns the presence or absence of breasts. Here again is an opportunity to emphasize a fundamental sex difference. You will point out to the girl that eventually she will have breasts like her mother's, and explain to the boy that this is an anatomical variation he will never have. This question is usually couched in terms of function, that is, "What are they for?" The function of breasts in the feeding of the newborn baby should be explained adequately to both boys and girls. Some girls, just prior to puberty, may be concerned because their breast development has not yet begun. They worry that they will not grow up to be women, or that if they do, they will never be able to have babies. Proper reassurance from the mother takes care of these transitory fears.

Another early question has to do with the origins of life. Where do babies come from? Most children are told that they "grew up in their mommy's tummy." The answer should be, "You were inside mother," without particular reference to "stomach" but with deliberate elaboration to specify that the child grew in a particular place inside the mother, a place that is there just for that purpose. It is necessary to emphasize again the difference in the sexes; the child should understand that a girl has a uterus and that a boy does not.

To give a child the idea that impregnation or the growth and delivery of the baby occurs within the gastrointestinal tract will confuse him badly. If the word "stomach" is used, then the stage is set for the child to believe that impregnation came by the oral route. When the word "seeds" is used, this misconception is compounded—the child thinks of apple or watermelon seeds that can be eaten. In other words, once you get this process into the gastrointestinal tract, you will have a terrible time getting it out! Even if you have to draw a picture on the kitchen blackboard, next to the reminders of what you need from the grocery store, make certain the children understand that there are two different tracts. Perhaps you can tell them that the stomach is just one little sac inside the abdomen and that this "special place" is another sac. Even if they don't understand the first time you tell them, you are laying the groundwork for later understanding.

"How did I get there?" This will probably be the next question. The answer will need to include the explanation of the origin of the child from an egg. The child should understand that the mother has these eggs inside her and that from time to time an egg grows into a baby. As I told you earlier, these early questions have nothing to do with sexual intercourse or the mechanics of how the seed got in there. What the children really are interested in is anatomy.

As any mother will attest, these questions probably will not be asked at a single sitting. There is a chain of questions which stem from "Where do babies come from?" A little later, you are almost certain to be told that whereas you said such and such, his friend Johnny said something else, and Johnny must be right because his mother said this, and she should know because her husband is a doctor! There will always be some collision with contrary information from outside the home, but here again, your matter-of-fact, straightforward answers will stand you in good stead.

It will be the rare child, however, who hears about the growth of a baby inside the mother's uterus without asking quite promptly, "How does he get out?" The necessary answer, of course, is that the baby, when old enough to live in the outside world, comes out of the mother's body by a special opening which the mother has for this purpose. If the previous lessons in anatomy have included information regarding the birth canal—that is, the opening of the uterus into the vagina through which the baby comes out—it will not be too difficult for the child to understand. Of course, it is necessary to explain that when the baby is ready to come out, this opening will stretch to allow for passage of the newborn. Great care should be taken to distinguish this "special opening" from the neighboring openings. You should not leave any confusion on this point.

One of the anxieties that a female child may develop centers on the birth process. The mother should make an effort not to associate pain and injury with the birth of a baby. She should be careful to point out that in the normal course of events, the mother is not operated upon, or her stomach opened up by the doctor, but the genital tract has a normal capacity to open enough to allow the baby to come out. This is also an opportunity to explain the usual presence of the doctor at the birth and the mother's stay in the hospital. You say that certain medicine can be given to ensure an easy birth and that the mother may be tired after childbirth and in need of a rest from the usual routine of the home. Perhaps you can say that although babies can easily be born at home and without a doctor present, it is best that a doctor be there to make certain that all goes well. It is important that notions of injury, trauma, and surgery be minimized.

In answer to direct questions or in anticipation of questions to come, it is usually necessary to explain carefully to the girl that babies are not "growing in her now." Her potential for having babies in the future is naturally dwelt upon. Little girls need to grow up before they actually are able to form babies. Since children are constantly comparing themselves in some way with older children, it usually suffices to say to the girl, "You have to be at least as big as a high school girl before the eggs are able to grow into babies." All girl children will ask sooner or later, "Do I have to be married to have babies?" To this, the truthful answer should be, "No, you don't *have* to be, but it is best in order that the child may have both a mother and a father to help bring him up." I think that at every opportunity in sex education the point should be made that very important values are associated with this whole business of sex, not only motherhood and fatherhood, but the companionship of the family, the protective shelter of homelife, the family's relations with the community, and the ties of kinship. Merely to play down negative association and feelings is not enough; one must also emphasize the positive features.

At some time, usually late in the series of questions a child asks, there will be pointed queries about the role of the father. At first, one may say that the father puts a seed into the mother and this seed starts the mother's egg growing. Later on, the child will want to know how the father puts the seed there. Then the facts of sexual intercourse for the purpose of fertilizing the egg should be given. Again, this can be done in medically and socially acceptable terms such as "sperm," "fertilization," "insertion of the penis," etc. Until a child is much older there will be no occasion to go into the details of passion and physical love.

Although many children can grasp these concepts on first hearing, one may occasionally encounter undue resistance. It is not at all unusual for a child to cling desperately to belief in the possibility of impregnation without sex, and some may revert to earlier faith in storks or other nonhuman agencies. It is often necessary to retell this tale a number of times.

Finally, is it better for the mother or father or an interested family member or family doctor to give this information? I believe that the main part of sex education will continue to be given by the mother, and, at least up to adolescence, only secondarily by the father. Many of the early questions will be asked in a setting where only the mother is at hand. Questions should be answered when they are asked or assurance given that they will be answered. Questions in adolescence or questions regarding problems allied to menstruation or masturbation can perhaps be answered more objectively by the family physician, though here again the secure child will probably be able to get adequate information from one or the other parent. Books can be used as supplementary material, but they certainly cannot take the place of the parent, and particularly the mother, as the prime purveyor of these important facts. It is not just that it is her duty; it seems a marvelous opportunity to cement a worthwhile and lasting relationship of confidence and openness between her and her children.

No one, of course, can outline ahead of time what the questions of the individual child in a particular family will be, nor can I outline the exact order in which these questions may arise. What I have tried to do is to raise some of the general principles that are involved so that you can figure out how to talk to your children. Your aim, of course, will be to prevent anxiety, fear, or shame from distorting the expression of this fundamental, instinctive drive.

QUESTIONS

Mrs. _____: My husband is a doctor and the children know he goes to the hospital each day to help sick people. I don't want them to think that because I'm having a baby I'm sick, so I tell them I'm going off to "the Baby House." With the great emphasis you place on telling the child the truth, I wonder if you would consider this an evasion of the truth?

Dr. G.: I have no objection at all. As a matter of fact, your suggestion may be a good one. Maybe our large maternity wards should not be designated as hospitals.

Mrs. _____: Perhaps it's a bit old-fashioned, but I think "the lying-in" is a rather nice way of putting it, and it doesn't have any of the connotations of sickness. When I leave for the hospital to have a baby, I try to go out in a great spurt of good health—even if I feel lousy—just so the children at home won't have to worry. Perhaps they could be told that there is a special section in the hospital where there are no sick people but where ladies go to have their babies.

Dr. G.: There is no question that children equate hospitals with sickness. Perhaps this last suggestion might put their minds at ease a bit. The questions about why you need a doctor and why you have to go to the hospital are ones they all ask. I think the only answer is that the mother needs to be somewhere where she can rest. For young children, the role of the doctor should probably be minimized because of their fears about injury and death and because it's difficult enough for them to be separated from Mother without any added burden.

Mrs. _____: The other day my little boy was talking to his eight-year-old sister and he announced that he was going to marry her when they grew up. She quickly said, "Oh no, Michael, you can't marry your sister, or your relatives or your cousins." Then he turned to me and said, "But why can't I marry my relatives if I want to?" I didn't quite know how to explain it to him. What should I have said?

Dr. G.: There isn't a satisfactory way to handle this without just giving them the most basic reason for it. Over the years, and for a long time past, people discovered that you should not marry a person closely related to you because it is possible that certain family physical traits that might be a little weak will be intensified and passed on to new generations.

Mrs. _____: We very early tell children that there are different kinds of love. We love our children in a different way than we love our husbands and wives. Why couldn't you just explain that what you feel for members of the family is a kind of family love and that this is quite different from the way you feel about the person you want to marry?

Dr. G.: That's another way of handling it. This question probably comes up most often with first cousins. It seems that either they are very attractive and you think you'd like to marry them or they are such brats that you can't stand them when they come to visit. I think the usual answer— but this doesn't really answer the question—is that you love your cousins, you play with them, go to the movies with them and all of that, but you don't marry them. This isn't a matter that will arouse much anxiety, so perhaps it's all right if the child doesn't get a complete answer. When they become adolescents, they will be old enough to understand something about genetics and the possibilities of compounding any familial weaknesses or tendencies to develop certain diseases.

Mrs. _____: Does the prohibition against marrying relatives come from the Bible?

Dr. G.: Taboos concerning kinship marriage have existed in many primitive societies. Our own originated, I believe, in the Judaic system of laws, and, as for so many of those laws, there was a good reason for it. The ancient dietary laws were very necessary. For instance, you might have been risking your life if you ate pork. Even now they find mummies that show evidence of trichinosis.

Mrs. _____: Perhaps you could use the example of a Boxer dog. They have a congenital hip abnormality which is supposed to come from inbreeding. You might not want to use animals to explain reproduction, but maybe it would work here.

Dr. G.: Well, this might pressure the point a bit. Clinically, I've never heard of this question causing too much trouble. We rarely see children who are heartbroken because they can't marry a sister or a cousin. Of course, I've seen more than a few who were heartbroken because they couldn't marry their mothers. Boys want to marry their mothers, and girls want to marry their fathers. This is a normal phase. We hope that we smooth this out in most cases.

Mrs. _____: You mentioned that occasionally a mother comes upon children who are experimenting or sort of learning a little bit more about anatomy. What is the best way to handle this? It doesn't seem quite right to say, "Go right ahead."

Dr. G.: Obviously, you can't go to that extreme, but I do hope you will view the situation with some sympathy. You can explain that you understand how interested they are in learning the differences between boys and girls, but this is not the way to find out these things. Then stress your willingness to answer any questions they may have.

Mrs. _____: You can always take them to a museum. There are lots of statues.

Dr. G.: Do you think they'd get much out of that? Those statues have a way of fooling you sometimes. Of course, the Museum of Science has a display which shows the whole reproductive system.

In all these matters of sex expression outside the home, be it in the form of exploring other children's bodies, open masturbation or whatever, we have to manage somehow to get across to the child some notion of the right of privacy. Though we may sanction certain of his activities within the home as nothing more than symptoms of a normal phase of development, we have to make sure he understands that society at large may take a quite different view, that he may in fact expose himself to rather rough treatment if he engages in those practices in the presence of outsiders. Now, this is a very delicate business, because we do not want him to get the idea that what we sanction at home is morally wrong or that the outsiders are morally wrong for objecting. There is an analogy here to our manner of safeguarding our beliefs in religion or politics. We do not insist upon intruding our beliefs into other people's lives against their wishes, but at the same time we conduct ourselves in a manner to stave off intrusions upon our own right to privacy. In the end, most of these conflicts do come down to intrusions upon someone's privacy. I suppose the answer, if there is an answer, is to be found in emphasis upon the *personal* nature of sex. Whether we agree or disagree with the prevailing moral code of our society, we have to accept society's insistence that these matters are not for public display, by us or by others.

Mrs. _____: My husband and I have been discussing another question that I would like to ask you about. As we read different things and talk to our friends, it seems that there are lots of different ways of approaching modesty within the home. Some say your child will have problems if you are always too prim and proper about being dressed, but others say that the other extreme can worry the child, too.

Dr. G.: This is a very good question. As in all of these matters, either extreme probably should be avoided. I do not advocate mothers and fathers running around the house without clothes on. The great differences between the child's body and the adult body may create anxieties. Some children, perhaps a good many, have very strong reactions to their first glimpse of pubic hair, for instance. The differences not only in appearance but in size of the adult sexual parts may upset some children. A naked adult body of the opposite sex may be entirely too stimulating for some children. I can't conceive that any great harm could come of a little girl's seeing her mother in the bathtub, but I would not be so sure about the father.

Thirty-five or more years ago, there grew up quite a cult for running around the home naked. Nowadays we are having some second thoughts about this, as about other matters. Of course, somebody might point to the nudist colonies as counterexamples, but I am not aware of any large-scale serious studies that have been made of the mental health of nudists or, perhaps more significantly, of any studies of the mental health of nudists before they decided to become nudists.

Mrs. _____: I remember when I first went away to school, I had trouble because I never hesitated to invite people in as I was dressing. It was just always the way we were at home. I had the impression that if the child saw the mother and father often like that, they just wouldn't think anything about it. My daughter a year old comes into the bathroom with me as I bathe. You say this isn't a good idea?

Dr. G.: When she gets to be two and a half or three years old it probably isn't such a good idea for her to go in while her father is bathing. Some anxieties that appear later on seem related to this kind of exposure.

Mrs. _____: What kind of anxieties?

Dr. G.: Well, the castration fears that I talked of earlier. But you cannot be totally rigid. If the child discovers you while you are undressed, you should just be as natural as you possibly can. If you make a federal case of the intrusion, you immediately start them thinking that there must really be something here that they are missing. One other problem is that there is some sexual pleasure in looking and seeing. There are other components, of course, such as touching and feeling and kissing, but this exposure may be too stimulating for a young child. Too much emphasis on any one component without the understanding that it is only a part of the total picture may accentuate its importance for a given individual.

Mrs. _____: Is this why most boys and girls sleep in different rooms?

Dr. G.: Yes, I would assume so.

Mrs. _____. But if you have a family of all girls and they never see their father, when are they ever going to know boys and girls are different?

Dr. G.: I've been asked this question a hundred times before, and I've never found a really good answer. I certainly do not suggest that the father parade around without his clothes to solve the problem. I suspect this isn't really much of a problem; there are always cousins and playmates. Someone will let them know about these differences, never fear!

Mrs. _____: What should you do when you find your young child masturbating?

Dr. G.: Well, here again the mother's response is very important. Any mother knows that these things happen. They know that children are curious and do experiment some and that they really should not be shocked or act as though this were a horrible, sinful activity. I think the best solution is to try to divert the attention to other things. There are, after all, different ways that children find pleasurable responses from their body. Thumb sucking and hair rubbing are a couple besides masturbation. Both from my clinical practice and from the statistics available, I have come to know that almost every child masturbates some. Of course, this becomes much more common in adolescence. It's important not to instill a feeling of guilt in a child about this. In the past, there have been many tales about the dire consequences of this activity, but we now know there is no harm either physically or mentally to the child except insofar as he is made to feel guilty and ashamed of his actions. When they are little, you more or less ignore it. Divert the attention by putting something into the child's hand. Let him pull a little truck or car across the rug, and he will refocus his attention.

Mrs. _____: How long will this go on?

Dr. G.: It will vary with the individual child, but in general it will go from early infancy up to school age. Sometimes a teacher will compound the difficulty. They are usually horrified!

Mrs. _____: No matter what you do at home, some other child or his mother will quickly let them know this isn't an activity that one should be engaging in out in public.

Dr. G.: You never can control these outside forces. Children never quite understand the differences in attitudes that adults have on any question. The important thing, as I have indicated, is that they can come to you without feeling ashamed when they have questions and know that you are a trustworthy source of information. I do not mean to say it is easy to feel relaxed in these discussions. It isn't. After all, here in Boston we have nine or ten generations of Puritans behind us. They had a rigid system where anything that had to do with any pleasure, not just sexual pleasure but any pleasure, was not to be condoned. They believed that people were here to work, and if you met the conditions, you would get your reward in heaven. It's not easy to live down these traditions. Some find it more difficult than others. It does seem this most recent generation is a little less tradition bound.

Mrs. _____: In everything you've said you've had the mother giving the sex instruction. Shouldn't the father have a part in this, too?

Dr. G.: By all means. Whenever a question is posed, it should be answered. There should not be a feeling that this topic can be discussed only with the parent of the same sex. Either parent should stand ready at all times. But by the nature of things it will be the mother who hears most of the questions when the children are little. As the children grow older, instruction by the parent of the same sex should be encouraged. In the case of menstruation, it will be natural for the mother to instruct the daughter, but the father should not attempt to sidestep any question on the subject. Keep all the lines of communications open; that's the way to build confidence.

Mrs.   · What should you do when children happen on evidence of menstruation or intercourse?

Dr. G.: It is important to stress the normality of the events. There's no need to go into details but only to reassure them. You don't want them to get the idea that anything harmful, destructive, or mutilating has occurred. Your handling of the situation will depend, of course, on the circumstances and the ages of the children. It is fairly obvious, I should think, that parents should make an effort to protect their privacy and keep children from stumbling into sexual situations. If by accident the child does observe this situation make sure that he does not take away with him ideas about fighting or physical assault or hostility in connection with the sexual act.

Really, the key to successful sex instruction is matter-of-factness and straightforwardness. Never put the questioner off. If the question comes at an inopportune time, in the checkout line at the supermarket, say, postpone it for the moment because you are too busy with money matters but give the answer as soon as you are in the car. Never give the impression that you are trying to be evasive. There is no question that sex instruction has its moments of difficulty, but it also offers a great opportunity to establish an atmosphere of openness and trust between parents and child.

Mrs. _____: We've talked mostly about explaining sex to young children. Since sexual mores seem to be changing, what *does* one say to teen-agers about premarital sex? If you take the old hard-and-fast line, does this just strengthen their conviction that you are unable to understand the "new morality"?

Dr. G.: As I think I have commented elsewhere, I don't think it's sensible to expect parents brought up in an earlier era to be able to accept the newer sexual code as outlined by present-day adolescent "revolutionaries." I think it is a false assumption to believe that parents can blithely go along with premarital experimentation by teen-agers. I am not arguing that the new code is good or bad, only the broad individual and social results of the application of it will determine that, but I don't think present-day parents will be able psychologically to condone these practices.

However, for what it may be worth to you in thinking about this seeming change in morality, it is my feeling that the major and central target of attack is hypocrisy. These young people are bothered by hypocrisy in respect to race relations, the practices of educational institutions, and hypocrisy in respect to the edicts of government. It is our alleged hypocrisy over this broad front of inequities and failures that is under attack. And our hypocrisy in respect to our avowed sexual code of ethics is being called into question, too. All parents must decide for themselves how best to handle this with their own children. My only advice is to be as honest and open with them as you can. It's not an easy matter with which to deal.

10

Understanding Death

How to explain a death in the family to a young child presents a very serious problem. From my own experience as a parent, and from all I have been able to glean from my professional work and from my colleagues, I have come to the conclusion that there is no single explanation of death that will be wholly satisfactory or that should be given to every child. If the mature adult cannot comprehend or accept the inevitability of death, how can we expect more of a young child? We know from observation that the young child exhibits great anxiety over any separation from a significant person, even for a relatively brief time. Our observation of this anxiety can only confirm our notions of the difficulties the child must undergo when he is faced with permanent loss of a loved one.

It is quite unusual for a child to reach the age of ten without having to face the death of a person or an animal known to him. The person may or may not be related to him; the animal may or may not belong to him, but these events will prompt for the first time his inquiry about death. The younger he is, the more difficult it is to give him a meaningful explanation. We hope to dispel his anxiety, but often this is not possible. It will take time for him to assimilate what he is told.

We have to seek answers for the inevitable questions our children are going to put to us. These answers, these explanations will, of course, depend upon, and have to be consonant with, the religious and cultural beliefs and customs that are important in our lives. The answers, consequently, will vary from one culture to another, from one religion or one socioeconomic group to another. One can offer some general guidelines, but even these will have to fit the age of the child and the nature of his questions. Only by listening carefully to the questions will we be able to detect the child's primary anxieties.

To the very young child, the analogue to death is permanent separation. It is in these terms that it can be explained, but the crucial difference between the two is that the individual or pet that has died will *never* return. This has to be stressed to the child. If it is not, the question of his return will be the very first the child asks. He should be told the truth. The fear of separation is one of the most basic fears of all children. The difference between "gone and coming back" and "gone and not coming back" is a vital element of his anxiety. When death is explained, considerable emphasis should be placed upon reassurance of the child about his own security. He must understand that he will not be without someone to care for and love him.

Without very compelling reasons to the contrary, the death of a relative should not be kept secret from a child. Beyond the ill effects from loss of confidence and trust, the child, like the adult, has the need gradually to work through his grief and anxiety. He must share the family grief and the family feelings, both positive and negative, about the deceased. He must be encouraged to contribute his recollections of the dead person and to take part with the family in contemplation of a future that will bring certain feelings of loss and emptiness. This sharing in the rituals of mourning is of foremost importance for children. No one can grieve healthfully without this outward expression of sorrow or without the sympathetic support and understanding of other persons.

The parent must stand ready to answer the child's questions as fully and as truthfully as he can, however poignant or distressing the questions may be. Often, the finality of the event will magnify the poignancy, for the adult himself has trouble accepting the finality.

The adult must be ever on the alert for questions suggesting in any way (1) that the child himself, by word or deed, was responsible for the death, (2) that the child may now have no one to care for him adequately, or (3) that the child, too, may die for his supposed misbehavior or as a result of his close contact with the person who has died. For lack of understanding, concerns like these may trouble a child deeply. He may ask such questions directly or he may only hint at his fears. Every effort should be exerted to dispel any feelings he may have of guilt or anxiety.

Childish fantasies about death, as about other subjects, can carry over into maturity. The fear of being buried alive, for instance, is a very common one. It is to be expected that burial or cremation will bring forth some hard questions. In replying to them, and to questions about heaven and hell, one should strive to be as simple and as clear as one can and to stress above all that death has brought an end to the sickness, pain, and suffering of the deceased. But one should never picture death as a process of "going to sleep." The words "sleep" and "death" should not be associated in the child's hearing. We die only once, but the child has to sleep every night. To establish a connection between the two in his mind can only be worrisome.

More specific fantasies related to death will be derived from the anxieties that they feel about the loss as it affects them. The fact of permanency is the most difficult to explain and for them to accept. The most frequently voiced fantasy, then, is that the person who died has *only* "gone away and will be back someday." Occasionally this fantasy will be buttressed by a claim that they actually "saw" or "talked to" the dead person, or that the person is "just asleep somewhere." Such fantasies are expressed by a child up to his ninth or tenth year. Presumably this wish-fulfilling type of fantasy is one method of working through the grief in an attempt to handle his sense of loss. It is not easy for an adult to know how to help the child but the greatest "help" in the long run is absolute honesty in discouraging whatever fantasies he has.

Adolescents have a particularly hard time accepting death. Indeed, many of the troublesome thoughts and daydreams in adolescence are centered around death. They are very concerned over the death or possible death of others and for the first time begin to realize the inevitability of their own death. As their experience and knowledge of the world increases, they no longer have recourse to the simple anxiety-reducing, wish-fulfilling fantasies of the younger child. The adolescent requires the long grieving period of the adult to master his sense of great loss and its attendant anxiety aroused in him. He should be encouraged to express and talk through his grief as an adult should. It must also be remembered that the adolescent, like the adult, may have some feelings of guilt about the person who has died. These feelings can range from feeling responsible for the death to simply having entertained angry thoughts about him while he was alive. They should be looked for, modified, and handled sympathetically by those around him.

The safest principle to bear in mind when telling children about a death is to beware of generalizations. In each family there will be particular conditions that will determine how the subject is to be approached. The age of the child, his nature, his previous experience of a loss must all be taken into account. For example, I know of a child who lost first his dog and then an uncle of whom he was very fond. Shortly afterward, his great-grandfather, to whom he was deeply attached, died. We have made the point of not keeping death in the family a secret from children, but should this child have been told about his great-grandfather? His parents thought not, and probably in these particular circumstances they were right. Let the child have a little time to recover from the loss of his dog and his favorite uncle before having to face up to the death of his great-grandfather. So, you see, almost every instance of a death in the family will present situations special to that family. And with this understanding, perhaps we can gain greater insight into the whole problem if we consider the details of other particular examples.

QUESTIONS

Mrs. _____: I have a sister who lost a son by drowning. It was just before his eighth birthday. He and two sisters, six and four, were together when it happened. The girls saw him drown. Now the question was, should the parents tell the sisters what happened to the boy? The father, who was not there when the accident happened, said to try to tell the children that Junior, which was what we all called him, had been sent away to school. They removed all his toys, clothes, everything, from his room. My sister wanted to tell them that the little boy had gone to heaven for she thought the girls were too young to know about death. They tried it both ways.

One day they tried to tell them the story about his going away to school. The little girls would never talk about him at all. The older sister would go to his chest of drawers, look through, see nothing, but she wouldn't say anything. We found out later that she had been calling a school friend and saying that Junior was dead. Then they changed their tactics and said that Junior had gone to heaven. About two weeks later, on his birthday, the girls asked if he was having his birthday in heaven. They were told that he would probably have his birthday there. A couple of months later, the girls still hadn't talked about him at all when one of them asked if Junior was still in the water. They don't talk about him directly, but now and then a question comes up. They ask a question and they look as if they know that what you're going to tell them is not true. We don't quite know how to deal with the situation. This happened over a year ago, but it's still not really been settled.

Dr. G.: In the first place, I think your sister was right in that she was not going to tell a fantastic story about the child having gone away to school. But, as I understand, these two children were there when the boy drowned? They know that he drowned?

Mrs. _____: Yes.

Dr. G.: Well then, their parents should have assumed that these children knew about it anyway, with the relative understanding or misunderstanding about death that a child or children at those ages would have and talked more openly with them about it.

You see, what's happening here is this: These children have never had the chance, nor has the family, to go through the normal and very beneficial period of mourning or grief over the loss of this child. They haven't been able to talk about it and face the issue, to go through a whole system of thinking and feeling that we know is very beneficial for people in the face of a loss of this sort.

Now, I think there are many things that could be happening to these children. In the first place, I am sure they know that this child died and is not just "away." Second, the faith which they're going to have in what their mother and father tell them in the future is going to be shaken. It's not going to be a full faith and confidence that they'll have. They will think, or even say to each other, "Who knows, maybe they are fooling us again? Maybe they are not telling us the truth?" Children don't like to be in this position. Lack of confidence in what their father and mother say to them very definitely can give them an insecure feeling, and this is an extremely important consequence of how these questions are handled with children. What to tell them now and how to make it stick as a correct answer will be difficult to decide.

Mrs. _____: What worries me is that I don't know whether the children still think their brother is in the water. They don't have any idea of burial. They didn't go to the funeral or anything like that. It seems to me that to think of the brother under the earth would be just as bad as thinking of him under the water.

Dr. G.: I would think that the thought that the brother may still be there in the water probably would be a very terrifying one, because if he's in the water, then someone didn't take him out.

Mrs. _____: Won't they think he's been taken out if he's gone to heaven?

Dr. G.: There's another factor here that may be very important. I don't know what the circumstances were, but it is quite possible that these children, in view of the actions surrounding the drowning, and all this camouflage and lack of truth, may in some way feel that they themselves are responsible for the death of the brother. They may not have mentioned their fears. This is a possibility when you try to fool children. It is always difficult to deal with the fact of death because young children just can't understand. The only reason you put in the heaven aspect of it, presumably, depending on the religious convictions of the family, is that you really are trying to tell the child what you hope he can understand, that is, that the person who died has gone away and will not be coming back. That is about as far as you can go in getting them to understand it. Gradually, talk of death becomes a more common thing. Often they pick it up in talking with friends. Children in the age group just ahead of them always educate them. The ten-year-old in the neighborhood will be educating the six-year-old, and the twelve-year-old will be educating the one who is ten. So it goes. I am sure that these children have a pretty good idea of what happened.

I think their great confusion at the moment may be why the mother and father had to handle it this way. There is the possibility that the children are assuming some guilt for their brother's death and assuming that the parents don't want to discuss this notion with them. There is a definite possibility also of the child's assumption that the parents have some guilt about the cause of this drowning. There may be all kinds of fantasies in regard to that. Should the adults have let him go into the water? Was he in a boat he shouldn't have been in, and was there no one there when there should have been? I don't know the circumstances, of course, but all these thoughts may be running through their minds, particularly in the mind of the six-year-old. Whatever is going on with her, I'll bet, in the quiet moments when they are together is being transported to the mind of the younger one.

There is a definite process, we have learned, in regard to grieving. It is a normal process. We should take advantage of all forms society offers to help one grieve and get used to the loss. First, you have to go through your memory and reevaluate the person who has died. This process of grieving involves a great sense of loss and a certain breakup of routine. Then come the positive feelings. Usually, even toward one's closest loved ones there is in some way a feeling of hostility with which you have to deal. There is the back-and-forth shift of thought regarding the dead person's "good and bad" features. "Why didn't he or she do this or that? Why did he leave me now?" Then comes the blaming of heaven itself or blaming the doctor or perhaps being hostile toward someone else who possibly could have been involved. The hostility may be directed toward the person who has died or toward some extraneous person. This is the "personalization" of one's anger, projecting it on someone else.

People go back and forth in the grieving process until they are eventually able to live with the positive and negative feelings they had toward the person who died. This accommodation takes time, and the point is that it should take time. It should be allowed to happen and things should be done to help it happen. The funeral, in and of itself, helps with this normal grieving process. The collection of all the neighbors in the house and the bringing of food after the funeral, the sharing on the part of other people—all these customs come down to us from centuries past and help in this process. My point is that I doubt that your sister and her husband have been able to get used to this loss either. If they had, would they have chosen to keep it concealed from themselves? They can't talk about it. If they could, they would be better able to sustain this terrible loss and, I feel, better able to turn to help their children to accept and bear it.

Mrs. _____: They talk about it to us but not to the children.

Dr. G.: It would be good for them if they could talk about it and good for the children, too. There is never, never any easy way of getting over this loss of a loved person. It is the most brutal problem and task of all those we have to face.

Mrs. _____: Do you think it would be too late now for

them to have a normal grieving period? Could the parents start it and then "trigger" it in the children?

Dr. G.: The parents will have talked through their own grief to some extent, I presume, but I can't see those efforts as more than a modified mourning because the whole family didn't share in it. Usually, in these situations the entire family, the neighbors, the church, and the social community —friends, local merchants, everyone the family has dealings with—help the bereaved through the crisis with the enormous support that genuine and widespread sympathy can give.

Mrs. _____: Well, this all went on, but always without the children. Where they live children don't go to funerals, and at the time of the normal mourning period, the children were staying with their grandmother. This is what happens in many families. You try to keep them away from death, especially violent death. The grandmother dies a normal death and you explain to them that the grandmother is gone, but in the case of this death they obviously thought the children were too young to be included.

Dr. G.: Yes, I know. If one could have chosen a best way, one would not have put such a blanket of silence around it, not letting the children know all that was going on. The customs in regard to death and funerals vary from culture to culture, but many of us who have worked with children favor the procedures that include children in the mourning.

Mrs. _____: Should the children participate in the actual funeral?

Dr. G.: Usually, but depending, of course, on the ages of the children. There are families who will feel as your sister's husband felt when he wanted the wall of silence. Some people do try this approach but not usually. They try their best to explain. They know they can't give an adequate explanation, but they do their best. What parents can tell their children will vary with the age of the child. You probably saw the funerals of President Kennedy and Senator Kennedy on TV. It seemed to me that both the widows were very, very wise in seeing to it that the children were involved. I think those funerals provided an excellent example for the rest of us, even though our situations will be by no means as public or as international in significance. Judgment has to be used, of course, but I think silence and denial are not a good solution.

And let me digress a moment here to suggest that the death of famous persons or of distant relatives can stir uneasy questions in a child's mind about the relation of death to his parents or to himself. With very careful handling of these questions, it is possible for parents to begin to prepare the child for the subsequent personally significant deaths he will have to live through. This preparation will never keep the fact of death from being difficult to deal with, but it can help.

Mrs. _____: To go back to the drowned child, didn't the other children ever ask their parents what had happened to their brother?

Mrs. _____: They did. The oldest one, in a very sly way. In the beginning, everybody was confused. The great shock was that they had seen this violent thing, and the immediate reaction of the parents and adult relatives was to try to wipe it from their minds and sort of make everything "nice." Then when the children had recovered a bit, the oldest already knew there was something wrong, and I am sure felt that in a way her asking about it would make it worse. She wouldn't come out with a direct question, but she was testing. The whole situation was very difficult. They were at home when it happened, and they went off for a holiday right away. This was all part of trying to make them forget. I think now, looking back, this made it worse, because when they got to my mother's house, it was just as if nothing had happened. The family said he had "gone to heaven" and things like that, and the girls simply accepted it. Then a couple of weeks later the oldest girl asked if Junior was still in the water. She didn't know what to believe. I think she still thinks he's there. This is what worries me.

Dr. G.: Would it be possible to take the children to visit the place where he is buried?

Mrs. _____: That is what I was wondering, whether it would be worse for them to think of him under the earth. I don't know whether they will believe that either because they saw him go under the water. You see, the nineteen-year-old girl who was caring for them drowned in trying to save him, so the two children were on the beach alone for half an hour after the two had disappeared.

Dr. G.: But they were not there when they took the bodies out?

Mrs. _____: No.

Dr. G.: I still think it probably is not too late to tell them the truth and to straighten them out, and certainly to tell them with repeated emphasis that their brother is not still in the water. The uncorrected supposition that their drowned brother and the drowned baby-sitter who tried to save him were left by the parents in the water could be terribly upsetting to these children. It could radically shake their feelings of security in their parents to continue to believe that they cared so little that they did not take the boy and the girl out.

All this is part of what I called "working through one's grief." You will remember I mentioned death as one of the facts, stresses, and crises which can have considerable effect upon child development. It will have a different effect on these two children because of their difference in age, the different stages of their personality development, and the different internal problems of growth they are facing.

Mrs. _____: The boy was a very gentle one and always looked after his sisters. After he died the oldest tried to do this for the younger one, tried to look after her.

Dr. G.: The fact they are both girls can make for all kinds of conflict, too, in regard to sibling position and preference, sex preference on the part of the parents, their own squabbles and fights. This entire problem is a very important one even though this particular instance has unusual features.

Mrs. _____: I have a related question. My father died last week in New York. We left my four-year-old in Boston because we didn't feel he should witness the grieving. My father was a very young man. We had planned to bring our son down after a few days, but he unfortunately got sick and so never got there. Since he was obviously most unhappy to be sick without his mother at hand, we came home. He hadn't been told about his grandfather because I hadn't wanted to tell him and then run off. I waited until I came home. I told him that grandfather wasn't there any more. "Well, where was he?" Since I am in the habit of being very straightforward I had to tell him the truth. This bothered him terribly. The second thing that bothers him and what he keeps asking is whether my mother and my brother, who is his uncle, are still there. He continually asks, "Are they still there? Am I still going to see Uncle Stephen again?" The third thing is that although he adores my mother, he doesn't want to talk to her on the telephone. As a matter of fact, he refuses to talk to her. We are going to see her at Thanksgiving, and he already has decided he "is not going." His behavior this past week has been very unusual. I don't know if it's because I left him or if it's a combination of that and the death of my father. I try to convince him every night to talk to my mother, but nothing works. I don't want to upset her and tell her that he doesn't want to talk to her, so I have to make excuses every night about where he is.

Dr. G.: I wouldn't make so much of a case out of his not wanting to talk to his grandmother. He must have some rather unusual notion in regard to her and your father's death. I wouldn't try to push him, I wouldn't try to do anything. Let him work through this himself. He will probably

feel better about the whole thing when he sees his grandmother and his uncle. You told the child the truth insofar as
you could and that was important.

Mrs. _____: Since I don't "believe" myself, I just can't
tell him that my father went to any "heaven." I just couldn't
say that, but I have tried to give him an idea of immortality,
about how we are not going to forget him and that sort of
thing.

Dr. G.: Was he close to this grandfather?

Mrs. _____: Yes he was, as close as you can be when you
are 250 miles apart. Another thing is that my grandfather
died last year. He was in his eighties. Our story then was
that when you get very old you die. But my father was only
fifty-three and an extremely young-looking man. David knew
my father was not old, so this required a new explanation.

Dr. G.: There is another thing to think about here. The
boy can accept the fact of the grandfather dying, but it's
getting a little closer to his own parents when death comes
at the age of your father. Now he might feel he cannot be sure
that something won't happen to you or to his father because
you and your husband are also young.

It is not a good idea to let children think that people die
only because they are old. They must learn that younger
people and even children die. Remember, children have a
very poor concept of time. The difference between the child's
age and the age of his parents is great. To him, they can be
just as "old" as the grandfather and, if he associates death
with age, just as threateningly liable to death. It is much
better to stress the illness of the deceased: He was in pain;
he would never have overcome the illness; if he had continued to live, he would not have been the same person the
child loved, and he could not have lived a normal life. Now
that he is dead, his sufferings are over.

Mrs. _____: When my grandfather died, we just went
for a day and came right back home again. The next day,
the boy didn't eat though eating is *not* one of his problems.

He didn't eat for a full day, and then he didn't eat breakfast the next morning. When he came home from nursery school, miserable from hunger, I made him lunch, but he still wouldn't eat it. After a half hour of questions—this was about a year ago when he was just three—he said that he wasn't eating, for if he didn't eat he wouldn't get to be a big boy and get married and have children; then my husband would never get to be a grandfather and so he would never die. In the end, we told him that if he didn't eat he would just grow up to be a very little man but that he would grow, so he finally ate.

Dr. G.: What he did, you see, was cling to his immaturity because it was dangerous to grow up. We meet unusual behavior like this in childhood. They refuse to grow up, or refuse to eat, or refuse to learn in school lest they go from grade to grade. Sometimes they seem to have a need to believe that if they grow up something unfortunate will happen to them or to someone else. These seem like unusual notions but they really aren't. We don't see this behavior or hear it expressed in words every day of the week, but we meet it quite frequently. This is one of the blocks to "thriving" and to maturity that have nothing to do with dietetics, or glands, or with metabolism either. The psychological fact is that when you behave in this way you are trying to hold on to a lower level of development because you feel more secure on that level. You also think, magically, if I keep little, my father will also be young. He won't be a grandfather, and in this way I can protect him from death. This is the type of thinking that children do. We have here an extraordinarily educational example of this sort of thought process. What this boy went through was not abnormal at all; indeed, it is not atypical for a child his age. This kind of thinking probably goes on quite frequently in the minds of our children though we rarely notice it or have an explanation for it. We just say, "Well, they are blue or discouraged and don't want to eat because they feel sad and sorrowful." But behind it, you see, is this construction of an entire extended theory which in the child's mind is a very logical one. I'm certain this sudden bizarre behavior puzzles and troubles you, doesn't it?

Mrs. _____: It's just his tears. He's not usually a crier. I spoke to his nursery school teacher, and she said he cries if you look at him cross-eyed. This is an example of what happens: I'll say, "David, get your shoes." "I can't find them." Then comes total hysteria.

Dr. G.: He is indeed grieving, in the way perhaps that children, not adults, grieve. I am afraid that anything you say may be interpreted by him to signify that he isn't worthwhile or that he isn't loved or something like that, even though you are doing exactly what you did before. Looking now at this first incident and realizing how complex his reasoning was, we have to wonder what he is thinking about now. If we could get at his present thoughts we probably would find them to be no less logical from his point of view and in the light of his meager understanding than were his reasons for his previous reaction. To us, his behavior may appear completely illogical, childlike and magical, but not to him. This is how complex behavior can get and it is difficult for us as adults to understand the kinds of childish thinking and feeling which we, ourselves, have long since forgotten.

Mrs. _____ · Now he talks about it. When somebody comes in the door, he says, "My grandfather died." It's the first thing he greets people with.

Dr. G.: This is really a part of his grieving process, and, in turn, it is certainly more adultlike. You talk about the person who is gone. You go into all his attributes, as I have mentioned, and review all the good and important things that went on during his life. You remember this and you remember that and you comment upon them. This reminiscence goes on in all families. It should go on if the survivors are finally to get a realistic picture of the person who has been lost, a picture with which they can live. For a satisfactory resolution of the grieving this process must take place. It is a normal process, but many people can never give themselves over to it. They go on for years at a very much lower level of efficiency in their work and in their relationships because they refuse to face all the positive and negative aspects of a situation of loss. They try denial. They will not talk, because they feel bad; they are ashamed to feel bad, and so it goes. In modern society it takes people a long while to get over grief. It is in a situation of just this sort that the absence of the old-time "extended family" is so sorely felt. The beneficial display of grief in loss is not available to us now that family members are so dispersed.

It might interest you to know that these remarks I have made in regard to this grieving process are based in part on studies that were made at the Massachusetts General Hospital by Dr. Erich Lindemann and his group on the people who lost relatives in the Coconut Grove disaster, in 1942. As you may remember, altogether 499 people died from burns or smoke when that night club burned to the ground. Dr. Lindemann had the opportunity to work with and study the relatives of a good many of those unfortunate people. Most of what we know in psychiatry about the grieving process is based on Dr. Lindemann's fundamental observations of the close relatives of these disaster victims and other relatives and people who escaped from the fire. We realize now that grieving is a normal process that has to be gone through and should not be interfered with. We had forgotten that the ceremonies and the rituals, however unusual, of the ages had been devised and carried out to help people in this process. We need a modern substitute of some kind for the rituals that have been put aside.

Mrs. _____: My problem now is that my son still refuses to go to New York to see his grandmother. He obviously is going because we're going, but I would rather not have to have a scene. I would rather try to work it out before we go so that we don't have a scene in the presence of my mother.

Dr. G.: I am not sure that you're going to be able to work it out entirely before you go, and I am not sure that you're going to avoid some type of "scene." I am not sure that the scene might not be good for him and for your mother and for all the others concerned. Of great significance and importance is the fact that he will know by going there that the other people in the family are still alive and available to him. Again, the reason for his reluctance to talk to your mother may be quite different from what you think. Children, you know, are the world's best "theory builders"! He may have a theory that your mother is in some way to blame for the death of his grandfather. People always look around for a villain at the time of crisis. When anything like this happens it's not deeply and thoroughly believed that an "accident" occurred to the loved one; it's not, for example, "disease" that got into the lungs and caused death. Human beings always try, in varying degree, to find a *person* to be responsible for events. This is one of the most primitive types of thinking that we see in normal people—they "personalize" an event which is really an act of nature. People fall back upon a more primitive response and ask *who*, not *what*, is to blame. I have a hunch that in some way the boy thinks somebody could have saved his grandfather but just didn't do it, so he doesn't want to have anything to do with these saviors who failed and this is why he does not want to go to New York. I wouldn't face him with this. Just leave him alone and take him down to New York. Listen to him now because it will be illuminating and helpful to find out just what his theories are that are troubling him so intensely. On the basis of what you learn from him you may be able to construct a plan to really help him. I wouldn't anticipate it however, and say, "Maybe you think Grandma had something to do with it." Don't do that. But if he should say it, don't be surprised, but *listen*—listen ever so sympathetically to any and all curious "theories." Don't rebuke him or belittle him for any of his ideas.

Mrs. _____: The last time we were there, my father was sick and David wouldn't go into his room. We were there for a week. The first couple of days he went to see my father, but after that when we would tell him to go say good morning to Grandpa, he just wouldn't go anywhere near the room. His room was across the hall, and he would walk straight ahead and then make a sharp right and not even look into the room. When we were ready to go home, he finally went in to say goodbye but under duress. It was only a goodbye. That was it, and he walked out the door.

Dr. G.: Obviously, he had a theory at that time regarding going into that room and what might happen. I don't know what the theory was. One can make all kinds of conjectures.

Mrs. _____: Could it have been a fear that his grandfather might be about to die, and now it might be the same thing with his grandmother?

Dr. G.: It is difficult to say with certainty, but, anyway, he's probably thinking now that *somebody* had something to do with it all. His reasoning may go in this fashion: "When I get sick my mother takes care of me and I get well. My grandfather gets sick. My grandmother took care of him and he didn't get well." It may be as primitive and as direct as that. I would leave him alone. Let him do his own talking. But I think it would be very good for him to see his grandmother and find out that she's still there.

Mrs. _____: That's why I thought if he talked to her on the telephone he would know that she was right there as always, but he's not interested. One thing I haven't mentioned is that two years ago I had a baby stillborn. He was well aware that I was going to have a baby and well aware that no baby ever came home. Last year, when I was pregnant again, I had the flu. He came home from school one day, and I was in bed. He wouldn't come upstairs. He just sat at the bottom of the stairs. "Is Mommy dead?" he asked. "Did the baby die?" He's had bad experiences and perhaps he's remembering these other episodes.

Dr. G.: I think he's had a number of crises, and again, although the whole affair is sad, it has been very instructive for us in our group. You see, the more you put the pieces in this jigsaw puzzle together for me and the other mothers, the stronger becomes the possibility that he may think mothers and grandmothers have the power of life and death over children. He probably wouldn't be as explicit as that, but this is a common response in children. We have had children in the out-patient clinic who responded similarly to a series of deaths in their families. Suppose there have been one or two deaths of boys, let's say, in the family where there is a remaining boy. We have seen this kind of problem. The remaining boy might be afraid that what happened to his brother or brothers will happen to him, whereas he may feel his sister is always more worthwhile in the mother's eyes and therefore nothing will ever happen to her. But by the very fact of being a male—maybe mothers have additional or magical powers over males—he is in danger. This is a very primitive way of thinking, but it is the way children think, depending, of course, on their particular stages of development. So this same rationalization may be in the background of this episode of his coming home and sitting at the bottom of the stairs. The main thing at the moment is for you not to worry. I wouldn't try to analyze this child too deeply if I were you, to search out every cause or motive for every thought or feeling. Don't try to probe deeply into what's going on. If he tells you, well and good. Death is a very important fact of life that parents have to cope with often. How it is met sometimes makes a great deal of difference in the child's future, his confidence, his security, and his faith in what his parents tell him. It will be interesting to hear what does happen when he goes to New York.

Mrs. _____: If we survive!

Dr. G.: You'll all survive, all right. I expect that *you'll* feel much better, and all of us are confident that you'll handle it in grand fashion! He may have a big scene. I wouldn't think it was bad if he and his grandmother did have a big scene. It might be very helpful, psychotherapeutically I mean, for both of them.

Mrs. _____: Should she prepare her mother for this?

Dr. G.: All you can say to your mother, it seems to me, is that he is so upset that he doesn't want to talk about the death or to see people who were close to his grandfather. Don't get your mother upset by even hinting that he may feel that she might be to blame for the death. Don't tell her all that you told me. This will only make her problems all the heavier. I give you this advice because you know that as a psychiatrist I am supposed to allay anxiety, not be a party to *causing* it.

Mrs. _____: The circumstances of this incident suggest another question. Should a child be told that a hopelessly ill member of the family is going to die?

Dr. G.: Again, I hesitate to lay down any specific answer. It will depend entirely on the conditions: the age of the child, his nature, his degree of maturity, whether he has experienced another loss recently or a succession of losses. Every case will be different. Bearing in mind the general principles we have developed, the parents will have to use their own judgment.

You will remember that in the first example I gave you the child's beloved dog had died and then a favorite uncle. I might not give the same advice regarding this child and the death of his great-grandfather that I would give regarding another child who had not experienced recent losses. To say it all depends may not be the most satisfactory answer, but at least it is an honest one and in the case of children and the fact of death a wise one.

Mrs. _____: You mentioned using the death of important persons as an opportunity to prepare children for death in their own families, and you link the death of a pet dog with the death of a favorite uncle in respect to the effects on a small child. Can the death of pets also be used to prepare children for facing the fact of death in the family?

Dr. G.: Yes, if one does not expect too much of it. The death of pets is likely, as I have said, to provoke self-directed or parent-directed associations in the child's mind, and parents must be careful in dealing with them.

Mrs. ———: Well, what about formalities of burial for pets? You know, people throw dead turtles or other small pets into the garbage or flush dead goldfish down the toilet. Is this casual disposal likely to upset children? Should parents make a point of seeing that dead pets are given a proper burial?

Dr. G.: I think so. We should do whatever we can to encourage reverence for life, and providing a decent burial for a loved pet should contribute to this attitude, besides helping to get the child through the grieving process. The grief many children feel for their dead pets is quite real and can be very poignant, you know. I can see that having a dead pet thrown in the garbage or down the toilet might lead to a process of childish logic running something like this: "If anything happened to me, I'd be worthless, too, and they'd just throw me in the garbage or down the toilet."

I never thought of it until just now, but there might possibly be an association here with some of the difficulties encountered in toilet training. Once in a while, we are handed a toilet-training problem for which no explanation can be found. Could it be that the child has seen a dead pet or some living thing flushed down the toilet and has had a strong reaction of fear? I don't recall having seen anything along this line in the technical literature. It would be worth looking into.

In connection with the death of pets it should be emphasized again that the familiar expressions "gone to sleep" or "put to sleep" are quite out of place. Death and sleep are not the same, and we should avoid establishing any connection between them in the child's mind.

Mrs. _____: My two-year-old is very upset if she sees either my husband or myself lying down with our eyes closed. Now, in the mind of a two-year-old is this associated with death, do you think?

Dr. G.: I would not want to be definite about this, for it is not unusual in children somewhat older to have a fear of this sort when they see their parents sleeping. "Are they going to wake up?" is their question. In general, however, I would think that a two-year-old would not be concerned about death, but a child of three and a half or four might very well be frightened on seeing his parents asleep and might wake them up to prove to himself that they are very much alive.

In this discussion we have considered in some detail the problems encountered by the child—and by you as mothers of children in the face of the inevitable death of a loved one. All psychiatrists consider loss through death to be *the* most fundamental problem faced by human beings, adults as well as children. It should be clear that various responses can be expected, and that different devices or suggestions can be offered to assist both children and their parents in dealing with this disaster. I should say, too, that the examples you mothers have given us for consideration have been extremely instructive, to me as well as to you, and pointedly illustrative of children's reactions to a loss through death.

In summary, let me say that it is always best to pursue a course of giving truthful explanations and answers. I realize this course can be terribly difficult for the parent to follow. The most important concern is the basic confidence the child has in his mother and father. His confidence will be founded on their unvarying adherence to the truth, as far as it can be determined by them, and in all matters will be vital to his basic sense of security in respect to the world about him.

Obviously, I cannot, as a professional, take the position that the ideas of immortality and heaven held by millions of people should not be advanced to assuage the child's great sense of loss in the death of a loved one. For me to do so would be an affront to the sincere religious convictions of many, many wonderful parents. Yet it is my clinical experience that children, even at the preschool age, are less and less comforted by this explanation. In the long run, it poses more unanswerable questions relative to the continued existence of the dead person than parents can reasonably handle. I know nothing of the individual religious convictions of you mothers, and so I feel that I should not pursue this subject. These beliefs are items of faith, of sincere conviction, and they embrace values which are extremely important to you. I rarely retreat from a discussion, but I am certain you will understand why I should wish to avoid this one. Nevertheless, the insights gained in my own clinical experience with children do not allow me to retreat from the basic conviction that in this matter and all other matters the truth will enhance the parent-child relationship and the feeling of security that is so vital to the child's full development.

11

Personality Development
in the Handicapped Child

DAY AFTER DAY, the parents of a handicapped child live in the reality of his limitations. As they watch other children at play or at the tasks of childhood, they cannot help comparing the differences in his pleasures and his accomplishments. It goes without saying that the child with a severe handicap, physical or mental, requires a different approach from that we take for his more fortunate brothers and sisters, but it is not always easy to get through the sadness and the compassion to the roots of various problems almost bound to arise.

In the first place, it is necessary to remind you that not all mothers view childbearing as a completely glorious fulfillment of their biological or psychosocial selves. Clinical experience has taught us that many women, who often turn out to be more than adequate mothers, approach motherhood with a high degree of ambivalence. This ambivalence may have its roots in the unconscious; that is, in the unconscious residue of experiences they have had with their own mothers and fathers. In the light of these experiences, they may enter their new role either with fear or with unconscious but strong doubts of their adequacy for maternal responsibilities.

If on top of this ambivalence, ambitions for careers in their own right should emerge, then their feelings about the nature and meaning of childbearing, their unconscious attitudes toward children, may be altered still further. One must keep in mind the present-day emphasis in America upon a new and accepted type of bisexual orientation. Today women of certain socioeconomic classes look upon motherhood as a time between periods of gainful employment or professional achievement. A new orientation is evidenced also in an increased instance that the father take a more and more prominent part in the actual day-to-day rearing of children. These accepted modifications of traditional roles have to be considered in our evaluation of today's parents and their attitudes toward children, normal or handicapped.

Second, in respect to the attitudes of mothers and fathers toward individual children, one always must take into account the significance the sex of the child will have for the particular parent. Again, we have learned that the unconscious attitudes of the mother toward male children may be markedly different from her attitudes toward girls. And a similar variation of attitude is to be expected of fathers. These variations again have their origins in the parents' favorable or unfavorable experiences in respect to their own parents or to older or younger siblings of the two sexes. One can expect to find and usually will find variations of some degree in a family's child-rearing practices, depending on the sex of the children. There may even be variations in the expectations for the child's success or failure in whatever he undertakes. It is not unusual for a mother who is able to do a creditable and even splendid job in the care and training of a girl to find herself utterly unable to help or to cope with a boy as he attempts to solve the various tasks in development that he encounters.

In the third place, it is unreasonable and inaccurate to assume that the attitudes of mothers and fathers toward their children will remain consistent throughout childhood and adolescence. It is not unusual to find marked variations in parental attitudes, both positive and negative, as the child progresses from infancy through the latency period and into adolescence. In other words, there are mothers who out of their own lifetime experiences and instinctual needs have the best possible attitude toward children as long as the children stay babies or preschoolers, but who find their reactions changing when the child goes to school or enters adolescence. In the extreme, these mothers may enjoy children only while the children remain babies and completely dependent. But when the child starts to show independence and secures many of his satisfactions from other adult figures or from members of his own peer group, then this attitude of the mother may change and there may be a sharp modification of her emotional investment. Of course, we do see mothers who get less satisfaction from or even dislike the child's dependency upon them, and do their best to accelerate his development to make him become independent sooner. Sometimes a child of this sort of mother becomes the so-called rejected child.

Finally, a mother's attitude toward an individual child in her family may differ, sometimes markedly, from her attitude toward all the other children in the family. Factors of immediate or prevailing significance in the life of the mother previous to the birth of each child determine these variations. The familial milieu at the time of conception and during gestation can be a powerful influence. Economic crisis, changed marital relations, sickness of the mother or other members of the family during this period—all have their effect. The feelings, or degrees of feeling, of both the mother and the father will be different for the child born in time of family crisis. The unconscious associations in the minds of the parents are different for each child, and these associations may be of special significance if a child is unfortunate enough to be born with a congenital handicap, or if an older child becomes handicapped at the same time the parents are trying to solve a crisis. It is not necessary to emphasize that the birth of a handicapped child, or the severe handicapping of a child later in childhood, constitutes one of the real crises that many persons in this world have to meet.

When the psychoanalyst evaluates life crisis, he takes a point of view somewhat apart from that of members of other medical disciplines or the population at large. Through his intensive, detailed explorations of basic personality structure, he has come to expect that all crisis situations will call forth all possible methods of defense against anxiety. This principle holds for him whether the crisis be developmental, such as those attendant upon the Oedipal situation, adolescence, or the menopause, or nondevelopmental. The defenses called forth may be of a quite infantile and regressive nature. He notes, too, that in times of crisis one can expect a temporary reactivation of powerful unresolved or partially solved emotional and interpersonal problems of early life. The presence of a handicapped child is such a crisis. Both the immediate reaction and the eventual adjustment to this hardship will be difficult.

If we are to understand the relationships between parents and handicapped children, we have to explore certain implications beneath the surface. First, we have to recognize that disease and defects, physical or mental, have unexpected unconscious meanings for a great number of people. These meanings are buried deep in the unconscious; they even have relevance to folklore handed down from generation to generation.

Foremost in importance is the unconscious, or even preconscious, notion that disease or defect is visited upon us or upon our children as punishment for our own impulses, regardless of how well we have controlled them, or for actions about which we feel guilty. The visitation of such catastrophes is looked upon by some in our society as the will of God. The counterpart for the less religious segments of our population is a belief that these accidents are the will of Fate or Fortune. In both instances, however, unconscious interpretation gives the misfortune the nature of a punishment.

Closely associated with this unconscious or preconscious attitude is an inevitable, but not necessarily realistic, conviction of "person-causation" of sickness and disease. By this I mean that a parent's first response to the handicap of the child is likely to be the disturbing thought that he has caused the condition by his own direct or indirect action. Or, failing to ascribe the disaster visited upon the child to any one person's act or acts, the parent may quite unrealistically lay it to omission of certain things that should have been done. To put it another way, the parent sees his or her own negligence to have been the alleged cause. One needs only to listen to mothers and fathers as they try to explain historically the onset or culmination of a child's sickness or injury. It is soon apparent where they place the blame. These attitudes are fairly universal throughout all classes in our society. In the minds of many men and women the fortuitous, uncontrollable event, or the essentially impersonal microorganism, is never wholly acceptable as a causative agent of disease or disability.

Associated with this tendency to *self*-accusation, there is also a tendency to project the conviction of guilt onto *someone else* in the immediate environment: another member of the family, a neighbor, or often the child of a neighbor.

In the case of congenital handicaps, there is a tendency,

even an insistence, to ascribe the disabilities to faulty inheritance handed down from immediate or remote ancestors on
one or the other side of the family. It may also be ascribed
to some sinful act immediately preceding the birth of this
particular child or to an assumed unworthiness inherent in
oneself. Again, in pursuing such ruminations, the parent
sometimes selects as the object for blame her family doctor,
her obstetrician, or the pediatrician caring for her child. The
unconscious corollary of the physician as an omniscient saint
is that of the physician as a potential evildoer; doctors learn
early in their professional life not to be too surprised or too
chagrined at having either of these polarities thrust upon
them!

These, then, are some of the meanings, attitudes, and
mechanisms of defense that arise within the individual at
the crisis of having to shoulder responsibility for the care
of a handicapped child. Variations on these themes can be
expected in accord with differences in family dynamics.

We should not find it difficult to understand why parents
rely so heavily upon the mechanism of denial in their attitudes toward the child's handicap. Only with great difficulty
can they allow themselves to assume—or, many times, allow
the child to assume—a fairly realistic attitude toward the
extent, the seriousness, or the permanence of the child's
handicap. The important word here is "realistic." Reliance on
denial turns mothers of handicapped youngsters into "as-if"
dreamers. The mother is eternally striving for adjustment,
for an inner emotional freedom from anxiety based on the
fiction that both she and the child can and should act and
plan "as if" the handicap were really no handicap at all.
Naturally, one hopes that the mother of a handicapped child
will do everything in her power to help the child exercise his
remaining potential for learning and development. This is
the healthy attitude we encourage, and one based upon realities squarely faced. The unhealthy denial reveals a lack of
reality so crippling that only more grief, disappointment,

failures, and bitterness can ensue as time goes on. Those of us who work with parents try to understand the need for this denial and through our understanding to guide the parents toward an effective modification of it.

The age at which a serious handicap is visited upon a child is another significant element in the relationship. The mother's performance in caring for the child will depend to some extent upon her unconscious feelings about childhood dependence. An early disability, perhaps from birth, that prolongs total, or almost total, dependency will bring forth in the mother a quite different response according to whether her unconscious desire is to keep her children dependent upon her for the shortest possible time or the longest possible time. These variations in attitude trouble many mothers. They feel extremely guilty about them.

The foregoing discussion of unconscious parental attitudes leads us quite directly to another defensive mechanism much favored unconsciously among mothers of handicapped children: namely, the defense of an almost obsessive overprotection of the child. To be sure, this defense also may spring from the deep unconscious need within the mother for the absolute dependency of the child. Not uncommonly, however, overcare may have its unconscious base in the guilt the mother may take from her feelings, however repressed, that the child is, in reality, an extreme burden, an inordinate care, and from her pessimistic view that the future can hold only limited opportunities for him. At the very deepest level, as we all recognize, the child regarded unconsciously as a burden may stir within the mother an unconscious wish for his death. And accompanying this obsessive overprotection may be other feelings of guilt for possible neglect of normal children in the family. These mothers may be quite unable to allow themselves normal expression or fulfillment of their own emotional needs.

Most often this guilt is an initial feeling, the usual accompaniment of what we in medicine term the "diagnostic shock." It comes as the parent has to face and accept the fact that his child is disabled. I cannot stress strongly enough, however, that these feelings need not continue. It is my conviction, after long experience, that this is the time when parents may benefit most from the guidance and support of a physician or a psychiatrist. He is able to understand the conflicting emotions and offer professional advice in which the conflict is recognized. Many of these feelings will be modified dramatically as the parent talks them through with an experienced, objective, yet sympathetic person.

The handicapped child becomes aware very early in childhood that he is different from other children his age. His own observations and his experiences with other children tell him this. He also learns this through the different way he is treated. He knows no one expects the same things from him as they do from other children. He knows he is excluded from certain activities because of his disability.

Handicapped children often fight their handicap. They become angry and aggressive toward those around them when it gets in their way. They deeply resent being different and being treated differently. They may also resent that their seemingly all-powerful parents are unable to overcome or correct their defect. The primary aim of anyone who is caring for a handicapped child is to indicate to him that his handicap makes no difference in his worth as a human being and that he is valued in the same way as the other children. He is loved because he is lovable. Strong positive relationships are vital to the child with a handicap in respect to his own personality development. Perhaps they are even more important to him than to the completely normal child.

A more serious response of the child who is handicapped is to withdraw from *all* activities because he is unable to participate in *some* of them. General withdrawal should be watched, and if it persists, advice from a professional counselor should be sought. Talking over his feelings about his disability with someone outside the family is often very helpful.

QUESTIONS

Mrs. _____: I wonder if you can suggest ways in which I can help my handicapped daughter to adjust, to understand that her condition may not change too much but to go ahead and make the most of the abilities she has.

Dr. G.: This is a very difficult problem for parents. What is the nature of the handicap?

Mrs. _____: Well, she's small. She's eight years old and in the third grade. She weighs only 25 pounds and is 35 inches tall. She is in a class with other eight-year-olds and they are about twice her size.

Dr. G.: Has the pediatrician found any particular reason for this?

Mrs. _____: They feel she has a thyroid problem. She's on medication, but we haven't seen any results yet. They have mentioned using growth hormones, but I don't know if they will decide to do this.

Dr. G.: I take it she is completely well otherwise? Would you say she's about as large as most four-year-olds?

Mrs. _____: Oh yes, she's very healthy. She wears a size 2 or 3 dress. She's not as big as a four-year-old.

Dr. G.: Does she give any indication of anxiety?

Mrs. _____: Well, she asks, "Why am I small?" I tell her that we're not always the same and that's why we take her to Children's Hospital to find out if something is wrong and what can be done about it. I don't know what else to tell her. She looks at those other kids and she wants to be like them so badly. It's really . . . it's hard. Then, of course, I have a problem of how other children react to her. They want to pick her up all the time because they think she's a baby. In fact, the teachers have problems with the other children who treat her as though she's a toy. They have to keep saying to the others, "Leave her alone. She's eight years old and she can manage for herself."

Dr. G.: And she does all right for herself?

Mrs. _____: Oh yes, she's very independent. How can I reassure her that it really doesn't matter that much to us? I think because the family has lived with the problem it isn't so much a problem for us as for the outside world. Just walking to and from school, other people see her and wonder why her mother lets her go out by herself.

Dr. G.: What other things happen? What other problems does the child herself run up against?

Mrs. _____: She can't reach anything at school. They had to make her a special desk. She goes to a public school, and they have been marvelous about the whole thing. They have made her a little desk that travels with her each year. She happened to grow a centimeter or so, and they raised the legs a little bit. But she is waiting for a new desk. She thought she was going to get an altogether new one, but they only boosted the legs a little. Opening those heavy swinging doors is a real problem.

Dr. G.: First, and I'm certain you've done this, you have to tell her that it's no disgrace to be small, that there are a lot of small people in this world and there's a place for small people. Her small stature doesn't detract from her worth the least bit.

You will have to be careful not to raise hopes that someday she is going to grow as tall as most of those around her. I think that you can just say that the doctors are doing their best to try to find out why some people are small and some people are tall "string beans." You can keep bolstering her image of herself by showing her how worthy you feel she is. The teachers seem to be cooperating, and that's important. You can't expect other children of the same age not to ask embarrassing questions of a handicapped child of any kind.

Sometimes they try to make scapegoats of them. They call them different or queer and point out that they can't do all that the rest can do. Children can be quite cruel. She will need an added amount of encouragement from you.

Mrs. _____: The other children call her a midget sometimes.

Dr. G.: Yes, I thought this might be the case.

Mrs. _____: Another thing I would like to know—do you think her father and I should discuss this problem in front of her? Should we leave everything out in the open or should we discuss it when she isn't around?

Dr. G.: It depends on what you're discussing. I would think that certain aspects of her condition and some of your own anxieties should be talked about just between you and your husband. I don't think they should be discussed in front of her. If she thinks you're worried about it, her own worry will intensify. She may then say to herself, "Look, my mother and father are terribly worried about this. There must be something terribly wrong with me." Some of her own anxieties would be confirmed. Don't hide things from her. When she asks questions, they must be answered truthfully. As I have said on other occasions, it is extremely important for her to feel she can trust you.

Mrs. _____: She was in the hospital for tests for ten days this year. As far as the doctors could tell, her adrenal gland is sluggish—whatever that means. Now I feel as if everything is at a standstill.

Dr. G.: Did she grow to a certain point and then just stop or has she always been very small? How much did she weigh as a baby?

Mrs. _____: She weighed 7 pounds and 10¾ ounces and was 21 inches long. She was my biggest baby! After she was three months old, she just seemed to stop growing. She was 21 inches long then and in eight years she's grown only 14 inches.

Dr. G.: She's just about a yard high. Are there any children in her class that come anywhere near her in height?

Mrs. _____: No. My second child is a boy and he is very, very thin for his age, but he is taller than his sister. He's the small fry in his class, too.

Dr. G.: We know there is no disgrace about being small, but it is hard for them to bear. I think it's harder on boys because girls do not have to compete athletically with their peer group as boys do. And I think being of small stature is a very heavy cross for a boy to carry. Boys are more cruel to boys than girls to girls.

Mrs. _____: Let me give you an example of just one of our problems. This is something that happened recently. We took her out to buy a coat. The small sizes that fit her always have a bonnet type hat. If she just sees the bonnet with the coat she refuses to try on that coat even though it may fit her. A lot of children have those "bench-warmer" coats. She wanted one, but try to find one to fit her! We finally found a size 4, three-quarter-length coat, and it fits her like a full-length coat, but she is happy because it is almost like the ones the other kids wear. At least, it didn't have a bonnet. It was a grown-up style.

Dr. G.: You certainly seem to be doing all one can do. Just keep on doing it and try to get across to her that size doesn't determine one's worth.

Mrs. _____: But it isn't enough sometimes.

Dr. G.: It probably can't ever be quite enough. Has she ever read about other people who have excelled in some way despite handicaps? Does she know that some men really prefer petite girls to big tall ones?

Mrs. _____: Since kindergarten little boys have been bringing her gifts. She reads everything in sight, so maybe I could find something like you suggest.

Dr. G.: Miles Standish was also a small fellow. I think he was 5 feet 3. Of course, there's Napoleon. I wonder if there are any famous short women? Go to the library and ask the librarian what she can find. That's her job.

Mrs. _____: As I said before, they used to talk about giving her growth hormones, but now since the tests, they don't seem to say much. I have every bit of confidence in them. My son is only six, but they feel he will make a spurt when he reaches adolescence. They don't feel this about her.

Dr. G.: I just remembered there was a great skier who was only 5 feet 3. She was a sensational jumper! Is she strong and capable of doing physical things?

Mrs. _____: Oh yes, absolutely. She's perfectly formed and in good proportion. She'd love to ride a two-wheel bike, but she can't reach the pedals. She can jump rope very well. My husband and I have been talking about trying those pedal extenders. They might help.

Dr. G.: How about ice skating or roller skating? Small, compact people do those things well. I think her morale might be given a real boost if she could succeed in one of those sports. From what I understand, the children are fond of her.

Mrs. _____: Yes, they love her too much!

Dr. G.: How can you be loved too much? Too much love is never enough!

Mrs. _____: She's excited now because she is beginning to lose her teeth, which she has been waiting for—to be like the other kids again. Everytime she feels one coming loose, she runs to me and wants me to take it out.

Dr. G.: How is her disposition? Is she friendly and outgoing?

Mrs. _____: She used to be very, very shy. When she started kindergarten she had real problems. When she had to draw a picture she would use only a black crayon. It was so discouraging. Then her first-grade teacher took over and she was just marvelous with her. She changed her from a shy, overly sensitive little girl into a very outgoing child.

Now she talks to people and is friendly. She seems to be coming along fine.

Dr. G.: Have you ever heard the way she answers children who ask her about her size?

Mrs. _____: Yes. She comes home and tells me about it. She'll say, "Oh, he called me a midget," or something like that.

Dr. G.: Does she cry?

Mrs. _____: No, she won't cry about it, but she asks questions and I know she is bothered.

Dr. G.: Other children will ask questions because of their own anxieties. If one child sees another with a handicap, the immediate reaction is, "Could this happen to me?" In your daughter's case they probably say, "Could I just stop growing, too?" They try to find out why this child is handicapped and then, as though their own concerns will disappear, they assume a superior, sometimes taunting attitude.

Mrs. _____: The teacher said that my daughter often stares at the other kids, and it is obvious she wishes she could be as big as they are.

Mrs. _____: I think this brings up a greater problem, too, a more general problem. How do parents protect children from some of the hurts which are going to come from other children because there's something a little different about them? They may be short or tall, or too thin or too heavy. They may wear glasses or a brace. It's hard for mothers to shield children from these realities of life.

Dr. G.: It's a very serious problem. Usually, the parents can't answer any direct questions and they're not there when the hurt occurs. Sometimes the tone of voice the other children have used in talking to them is what hurts. I think it's a very good thing that she comes home and tells you about these incidents. Some children just take them into themselves and never mention them—they are much worse off. As long as she comes home and tells you, you can keep on explaining things to her.

Mrs. _____: I'd also like to mention something about her ten days in the hospital. I was under the impression you should always prepare children when they are going to the hospital, at least a week or two ahead of time. We're a large family and we thought we would all work at it. If we know something is going to happen, we try to get the child to accept it long before it happens. But the doctor said, "No, don't tell her yet. Tell her a day or two before she comes in." Well, my daughter didn't complain while she was in the hospital. She just took everything. She was very sad, but she didn't say anything the whole ten days she was there. My son, if they did something he didn't like, just squawked. He cried. I think he accepted it better. Now, if my daughter and I have a disagreement over something, she'll say to me, "You didn't come to see me those ten days I was in the hospital." I did. I used to come twice a day, and I don't understand how she can feel that I didn't.

Dr. G.: How old was she?

Mrs. _____: She was seven then.

Dr. G.: She maintains you didn't come at all?

Mrs. _____: Yes. Is this her way of telling me that she just didn't like those ten days?

Dr. G.: Oh, I think so. She must have some memory of your coming, and you probably took her a present, too. But you know, a day in a hospital is like a week to a child. It would be very easy for a child to say that there were days when you never came, but to say you didn't come at all is unusual.

Mrs. _____: Should you tell a child way in advance that something like this is going to happen and that there may be things that happen that are unpleasant?

Dr. G.: Well, I don't know about way in advance. I don't think it's necessary to tell them more than a week ahead of time, because then they start getting anxious about it and they won't talk about anything else. However, you have to tell them soon enough so they can work at it in their minds or in their feelings or perhaps play it out with dolls. It makes a difference, I think, that they know what's going to happen. We're having a great deal of difficulty in some hospitals in regard to serious operations on children where the doctor doesn't want the child to know until the night before the operation. We psychiatrists don't like this idea at all. The child comes in, they do tests for two or three days, and then they decide to operate. Some surgeons will not let you talk it over with the child. Often the nurses know that the child is going to be operated on, and the mother and father know, but everybody has to keep it quiet. Then, the night before the operation someone comes in and tells the child. They give him a sedative, let him sleep, and then take him to the operating room. This somehow seems to me to be altogether too short notice. The child doesn't get any chance to cope with the anxiety he has. It's almost like not telling him at all. Still, if you tell them two weeks ahead, depending upon what the operation is and how old they are, I think that's too long for them to be fretting over it. Again, a day is a week to a child, and if you look at it that way, you can see having to worry for ten weeks or so would just be too much.

Mrs. _____: There was one good thing they did in the hospital. They did prepare the children the night before for the tests they were going to do the following day. They would tell them exactly what was going to happen. I think they were marvelous to the children. They gave a lot of attention to them. They were on a special research ward.

Mrs. _____: I think, too, that some children can accept things they can understand. If they see someone has fallen down and broken an arm and has a cast, they can accept it. Some of these things aren't quite so easy to understand. We had a recent experience with our youngest child who is ten. She'd had a recent checkup but somehow didn't seem herself, so I took her to see the pediatrician. He found her thyroid gland had enlarged to about twice its normal size in just a short period of time. He talked about it in front of her and as she was sitting there, I could see her becoming increasingly upset. She has heard about glands, but she didn't really understand what the glands do. By the time we got out to the car, where I could talk to her and explain it a little bit more thoroughly, she was really very concerned. We went on to see a specialist and he feels there's probably not going to be a long-term problem. As it happens, I was eleven when I developed a bit of a goiter, and apparently this can happen around the time of puberty. Glands are hard to explain to children. You know, bones and muscles they can understand.

Dr. G.: What had you told her or what had she heard about glands?

Mrs. _____: That's just it. I can't quite remember what I had told her. I think perhaps in explaining to her some of the facts of life, I probably told her that the glands play a part in this development. I think this may be something else that's important here. I've noticed that recently she has more questions about her own development. She wonders when she'll begin to see some changes in herself.

Dr. G.: I'm glad you brought this up at this point. Why don't we just assume that this is what's happening in the case of both these girls, that one of their fundamental anxieties may be that they are not going to grow up and have babies? You can say that this is far-fetched and doesn't ring true, but I have a feeling that this may be one of the worries.

Mrs. _____: You know, now that I think of it, I recently asked my daughter what she wanted to be when she grew up. She said, "I want to be a mommy—just like you!" She couldn't think of anything else that she wanted to be.

Dr. G.: You see what has happened in this situation. I'm certain this may be one of her worries about not growing. When the question of her becoming a grown-up woman comes up again I think I would just say that you don't have to be big to do lots of things. You don't have to be big to be a good teacher, or a good skater, or a good dancer. You don't have to be big to get married and be a good mother. I would bring this up deliberately and see what comes of it. If you can put her mind at rest on this it may be very helpful. I would say that there are plenty of small ladies in this world who have babies.

I'll bet she is worried about other future female roles. Whether she is going to have boyfriends and get married is just as important in her thoughts about the future as whether she is going to be able to ride a bicycle. We're approaching Christmas and that's a natural time to talk about birth. Maybe she'll say something about this, and you'll have an opening. If she has this security, she may not feel so different from the other girls. I think it's worth a try.

This talk about operations reminds me. It's been my experience—I mentioned this in earlier discussions—that children who have become emotionally upset often have a history of early surgery. It is not unusual for these children, particularly girls, to assume that something was done inside them that will prevent their having babies. I try to urge upon mothers that they specifically tell children about to undergo abdominal operations that this surgery will have nothing to do with becoming a mother later on. You would be surprised to hear how many girls have this notion. They are convinced the surgery must have something to do with the place where the baby grows or with the glands that produce eggs. I think it's well to assume these worries exist and to go ahead and reassure the girls.

Mrs. _____: Everyone says it's best to treat the handicapped child just as if he was like any other child. But this really isn't so. Shouldn't he learn that he is different and adjust to the fact?

Dr. G.: Parents should not convince themselves that it is best to treat a handicapped child as if he has no handicap. Both they and the child know this isn't so. No matter what the child is told, he knows he is different. We want him to face and master the reality—not avoid it. Denial as a defense is understandable but unworkable. Some things in life—and handicaps are among them—just will not be denied. Of more importance, perhaps, is that the denial makes it unlikely that a positive and constructive solution to his problem will be found. We want for him the fullest possible development and growth despite his handicap, and that will require a realistic approach to what he can and cannot do.

Mrs. _____: What about the child who is born blind? Is he better off at home or in a school for the blind?

Dr. G.: In answering your question I think I will reflect the feelings and opinions of experts who deal with children born blind. Most of them feel it is far better for these children to remain at home than to be sent to a residential school. This is particularly true for the infant and preschooler and even the elementary-school-age child. As I've stressed before, these children face the same tasks in early personality development that the sighted child faces. All of these are easier to solve as a member of an intact family group. When the blind child reaches the preadolescent or adolescent stage, serious consideration should be given to his enrollment in a specialized school where the facilities for his special needs are available.

Of course, the circumstances within each home, school, and community will need to be evaluated. Of great and continuing importance is the need for the parents of a blind child to be in touch with some counseling agency whose professionals can advise and assist them in their planning for the individual child.

Mrs. _____: My neighbor has a sixteen-year-old son who developed diabetes two years ago. He just hasn't been able to accept it and refuses to take good care of himself. He had always seemed to be such a stable boy, but his personality has really changed. He's rebellious and sullen. Would his adjustment have been easier if he'd been younger when it developed?

Dr. G.: It is not difficult to understand the severity of the blow this boy has had. He has developed a physical problem that not only will limit some of his usual activities but also means he will have to guard and be concerned with his health for the rest of his life. He will have to reformulate and live with a very different image of his own body. This new image may convey to him a deep sense of inadequacy. He will be dependent on medication for the preservation of not just his health but his very life. His whole life style will have to be altered to permit a somewhat rigid, closely adhered to schedule. Even in his future vocational choices, he will need to take his diabetes into consideration. In the light of all these imposed changes I can certainly understand his becoming rebellious and sullen. He must be basically very depressed.

His refusal to take good care of himself is probably another form of defense by denial. He would wish to deny that there is anything at all wrong with him. This is a primitive type of defense utilized by many people when they initially face a serious illness. At his age, it is quite possible that he has acquired a considerable amount of information about diabetes and he may have been told that the condition tends to run in families. If so, some of his rebelliousness may be directed at his parents who he feels have passed on this condition.

In a younger child the acceptance of and adjustment to this condition is not necessarily easier. It may be more difficult for both the young child and his parents because he cannot understand the nature of the illness. However, he may be at a more level period in his development than the adolescent, who is facing turbulence on so many fronts. We just have to hope that this boy can be kept in good physical shape until he gets his feelings under better control.

I would like to make a few final points. Let me emphasize that all the developmental tasks facing the average child also face the child with a handicap. His solution of these tasks of orderly interpersonal development are just as important for him as for any other child. I would like to speak particularly about this in relation to the mentally retarded child.

It has been particularly distressing to me as a child psychoanalyst to note that in the recent valuable emphasis, local and national, upon the long-neglected needs of the mentally handicapped child, little or no attention is being paid to one obvious fact: The handicapped child and the normal child have the same emotional or personality-development factors to deal with.

As I see it, the mentally retarded child faces all the problems inherent in the usual development tasks, threats, and crises of normal or physically handicapped childhood. To set the retarded apart as needing only *educational* help constitutes another deprivation that should be corrected. The parents of these children should have available to them all the benefits of the experience of the child psychiatrists, psychologist, and social worker.

That parents of *mentally* handicapped children—and the leaders in the professional and parent groups—should have disavowed any need for clinical psychiatric help for their children and for themselves is not too difficult to understand. There is, I suppose, the ancient fear generated among them that mental retardation might be associated with "mental illness," and they are hopeful of avoiding such implications.

Whatever may be the reasons for their attitude, this lack of concern constitutes a crucial block to the attainment of really *comprehensive* care for the mentally retarded and shuts off beneficial guidance of the parents.

Finally, may I say that we in the psychoeducational clinics have discovered that a fair proportion of nonlearners—and indeed, some of those designated by schools and outside agencies as "mentally retarded"—are not suffering from intellectual defects but from nonorganic emotional blocks to learning.

It is my own professional belief that *all* children who show educational retardation, including organically determined "mental retardation," should have at least the diagnostic help offered by psychiatrists and their associated mental-health workers. And the parents should have professional guidance as well.

For the handicapped child, as for any child, every opportunity to enrich experience should be seized and exploited. One must be alert to make the most of the capabilities that are untouched by the handicap. Most important, of course, is to include the handicapped child, whenever possible, in the family routines, conversations, and plans. Familiarity with the activities of the rest of the family will broaden the handicapped child's world. This deliberate attempt to spread the boundaries of a limited existence will call for a different prescription for each child, depending on the nature and extent of his handicap and upon his age. One last word of caution is necessary here: At all times, these attempts must be kept in a realistic perspective, in which the handicapped child's abilities and limitations are clearly seen and the special efforts in his behalf are kept in balance with the real needs of the rest of the family.

Index

person recognition by, 18–19
pleasure-pain principle in, 9–11, 19–20
Insecurity
aggression stimulated by, 110
learning difficulties due to, 132–34
Intelligence, 155
I.Q., 155–56

Jealousy, Oedipal complex and, 47–48
Jefferson, Thomas, 95

Kennedy, John F., 212, 248
Kennedy, Robert F., 212, 248
Kindness, 127–28
King, Martin Luther, 212

"Ladders of development," 5, 14–15, 154
See also Growth
Language, 144
early use of, 40–42
"Late bloomer," 158–59
Learning
aggression in, 136
attention in, 134–35
curiosity and, 139
difficulties in, 131–38, 141, 143–44
emotional problems and, 159–60
environment affecting, 142
excitement of, 38–39
family affecting, 139–40
fantasy in motivating, 113
heredity and, 142
neurological problems interfering with, 158
praise for, 123–24
"precision," 38, 40, 56, 102–103, 130, 134, 138–39, 145–46
reading problems in, 156–57

reinforcement in, 41–42
"romantic," 38–39, 102–103, 198
rules and regulations in, 56–57, 129, 138–39, 144–46
words and, 130–31, 143
Lindemann, Dr. Erich, 255
"Loner" child, 126–27
Lying, children's, 45–46

Marriage
close relatives and, 230–31
interracial, 184–85, 187–88
Masturbation, 228–29, 232, 235
Maturity, 136–37
Menopause, 266
Menstruation, 228–29, 236
Mental retardation, 105, 159–60, 283–84
Mesomorph, 28–29, 31
Misbehavior
adolescent, 193–94
attention and, 88–89
"Mixed dominance," 156–58
Montessori, Madame, 160–62
Moral development, *see* Conscience
Mothers
attitudes toward children in, 265–66
childbearing views of, 263–64
childrearing guidelines for, 26–28
death and, 258
infant valuation of, 12–13
intuition of, 26, 145
sex education role of, 225–27
See also Parents
Mouth, 39
infant pleasures derived from, 12

Negativism, preschool, 47
Nudity, 233–34

Rules and regulations, 44
pre-adolescent role of, 102–103
role in learning of, 56–57, 129,
138–39, 144–46
social conduct, 138
toilet training and, 78–79, 138

Santa Claus, 203–204
School, 186–88
adolescent attitudes toward,
172–73
mixed religious celebrations at,
200–202
specialized, 281
See also College; School, nursery
School, nursery, 144, 146
aggression helped by, 64
Montessori system of, 160–62
Self-discipline
corporal punishment and, 85–
86
establishment of, 84–85
Sensitivity, 121–22
Separation, anxiety arising from,
6–7, 239–40
Sex
children's experimentation with,
231–32
pre-marital, 237–38
retribution fantasies concerning, 51–52
Sex, differences in
childrearing affected by, 264–
65
children's curiosity about, 221–
22
development affected by, 4–5,
16, 81–82, 132–33, 136–37,
140–42
Sexes
adolescent companionship between, 173–74
pre-adolescent division between, 112

Sexual drive, 218
stealing as substitute for, 116
Sexuality, teaching of
anatomical differences in, 224–
25
animal and plant analogies in,
222–24
comfortable attitude in, 220–
22
doctor's role in, 228
explanation of birth in, 225–27
father's role in, 236
marriage values stressed in,
227–28
modesty in, 233–34
mother's role in, 226
origins of life questions in, 225–
26
parental inadequacies in, 218–
19
scientific terms for sex organs
in, 219–20
sexual intercourse and, 228,
236–37
truth in, 220–22, 229
vocabulary in, 225–26
Sharing, 53–54
difficulties in learning, 60–61
Shyness, 127
Sibling group, ordinal position in,
120–23
Sibling rivalry, 33–34, 105–106
aggression in, 54–55, 62–63,
67–68
lying due to, 46
middle child's problems in,
122–24
parental solutions to, 64–65
regressive behavior due to, 46,
61–62, 66–68, 107–108
sharing difficulties due to, 60–
61
Spanking, 30
children's guilt feelings and,
88